4/03

Red Matters

Rethinking the Americas

Series Editors

Houston A. Baker, Jr.
Eric Cheyfitz
Joan Dayan
Farah Griffin

Red Matters

Native American Studies

Arnold Krupat

PENN

University of Pennsylvania Press

Philadelphia

Copyright © 2002 University of Pennsylvania Press
All rights reserved
Printed in the United States of America on acid-free paper

10 9 8 7 6 5 4 3 2 1

Published by
University of Pennsylvania Press
Philadelphia, Pennsylvania 19104-4011

Library of Congress Cataloging-in-Publication Data
Krupat, Arnold.
    Red matters : Native American studies / Arnold Krupat.
        p.   cm.
    ISBN 0-8122-3649-1 (cloth : alk. paper).
    ISBN 0-8122-1803-5 (paper : alk. paper)
    Includes bibliographical references and index.
    1. Indian literature—United States—History and criticism.
2. American literature—Indian authors—History and criticism.
3. Indians of North America—Historiography.
PM238.K78   2002
810.9′897—dc21   2001052539

Contents

Preface

The title I've chosen for this book is neither original[1] nor, strictly speaking, adequately descriptive of what the reader will find here. Nonetheless, I've chosen *Red Matters* because red has not much mattered as yet, not in the aura of the postcolonial, gender and race, borderlands, cultural, or subaltern studies. Although there exists at present a solid body of criticism demonstrating the importance of Native American literature in its own right and in relation to ethnic, minority, or difference literature of a variety of kinds, Native materials still continue to be badly neglected.

This is not the place to elaborate on just why this might be, although I do want to offer a few brief remarks. That Native people are largely ignored as part of the political and social fabric of American life results from a persistent inattention to them in the media. And media inattention, I believe, is the consequence of the fact that Native people, in particular the most traditional Native people, have generally avoided the sort of confrontational or performative politics on which the media thrive. That Native people and their cultural expression are ignored in the academy results from a lack of numbers, of both students and professors, on the part of Native people (and of others interested in Native culture).

Exceptions to the first of my generalizations were provided by the takeover, in the late 1960s, of Alcatraz Island and the Bureau of Indian Affairs in Washington, and as well by the violent events at Wounded Knee in 1973, actions we shall consider further in the final chapter of this book. But Native American protest against treaty violations and broken promises did not usually take such visible and vocal forms in the last quarter of the twentieth century. As for academic mass, given the horrendous situation of Indian peoples in terms of health, jobs, and education, one can readily understand why young persons, Native and not, interested in American Indians would choose to enter the fields of public health, medicine, and nursing, substance abuse and employment counseling, early childhood and adult education, rather than to go into cultural studies or literature. Surely the need for Indian health service workers and Indian rights' lawyers has been and probably continues to be easily as great as the need for Indian text or performance explicators. But—to speak only to the academic issue—the number of students and the number of scholars working on Indian cultures and literatures does seem now to be increasing. For the short term they are still likely to be ignored or marginalized by most of those with hiring and curricular power, but for the long term I believe their prospects are bright.

This is because, as Malcolm X famously said, the chickens will come home to roost: or, as, I am saying, you just can't understand America, more specifically, the United States, without coming to terms with the indigenous presence on this continent. Americans, as William Carlos Williams lamented in 1925, "do not believe that they have sprung from anything: bone, thought, and action. . . . Their history is to them an enigma" (113). The Puritans, Williams insisted, "never realized the Indian in the least save as an unformed PURITAN" (113). In the same year, D. H. Lawrence wrote that "every continent has its own great spirit of place. Every people is polarized in some particular locality, which is home, the homeland" (5–6). For all the mystified nature of Lawrence's philosophy, one may take very seriously his contention that "the spirit of place is a great reality," and that, just as "China produces the Chinese and will go on doing so" (6), so, too, has America produced its own Native people and will go on doing so. This is something the Euramerican invader-settlers still have to recognize, as they must also recognize the need to come to terms with whatever "place" they—we—have not as yet befouled or destroyed.

To state the obvious, Native people were here first, and, for all that they suffered near genocide, they have not and will not vanish. Despite the appalling conditions under which Native people continue to live as a consequence of ongoing domestic imperialism, it is a matter of fact not prognostication to say that they are going to persevere and thrive. That means that Native literature and culture will also thrive and in its thriving bring forth an adequate cohort of critics to provide appropriate critical response. Again, these developments seem to me currently very much in active progress.

Paul Gilroy has written that, although the Holocaust is finally coming to be understood as not just an issue for Jews but "a part of the ethical and intellectual heritage of the West as a whole" (49), slavery continues to be treated as an issue only for black people. Gilroy does not mention Indians, but that is only one further illustration of the fact that when it comes to the indigenous people of the present-day United States, there is no awareness, not only that the history of genocidal devastation is a "part of the ethical and intellectual heritage of the West as a whole," but even that it is an issue for Indians. There is simply no awareness at all. (And Gilroy is someone very broadly and sensitively aware.)

This lack of awareness most immediately and directly hurts Native people. But I want to state as strongly as I can that this lack of awareness also hurts Americans in general. This is because it is simply not possible to achieve any remotely adequate understanding of the "ethical and intellectual heritage of the West as a whole," or, locally, that enormously powerful offshoot of "the West" known as the United States of America, without engaging ethically and intellectually the treatment here of blacks and Indians. This would be like trying to understand Europe without engaging its treatment of Jews. Or, to put it another way, it would be like trying to understand Shakespeare while ignoring the existence of Shylock, Othello, and Caliban.

In a discussion of diaspora and the presently difficult relations between blacks and Jews, Gilroy notes "the manner in which carefully preserved social histories of ethnocidal suffering can function to supply ethical and political legitimacy," to debates about "the status of ethnic identity" and "the power of cultural nationalism" (207). Surely the narrative of "ethnocidal suffering" in America must include the experience of the indigenes and their descendants. There is important work, here, that remains to be done.

*   *   *

In what follows, I develop the cross-cultural practice of what I have formerly called ethnocriticism,[2] and what I will here elaborate as cosmopolitan comparativism. I argue in Chapter 1 that criticism of Native American literature today proceeds from either a nationalist, indigenist, or cosmopolitan perspective. The nationalist grounds her criticism in the concept of the nation and uses tribal/national sovereignty, a legal and political category, to guide her examination of Native cultural production. The indigenist foregrounds what is instantiated as a pan-Indian geocentric epistemology, a knowledge different from that of dispersed Europeans and other wanderer-settlers. It is this Other knowledge that subtends the indigenist's critical perspective. The cosmopolitan is more nearly—to coin an oxymoron—a well-organized *bricoleur*. Aware that casual eclecticism can lead to critical and political irresponsibility, and doubting the flexibility of a true *ingénieur*'s systematicity, the cosmopolitan would cobble her criticism out of a variety of perspectival possibilities.

Thus the cosmopolitan takes very seriously nationalist and indigenist insights, although her own position is that it is unwise to be bound too rigorously by either the nation or traditional knowledge. Nonetheless, I will argue, it is not only the case that the cosmopolitan needs the perspectives of the nationalist and indigenist, but that the nationalist and the indigenist also need the cosmopolitan. Each of these perspectives requires the others to achieve its full discursive effectivity.

As a type of the ethnocritic, the cosmopolitan must be committed to cross-cultural translation. Translation is a subject that has been of wide-ranging theoretical, critical, and scholarly concern of late, and Chapter 2 considers historical attempts to translate traditional Native American oral song and story into a variety of types of English, arranged on the page as verse or prose, and with differing sorts of syntax and diction. Currently existing translations, and, indeed, all future translations, I believe, must align themselves on the axis of what I call identity and difference in relation to the poetry and prose of the dominant culture. This is to say that translators whose interests are strongly literary will translate in such a way that the Native performance appears on the page as *like* (identity) what We[3] recognize as literature. By so doing, these translators risk obscuring the difference — the aspects that don't at all look like literature to us — of Native song or story. Translators whose interests are more nearly scientific — anthropologists, linguists — will render the Native song or story on the page in English in as exact and accurate a manner as possible, conveying the genuine difference of Their expressive performance. But this runs the risk of obscuring the artful, poetic, or literary aspects of the Native song or story. This is a version, to be sure, of the age-old argument between *sensum* and *verbum,* translation for the sense or the spirit, or translation for the strict and literal meaning — but with a very specific cultural difference.

The third chapter treats translation in a more nearly figurative than literal sense, and shifts from the category of literature to that of history. Euramericans classify texts discursively as "history" on the basis of their empirical accuracy. Although we know at least since the work of Hayden White that precognitive tropological preferences on the part of any given historian will lead her to narrativize the "facts" very differently from the way in which they might be storied by another historian; although we know, therefore, that the *meaning* of the history written by one hand will interpretatively vary from the "same" history set down by another hand, nonetheless, the facts of the matter, at this level of analysis, are not especially at issue. Everyone is playing by the same rules, or, as I want to say, everyone is speaking the same historical language.

While the second half of the twentieth century saw the appearance of a number of histories by Native and non-Native historians who approached the facts of the matter from a perspective other than that of the victors, these historians also were — these historians are still — more or less speaking the same historical language as that of the post-Enlightenment West.

But for traditional Native people, history is not measured by its empirical verifiability and/or accuracy. (This does *not* mean, let me quickly add, that traditional Native history is never factually accurate.) As we shall see further, for traditional people, history is a culturally and socially agreed-upon account of the past. It is what the elders and those with authority to speak have recounted as what happened. Their account presents the truth of the matter, a truth that may on occasion contradict what seem to be the facts. Usually, when this is the case, We call Their history myth; fetishizing fact, we neither accept their historical criteria as consistent with truth, nor do we translatively mediate between their language and our own. Meanwhile, they have for long translated Our history into terms more or less comprehensible to them without demoting it to some category of lesser import. Now it is more than time for us to translate Their history into terms more or less comprehensible to Us as history. I consider several instances of Native history in light of these concerns, and argue against the well-intended but, I think, pernicious notion that Their history and Ours are incommensurable and mutually untranslatable.

Chapters 4 and 5 take up literary works, two novels, one from early and one from late in the twentieth century. Chapter 4 offers a detailed reading of Mourning Dove's *Cogewea the Halfblood* (1927), the first novel of the twentieth century by a Native woman, in relation to the vexed category of "Indian blood," roughly parallel to the concept of "race," itself construed at that time both culturally—behavior that is learned and performed—and also biologically—behavior that is determined by "blood."

To situate Cogewea's dilemma as what we would now call a mixed race person, I consider some of the work of the foremost Native intellectuals of the years just before and after the First World War on the subject of Indian identity and compare it to W. E. B. Du Bois's conceptualization of what, for African American identity, DuBois called "double consciousness." Just as DuBois theorizes the attempt of the black person to be both a Negro and an American, so, too, does the "half-blood" Cogewea encounter the difficulty of one who would live a life of both/and—to be both an Indian and a "civilized" member of the dominant society—in a time that insists upon either/or. In this period, Indians are seen as having no social and cultural future as Indians. They must, it was thought, become "white" and "civilized," if they would not utterly vanish as human beings. Difficult as this made the situation of Native people unwilling to give up ancient and valued lifeways, the situation was equally difficult for those who, in whatever measure, did try to assimilate, for they faced the stubborn and pervasive fact of white prejudice. Although Mourning Dove could not solve Cogewea's dilemma—indeed, no one in the period could quite solve it—I think she did, at least for a moment, imagine a time when the despised "half-blood" would be celebrated as a "mixedblood" individual, in our current terminology, a *hybrid* person—yet an Indian nonetheless.

The fifth chapter brings me very nearly to the present as I contextualize Sherman Alexie's novel *Indian Killer* in relation to what—once more with reference to African Americans—I am calling "the rage stage." Alexie's novel takes as its subject the fact that Indians are very, very angry with whites who continue to assault, insult, and generally oppress them, and it imagines this anger finding an expression in violence, specifically, in the random and perhaps wholesale killing of whites. The ominous final chapter of the book seems actually to envision the further murder of whites in a celebratory fashion.

African American writing, at least since 1940 and Richard Wright's *Native Son* and up through the 1960s, had frequently recognized the existence of black rage. But Native American fiction of this latter period, the period, to be sure, of the so-called "Native American Renaissance" in literature, while expressing fully the harm done to Indians by the dominant society, tended to see the expression of rage in violent action as counterproductive, indeed, destructive to the individual and the community. Alexie's novel is very different in this regard. It also breaks with Native fiction of an earlier period in its general lack of interest in what had been a prominent if not preeminent concern of that prior fiction, the subject of Indian *identity*. I try to contextualize *Indian Killer* in social and literary terms, to examine, that is, its politics of violence and its poetics—of whatever beyond violence the novel might suggest.

Acknowledgments

I come now to the pleasant task of thanking those who, in many and various ways, have sustained my work and in a variety of ways have contributed to the making of this book. I've chosen to dedicate specific chapters to specific persons rather than to offer a dedication to the book as a whole. Their names, and those of other friends, colleagues, and co-workers who helped along the way, I list here: Karen Blu, Helmbrecht Breinig, Bella Brodzki, Eric Cheyfitz, Thomas Claviez, Michael Elliott, Winfried Fluck, Patricia Penn Hilden, Michael Hittman, Shari Huhndorf, Maria Moss, David Murray, Barry O'Connell, Chikwenye Ogunyemi, Louis Owens, W. S. Penn, Gerald Vizenor, Peter Whiteley, Shamoon Zamir. My student research assistants, Corinna Buchholz, Kate Reilly, and Hutch Hill, made life easier in a great many ways. My thanks as well go to the librarians of Sarah Lawrence College, in particular Cha Fagan and Judy Kicinski, without whose diligence and good cheer very little could have been done. My editor, Jerome Singerman, at the University of Pennsylvania Press, offered reassurance and support at just the right moments, for which I am grateful.

I offer special thanks to Tanya Krupat and Andrea Ferster.

A very brief and much earlier version of Chapter 1 appeared in the *Centennial Review* after its presentation as a talk at Michigan State University. In less brief and slightly later form, it was then given as a talk at the John F. Kennedy Institut in Berlin, and published in *Mirror Writing: (Re-)Constructions of Native American Identity*, edited by Thomas Claviez and Maria Moss. I am grateful to those who invited me to offer these talks and to the editors who published them for permission to reprint parts of those earlier versions. The present version, much expanded and revised, appears here for the first time.

Chapter 2 was first published as the lead essay in Brian Swann's volume *On the Translation of Native American Literatures* (Washington, D.C.: Smithsonian Institution Press, 1992). Although ten years have passed since its publication and many fine, new translations of Native American song and story have appeared, I have not altered or updated the material in this chapter. The theoretical principle of identity and difference that guides my historical account of actual translations should apply to the newer work as well as to the work I discussed. I am grateful to the Smithsonian Institution Press for permission to reprint.

A very different version of Chapter 3 first appeared as "America's Histories" in *American Literary History* 10, 1 (1998): 124–46, used by permission of Oxford University Press. For this book, I have not only revised and considerably expanded the original essay, but, indeed, I have had a definite change of mind. *Then* it seemed to me that those forms of traditional Native history that looked to Us more like "myth" than like "history" could nonetheless be accorded a measure of historical value in figurative translation. But I was not prepared to allow that one could legitimately speak of the *culturally sanctioned truth* of the matter as historical (rather than mythical) when that truth did not accord with the historical facts of the matter. While I continue to think that translation is often necessary for an understanding of some types of traditional American Indian history as history—no one can wholly step out of his cultural conditioning entirely, after all, and my conditioning has been Western—I *now* also think that traditional Native history has a legitimate claim to historicity on its own terms, and that the truth of the matter may indeed be as important or more important *historically* than the facts of the matter. How and why I think so is developed for the first time here. I am grateful to the editor of American Literary History for permission to reprint those parts of the chapter that first appeared there.

The study of *Cogewea* in Chapter 4 appeared in different form in a special issue of *Modern Fiction Studies* 45, 1 (Spring 1999): 120–45 on Native American literature. For its appearance in this book, I have expanded a good many of the discussions dealing with race and culture, and added to and revised the commentary on *Cogewea*. I am grateful to the editors of *Modern Fiction Studies* for permission to reprint material from the essay originally published there.

Chapter 5, contextualizing Sherman Alexie's *Indian Killer*, was presented in oral form at the Ethnohistory Conference at Mashantucket, Connecticut in fall 2000, and again at the American Indian Workshop of the European Association of American Studies meeting in Bordeaux, in spring 2001. It appears here in much expanded form for the first time.

Chapter 1
Nationalism, Indigenism, Cosmopolitanism

Three Perspectives on Native American Literatures

For David Murray and Shamoon Zamir

Criticism of Native American literatures today proceeds from one or another of the critical perspectives I call nationalist, indigenist, and cosmopolitan. The nationalist and indigenist positions sometimes overlap, and both nationalists and indigenists tend to see themselves as apart from and in opposition to the cosmopolitans. Nonetheless, as I will try to show, nationalist, indigenist, and cosmopolitan positions are all overlapping and interlinked so that each can only achieve its full coherence and effectiveness in relation to the others. All three positions may be enlisted for the project of an anticolonial criticism, as all three may also operate to reproduce colonial dominance under other names.

I am concerned with nationalism, indigenism, and cosmopolitanism as *critical* perspectives. But it would be foolish not to acknowledge that they have been taken as perspectives undergirding *identity* rather than criticism. One might think that identities and critical perspectives are related as cause to effect; it would therefore come as no surprise to discover that a non-Native person like myself would occupy a cosmopolitan critical position: I am a cosmopolitan critic *because* of "who I am." But this would be a gross oversimplification.

Neither identities nor critical perspectives are given by birth; neither identities nor critical perspectives are "in the blood" or produced by descent alone. This is not quite to say—as Werner Sollors once seemed to say—that identities are entirely a matter of consent. We know perfectly well that non-whiteness in the United States disqualifies or severely constrains certain choices of identity. And it is most certainly not to say, as Scott Michaelsen recently has said, that there can be no real difference between Indian and white identities. Michaelsen writes that "as soon as Indians begin to conceptualize whites (and themselves), it is already too late to imagine a real difference" (32), so that the "project of legitimation," the concern to determine "who is an authentic Amerindian, what is authentic Amerindian culture, and, perforce, what is not" (113–14) should simply be abandoned.

Rather, I am claiming, first, that what it means to be identified and accepted as an Indian person by other Indian persons is complex and subject to cultural, social, and historical forces—none of which, in my view, entirely extinguish personal agency. Second, I am claiming that an Indian or non-Indian identity does not in and of itself determine critical perspective. (Although critical perspective, as we shall see further in Chapter 5, may indeed partly serve to define the particular sort of Indian identity one might claim.) One might reasonably think it likely that the non-Native or outsider critic like myself would be drawn to cosmopolitanism, but this likelihood is by no means an inevitability. There are many non-Indian culture-workers who are committed to what might well be called a nationalist perspective, and there are others—many eco-critics among them—who foreground an indigenist perspective. No one of these scholars pretends to an Indian *identity* as somehow necessary to legitimate his or her critical perspective.

In what follows, I will comment as well, although briefly, on nationalist, indigenist, and cosmopolitan preferences for the textual and institutional locations for teaching Native American literatures, and the critical methods for writing about them.

*   *   *

The nationalist bases her critical position foremost upon her understanding of the term *sovereignty.* As Russell Means and Ward Churchill[1] have written in their brochure, "TREATY: A Platform for Nationhood": "Within the understandings of International Law, it is the right of *all* sovereign nations and sovereign peoples to enter into treaty relationships with other sovereign nations and peoples. Conversely, *only* sovereign nations and peoples are entitled to enter into such relationships (3). Thus Native "nations and peoples" were and are sovereigns inasmuch as, according to Pauline Turner Strong and Barrik van Winkle, between 1607 and 1775 the Crown and the various colonies entered into at least 185 treaties with Indian peoples . . . , treating them as sovereign political entities, if only to limit their sovereignty" (1993: 11).

Once the United States achieved its own independent existence as a "sovereign political entity," for almost one hundred years, from 1776 until 1871 (when Congress ended the treaty-making practice), it continued to enter into nation-to-nation treaties with the tribes. Since that time, some Native communities that had not signed treaties with the government have still been able to meet the (changing) requirements for "federal recognition" as tribal nations. "Nation," here, although it is synonymous with "tribe," is not synonymous with "state"; as we shall see further, Native people typically think in terms of the *nation-people* rather than the *nation-state*. The "sovereign political entities" that Native nations were and continue to be were not and are not *states*.

As Charles Wilkinson and Sidney Harring have shown, there is a strong line of cases from Chief Justice John Marshall's well-known 1832 ruling in *Worcester v. Georgia*, through *Crow Dog* of 1883 and *Talton v. Mayes* of 1896, up to *Williams v. Lee* of 1959, among others, that clearly supports the view that Native peoples were and continue to be competent self-governing entities—that they are indeed sovereign. (There is, to be sure, a contrary set of rulings from the decision in *Corn Tassel* in 1830, to *Kagama* of 1886, which introduces the "plenary power doctrine," effectively granting Congress the power simply to do as it pleases with tribal nations.)[2] Extending the scope of their paradoxical condition as "dependent sovereigns" (cf. Resnik)—extending sovereignty—is the foremost political task Native nations face today.

Native people who identify themselves as Lakota, or Ho-Chunk, Mohawk, or Miwok, if they follow Means and Churchill and regard tribal membership as comparable to citizenship,[3] may be opposed to the idea of their citizens holding dual citizenship. Means and Churchill, for example, believe that citizens of the Lakota nation are not U.S. citizens, and U.S. citizens residing in Lakota territory have the status of resident aliens. They may apply for Lakota citizenship—which, if it is granted, will require them to renounce their U.S. citizenship.

That the terms employed by Means, Churchill, and many other nationalist critics—"sovereignty," "citizenship," or "nation," for example—are obviously European terms does not compromise the case being made or the very real stakes involved. As Craig Womack has forcefully reminded us, nationhood and sovereignty undoubtedly had their own indigenous forms before the arrival of the European invaders (17). And "Before the Europeans arrived," as Mark Trahant clearly puts it, "indigenous people governed themselves. It's that simple. It doesn't matter what the governments were called: A tribe, band, or pueblo. The fact is that a self-governing community was here first with a unique political framework" (3). Indeed, many of the court rulings acknowledge this "simple" fact.

But perhaps it is worth a pause here to note Gerald Vizenor's recent attempts to find a way a way around the European vocabulary, a way to

speak of Native sovereignty as distinct from "treaty sovereignty" or territorial sovereignty "in the sense of colonialism and nationalism." (1998 188
and 183) Vizenor offers the neologisms "sovenance" and "transmotion"
as terms that might substitute for the usual Euramerican vocabulary for
and conceptualization of issues of sovereignty. "Sovenance" is "the sense
of presence in remembrance, that trace of creation and natural reason
in native stories." As for "transmotion," "Native stories of survivance are
the creases of transmotion and sovereignty" (15). These two quotations
are the clearest I can find to define "sovenance" and "transmotion," although it will be apparent that "transmotion" is part of the definition
of "transmotion." This is often the case with Vizenor's neologisms, the
consequence of a determination always to keep meanings and possibilities open.

Although Vizenor is not, as we shall see further, a nationalist, the position he develops here does more or less resemble that of the cultural
nationalist. Stories, pictographs and maps, ledger book art, and the continuous history of Native presence on this continent (constituting a "narrative") are what testify to the sovereignty of Native peoples; it is Native
cultural integrity that underpins Indian claims to autonomy and political
self-determination.

I think this is not far different from Vine Deloria, Jr.'s earlier sense that
"inherent in their peculiar experience on this continent is hidden the
basic recognition of [the tribes'] power and sovereignty" (1970: 115). Thus
as Scott Richard Lyons, citing Deloria, affirms,

the making of political decisions by Indian people hasn't been the work of a
nation-state so much as that of a *nation-people*. The sovereignty of individuals and
the privileging of procedure are less important in the logic of a nation-people,
which takes as its supreme charge the sovereignty of the group through a privileging of its traditions and culture and continuity. (Lyons 455)

These latter are tied to "power from the *land*" (477).

But even when Native invocations of nationalism today *do* seem in
some measure "derivative of European nationalist ideologies" (Lazarus
85), they are nonetheless also marked by post-World War II anticolonial nationalism. And this sort of nationalism, as Neil Lazarus notes,
"merely by virtue of its specificity as anticolonial nationalism, [is] obliged
to go beyond" (85, my emphasis) the older nationalisms of Europe and
the U.S. Anticolonial nationalism, therefore, does not strictly imitate
nor does it (in the complex and antinationalist senses of Homi Bhabha) merely mimic European nationalism. Lazarus remarks that " 'the
people' "—Natives or indigenes—in anticolonial movements around the
world "could or would not have spoken the language of nationalism with-

out transforming it at least to some degree into a discourse capable of expressing their own [other-than-European] aspirations" (86). Indeed, as Partha Chatterjee writes, so far as it has been successful, anticolonial nationalism "produces a different discourse. . . . Its problematic forces it relentlessly to demarcate itself from the discourse of colonialism. Thus [anticolonial] nationalist thinking is necessarily a struggle with an entire body of systematic knowledge" (in Lazarus 86). It is this "struggle with an entire body of systematic knowledge" that will lead the anticolonial Native American nationalist to the indigenist who, as we shall see, defines her position precisely in terms of Other bodies of knowledge. And this "struggle" will also lead the anticolonial Native American nationalist as well to the cosmopolitan whose worldliness requires expertise in the translation of Other knowledges, what I shall further describe as anti-imperial translation.[4]

Native American nationalisms—there are many Native nations and as well a "pan-Indian" nationalism—differ from other nationalisms, as we have noted, in that they do not seek the creation of postcolonial states. The "twin pillars of sovereignty," as Scott Lyons writes, are "the power to self-govern and the affirmation of peoplehood" (456). This means a decrease in the "dependency" of Native nations on the federal government and a greater degree of "autonomy." But it is not clear just what political *forms* expanded sovereignty for the people—as the "agency that lays claim to a monopoly of decision-making power," the "single center of legitimate collective self-knowledge and self-control," and the sole possessor of "legitimate force" (Ree 87)—might actually take.[5]

As Rennard Strickland writes, "Sovereignty is not a state of salvation that magically erases all troubles. . . . Our challenge—the challenge of Indian law—is to forge the sword of sovereignty into a weapon capable of attacking the basic human problems of Indian people" (52). This "challenge" is currently being met in a variety of ways, but, inasmuch as my focus is on *critical* nationalism, I will, with all due apologies, excuse myself from the task of specifying these ways further here.

For Native American nationalist *criticism*, the attempt to extend the political meanings of sovereignty to the realm of culture—to Native literary expression—has also occasionally meant the assertion of a "sovereign" critical stance in the sense of an exclusivist or separatist stance. Thus, the Native artist-activist Loretta Todd writes,

In the modernist period, it was the lands and resources they sought; in the postmodern it is the experiences, the sensation they want. Nothing is authentic or autonomous, therefore everything is fair game. Couple this with a still-vague yearning for meaning and the past and what do you get? Most often, appropriation of "tribal" cultures throughout the world. (74)

To resist this, Cecil King, an Odawa, insists that Native people "be consulted and respected as not only human beings, at the very least, but as independent nations with the right to determine what transpires within our boundaries. We want to say who comes to our world, what they should see, hear, and take away" (118). Speaking to anthropologists, King does not seem to be recommending that anthropologists and those they wish to study consult as equals (what others have recommended), but, rather, that there occur a straightforward turning of the tables: where once *anybody* came, saw, heard, and took away whatever he or she pleased, now *We* will say who can come, "what they should see, hear, and take away." As a title of Vine Deloria's put it, for now, "We Talk, You Listen." (But Deloria has never been a separatist.)

King's position in relation to Native culture and non-Native anthropologists (Native anthropologists, I think, would also be subject to the We of the Tribal Council or Cultural Preservation or Intellectual Property Offices of a given Native nation) has been extended to literature as well, most powerfully of late in the subtitle of Craig Womack's book, *Red on Red, Native American Literary Separatism*. Separatism, indeed exclusionism, is the theme of the "dream" King reported in his talk. In his dream, King saw that

all the peoples of the world were together in one place. The place was cold. Everyone was shivering. . . . Then someone said that in the middle of the gathering of Indians, what was left of the fire had been found. It was a very, very small flame. . . . All the Indians banded together to protect the flame . . . adding minuscule shavings from small pieces of wood to feed it.

When others learn that the "The Indians have a fire," they rush toward it, claiming that "it was our responsibility to share the flame with them." To them, King replies,

"It is our responsibility to preserve the flame for humanity, and at the moment it is too weak to be shared, but if we are all still and protect the flame it will grow and thrive in the caring hands of those who hold it. In time we can all warm ourselves at the fire. But now we have to nurture the flame or we will all lose the gift." (119)

Maybe later; but assuredly not now. Perhaps, as Peter Whiteley has developed the matter, this does mean "the end of anthropology"—at Hopi and elsewhere. And perhaps—given the violence done to Native cultures then and now by anthropologists and by those, not only collectors and New Agers but literary scholars as well, who have followed after—it *is* time to leave the "flame" in the hands of the Indians. As Whiteley puts it, "if anthropologists are not interested in the fates of their subjects, then what use can their knowledge have, either to the community itself or to any genuine 'science of man'?" (197). But he also offers five propositions (we will consider them in detail in Chapter 3) which might restructure the relationship between researcher and researched. Nonetheless, it may perhaps be too late for consultation, at least "in the field"; perhaps, at least for a while, separation must be the order of the day.[6]

In any case, it seems to me that so far as any critical account of Native American literature would be anticolonial in its possible effect, that account at this historical juncture must acknowledge and legitimate invocations of the nation in opposition to oppression;[7] it cannot, therefore, stand apart from some form of nationalism. Here I need to repeat that nationalist positions also need other positions, those of indigenists (as persons with different bodies of systematic knowledge) and cosmopolitans (as persons who can translate between different bodies of knowledge), for their anticolonial projects to succeed (for them not to replicate colonialism under another name or to become "neurotic" entities).

Separatism, for literary studies as for all else, is hardly possible in the world today; were it possible, moreover, it would deprive itself of important opportunities. As Michael Geyer has written, "we paralyze ourselves by proscribing thought on humanity, because it has been the mainstay of a Eurocentric imaginary before" (526–27). As Frantz Fanon saw the matter, "national liberation . . . leads the nation to play its part on the stage of history" (in Lazarus 72; Fanon 247–48). "It is at the heart of national consciousness," Fanon insisted, "that international consciousness lives and grows." Rather than nationalism as separatism, it is important to theorize Fanon's alternative nationalism, a "liberationist, anti-imperialist, nationalist internationalism" (Lazarus 72), what Anouar Abdel-Malek has called a "nationalitarian" position. We shall take this up further in the discussion of cosmopolitanism below, and note that varieties of "thought on humanity" and "international consciousness" have been very much present beyond Europe: in Africa, in the Middle East and South Asia, and on the North American continent as well.

I will turn here to the particular sort of inquiries a nationalist orientation to the criticism of Native American literatures might advance with *sovereignty* at the center of its concerns. Most of the work I know has been with traditional oral narrative of a variety of types; some of this work is now being applied to written work in English by Native Americans.[8]

Because questions about sovereignty, as Elaine Jahner notes in a recent article, are "questions about the boundaries of communities," it has been possible to demonstrate the way in which communities use the transmission and reception of particular narratives[9] as a way of defining their distinctive, bounded identity. Examining Lakota Stone Boy narratives, Jahner shows how Lakota people assert their "communal identity" (6) by the transmission and reception of these stories over the years. The historical process of selecting certain stories and story versions rather than others is, in Jahner's words, itself "an exercise in sovereignty" (7), that is, the right to independence and self-governance as a nation or people. (This would seem very nearly an illustration of the sort of thing Vizenor, as cited above, has in mind.)

Craig Womack, studying Philip Deere's Creek migration story and Linda Alexander's Creek narrative of how turtle got his shell busted, draws conclusions similar to Jahner's. As Womack states it, "When Creek people assume they have the inherent right to interpret their own literature and history . . . they are setting themselves apart as a nation of people with distinctive worldviews that deserve to be taken seriously. This is an important exercise in sovereignty" (29). To borrow a phrase from Julie Cruikshank, Native communities "*negotiate* with narrative" to "establish . . . cultural identity," an identity that undergirds a particular sense of distinctiveness connected to a particular geoscape, and implies autonomy and a full capacity for self-governance. Storytelling, as Cruikshank makes clear, can be understood "as communication-based social action" (2000:155). She examines the way in which "each speaker" at the Yukon International Storytelling Festival, "structures his or her narrative to convey themes of identity by linking social institutions, land, and social history" (58). The sense of the "land" at issue here is, to be sure, spiritual, in a manner we shall soon consider, but it is also legal and political, involving "land ownership" (60) and control—*sovereignty*. In similar fashion, Womack's study of Alex Posey's Fus Fixico letters, a written literature mimetic of speech, shows how they, too, are political in ways that complement their expressive aspects rather than conflicting with them.[10]

Perhaps this is the place to repeat my sense that (as with Jahner and Cruikshank) the critic or ethnographer need not be a member of the nation in question in order to choose to foreground the issue of sovereignty as a process by which narrating communities define themselves, positioning herself, therefore, among the nationalists.

Let us now look briefly at nationalist preferences for the textual location of Native American literatures. Nationalists tend to see the inclusion of Native American texts in anthologies of *American* literature as appropriation; they would rather restrict them to anthologies of Native literature only, or, even better, collections of Lakota or Cherokee or Navajo texts. Craig Womack, consistent with his separatist approach, insists on opposing "an argument for inclusion . . . saying with all the bias I can muster that *our* American canon, the Native literary canon of the Americas, predates *their* American canon. I see them as two separate canons" (7). In view of a five-hundred-year history of contact, one may wonder about the *degree* of separation that Womack can actually "see" between Native canons, then or now, and the settler canon, less than two hundred years old and lately open to revision.

For all that I cannot support Womack's logic of "literary separatism," I can understand the importance of its rhetorical instantiation: inasmuch as the "spirit" or "essence" of a nation (to invoke a nineteenth-century construction which nonetheless retains a certain residual force today) is expressed through its literature, national sovereignty requires literary sovereignty—as, indeed, literary sovereignty ("our" canon is "separate" from "their" canon) can be taken as evidence of national sovereignty. This is a version of the cultural nationalist position I mentioned above.[11] (But Womack, unlike Vizenor, is a political nationalist as well; his nation is Creek.)

Nationalists do seem willing to permit Native American literatures to appear in anthologies of anticolonial "resistance literature," where nationalism as a force—as in Africa, the Indian subcontinent, and elsewhere—is specifically marshaled, although they are concerned—with good reason—lest the very particular nature of Native American resistance be obscured by such comparativism.

Regarding institutional locations for pedagogy, nationalists are leery of Native literatures being taught in the context of general American literature courses or surveys, most likely to be offered by departments of English or American studies in the United States. They would reserve the teaching of Native literature to courses like "The Oral Tradition," "Contemporary Native Fiction and Poetry," or, again, "Indigenous Resistance," most likely to be offered by Native Studies or American Indian Studies departments or programs. Better yet would be courses in "Lakota Literature" or "Navajo Literature," and perhaps best would be these courses as taught in the tribal colleges, where instruction would proceed in a manner consistent with a particular institution's understanding of the Lakota or Navajo "way" or worldview.

As for critical methods, nationalists are again wary of "foreign" perspectives of the sort likely to be employed by cosmopolitan critics. Following the lead of Elizabeth Cook-Lynn, nationalists insist upon "Reference to the body of nationalistic myths, legends, metaphors, symbols, historical persons and events, writers and their writings [as forming] the basis of the critical discourse that functions in the name of the people; the presence of the Indian nation as cultural force [as] a matter of principle" (Cook-Lynn 84–85). Although this may at first appear clear, even self-evident, I think, rather, that it is badly confused. This is to say that "the Indian nation as cultural force" is not a "presence" that may be discovered in any given text. Rather, it must be determined *which* cultural "forces" in expressive forms—"myths, legends, metaphors"—might be said to operate in a manner consistent with what is today meant by "the Indian nation"—unless, of course, one categorically insists that *anything* Lakota "functions in the name of the people," that *all* things Lakota of ne-

cessity assert "the presence of the Indian nation as cultural force." Even
were one to grant this, it still seems unlikely to be the case that *all* Lakota
"writers and their writings," *all* Lakota "historical persons and events" of
necessity function as "cultural force[s]" specifically affirming the people
and the nation. (And there are dangers, as a number of writers have
pointed out, in treating the "people" or the "nation" as a unitary force
or indivisible essence.)

Womack cites this passage of Cook-Lynn's approvingly, although his
formulation of the matter is more clear. For Womack, the most important thing in any approach to Native literatures "should be a study of
the primary culture that produces them" (25). Here, one might ask—as
also with Cook-Lynn—whether culture and nation are synonymous, or
whether one precedes or determines the other. Womack reasonably suggests that a particular body of Native oral and written materials "must
surely provide models for interpretation and principles of literary esthet-
ics" (76), that criticism should be text- or performance-specific. And, indeed, his own studies of Creek literature have importantly begun to indicate just what those "models" and "principles" might be. Nonetheless,
it is necessary to point out that the "models" or "principles" any "body"
of "materials" may provide are not inherent in those materials. Critical
models and principles are constructs; like so much else, they are the conjunctural products of an encounter between an individual mind and a
cultural corpus. Womack has in the past expressed exasperation with observations such as this, seeing them as hairsplitting designed to miss or
evade the force of his point. To the contrary, however, one can only offer
such observations when one has taken his point with nothing less than
the utmost seriousness.

*   *   *

From an indigenist perspective, it is not the nation, but the "earth" that
is the source of the values on which a critical perspective must be based.
Thus, in Linda Hogan's novel *Power* (1998), Omishto, the narrator, re-
members a time when "The whole earth loved the human people" (229).
Power concludes with Omishto dancing, while "someone sings the song
that says the world will go on living" (235). The "world," here, is obviously
not the world of nations and nationalisms; rather, it is the animate and
sentient earth. Indigenists look to a particular relation to the earth as
underlying a worldview that can be called traditional or tribal. It is this
worldview that determines one's perspective on literature as on all else,
often regardless of national allegiances or statuses (e.g., whether one is
or is not a "citizen" of a particular Native nation or one of the people;
whether one's community has greater or lesser amounts of sovereignty).

These are the "local knowledges" or ethnic epistemes ("ethnicities") that daily and immediately "struggle with an entire body of systematic knowledge" (Chatterjee in Lazarus 86, and above), and it is these knowledges that give to nationalism its values and that underpin a *different* politics. If it should be the case, as Michael Geyer somberly observes, that "Beyond any metaphysics of place, Western practices effectively and pragmatically constitute global norms" (524), the burden on these knowledges and the politics to which they give rise is substantial indeed.

Winona Stevenson, a Cree woman, has recently quoted her mother as saying to her, "You are of this land, you are Indigenous, and that's what makes you different from everybody else" (37)—from "ethnic" persons or other Canadians, that is to say. Ward Churchill explains his indigenism as founded "upon the traditions—the bodies of knowledge and corresponding codes of values—evolved over many thousands of years by native peoples the world over" (403). The late Michael Dorris suggested that "a shared consciousness, an inherently identifiable world-view" would have to exist among Native peoples for the general category of "Native American literature" to exist. Quoting Dorris, Louis Owens writes that today, "in spite of the fact that Indian authors write from very diverse tribal and cultural backgrounds, there *is* to a remarkable degree a shared consciousness and identifiable worldview reflected in novels by American Indian authors" (1992: 20, my emphasis).[12] And José Barreiro affirms that "the principles that guide Native cultures bear a remarkable resemblance to one another" (in Whitt 225). These "principles," "bodies of knowledge," and "codes of value," this "shared consciousness" and "worldview," as I have noted, are said to derive from the special relationship to the land that indigenous peoples everywhere are presumed to share—again, regardless of their political relation to the dominant settler states that surround them.

In these regards, we may consider another quotation from Stevenson that is typical of indigenist discourse. She writes that indigenous people "are spiritually attached to [a particular] place . . . we never left the bones of our ancestors behind. Every hill, mountain, river, coulee, and forest has ancient stories that tell us how we are related to it and to each other" (42).

The latter part of Stevenson's statement, as Keith Basso has shown for the Western Apache and others have shown for other peoples, would seem to be accurate—although, as Cruikshank has made clear, land ownership "claims made by adjacent First Nations inevitably overlap, forcing communities into competition with one another" (2000: 53). This is to say that the "ancient stories" a mountain, river, or hill may tell one Native narrating community may not be exactly the same story it tells another.

Meanwhile, the first part of Stevenson's statement can only be true, in point of fact, for long-time residents of northeast Africa. Although *they* might literally claim "never" to have "left the bones of [their] ancestors behind," the historical record indicates that almost everyone has come from somewhere else (indeed, from *there*). Thus the question—a highly political question—arises of just how long it takes to *become* indigenous. In Hawai'i, for example, some claim indigenousness after seven generations of residence, while others would require 150. In the southwest, the Hopi claim to indigenousness rests on a presence dating back some hundred generations. But Navajo people in place for perhaps thirty generations can hardly imagine themselves as anything but indigenous to the landscape they know so well, and to which they are "spiritually attached."

Considerations of this sort would make indigenousness as defined by literal relation to landscape more difficult to achieve for those Native writers who grew up in the cities, or far from the home-places of their people. I note this not to impugn anyone's claim to indigenousness, but only to indicate the complexities of the issue—and to suggest that some indigenists (along with some nationalists) could equally well be called "cosmopolitan patriots," an apparently oxymoronic category proposed by Kwame Anthony Appiah, to which we shall return. All three of the positions I have named are imbricated, but this observation should in no way be thought to undermine the distinctive and necessary claim of the nationalists to speak on behalf of the sovereignty of native nations, nor of the indigenists to speak on behalf of those whose knowledge *differs.*

Indigenists base their politics on the epistemology and ethics of their geocentric worldview.[13] As Arif Dirlik has written, the indigenist's

insistence on a special relationship to the land as the basis for indigenous identity is not merely spiritual, an affirmation of an ecological sensibility, . . . [it] also calls for a transformation of the spatial arrangements of colonialism or postcolonialism. Indigenism . . . challenges . . . the system of economic relations that provides the ultimate context for social and political relationships: capitalist or state socialist. (21)

Indigenist geogenic knowledge, as I have said, may thus contribute to the nationalist's "struggle with an entire body of knowledge"—the knowledge that sustains colonialism—and provide a basis on which to construct both an-Other discourse and, as Dirlik claims, an-Other set of "social and political relations." It is the combination of indigenous "local knowledge" and the knowledge produced by turning a European-derived nationalism against colonialism that gives to Native nationalism its positivity, rendering it more than a force against or in-reaction-to. And just as the nationalist needs the indigenist for her anticolonial project, so, too, does the indigenist need the nationalist, for it is only in terms of the nation that "the spatial arrangements of colonialism or postcolonialism" can be transformed in such a way as to respond to local needs.

Non-Natives will not, of course, be able to claim an "indigenous identity," but some may indeed serve to help expound indigenous understandings. I return, here, to Peter Whiteley's sense—he is speaking specifically of Hopi people, but his remarks pertain more broadly—that "what is badly needed in ethnographic description are Hopi perspectives—social, cultural, critical, historical, ecological, and so on" (in Biolsi and Zimmerman 195). Rather than just "speaking for" Hopis, "anthropologists should start explaining to their audience, in a socially constructive way, how Hopis situate, evaluate, and feel about their actions in contemporary perspective"; and, regarding Hopi ritual, Whiteley's specific subject, they should convey to their audience "why privacy needs to be respected, why many accounts of ritual are subversive, and that Hopis want members of the dominant society to appreciate and learn from Hopi practice but without desecrating it" (196).

As we shall discuss the matter in Chapter 3, this will involve complex acts of *translation* of a sort that can lead to the radical *transformation* of the translator's own sense of his or her "proper" speech or "native language." I am suggesting—with full awareness of a certain utopianism or overreach—that the non-Native who begins by learning to understand the language and so the knowledge of another and who then attempts to "explain" it by translation, may occasionally or partly find his own tongue changed by it. This sort of translation, what I have several times called anti-imperial translation, is very different from acts of translation historically, which, as Eric Cheyfitz has powerfully shown, have been acts of appropriation. If an older universalism once engaged in imperial translation, perhaps a newer cosmopolitanism may engage in anti-imperial translation.

Outside a postcolonial, *responsible* anthropology, although by no means independent of it, we may also note the extraordinary development of "ecocriticism." Ecocritics may be persons with no claim to indigenousness as an identity but who nonetheless work from a deep sense of what David Abrams names the sensuous "surround"[14] as a source of vision and value. And we shall later speak of that cosmopolitanism which has shifted from an emphasis on "world citizenship" to an emphasis on world humanity or an ethics of earth, what Richard Falk calls "globalization-from-below" (59). This, as already will be apparent, is in no way a cosmopolitanism committed to overriding indigenous knowledges.

Indigenists would probably disperse Native literary expression among anthologies and departmental or institutional locations. Fourth and Fifth World anthologies comprising literature from indigenous persons around the globe would be suitable, in their eyes, for Native literature, or anthologies like *The Indigenous Voice*.[15] Like many nationalists, indigenists would also include Native literary expression in anthologies of "resistance" literature, foregrounding epistemological difference and value rather than the national category. But, again, this is a matter of emphasis. The nationalist struggle for power is a struggle for power in the interest of a different kind of life, based—to say this yet once more—on different understandings, and, as noted above, this different kind of life can only express itself at the level of the people, whatever (nonstatist) political form Native nation-peoples of the twenty-first century may construct in order to materialize an expanded sovereignty.

As for courses in which Native literatures might best appear, indigenists might offer such things as "Epistemological Pluralism," "Nonanthropocentrism," or "Environmental Ethics."[16] So far as critical methods are concerned, indigenists would turn to a number of recent efforts to consider such matters as how and to what degree language use in the English texts of some Native writers might parallel usage in tribal languages— this, of course, for writers who speak or know a tribal language. Or how imagery and description in a given text—its reference to colors, numbers, plants, animals—might reflect specifics of one or another traditional culture. Similarly, texts by Native writers have begun to be examined to see whether and how their constructions of the self or person, the family or community, or, indeed, the meaning and function of gift giving and exchange[17] might derive in significant measure from traditional, indigenous understandings of these matters. Julie Cruikshank's *Life Lived like a Story: Life Stories of Three Yukon Native Elders* is a model of such work with contemporary traditional people.

*   *   *

Just as Winona Stevenson's mother encouraged her to "remember that you are of this land," so did Kwame Anthony Appiah's father urge his children to "Remember that you are citizens of the world" (1997: 91), a cosmopolitan perspective. The "world" invoked by contemporary cosmopolitans has a long history, going back to strands of the Classical and early Christian traditions as these are revived in the Renaissance and substantially developed in Enlightenment thought.

Before going further, it must be noted that Anthony Appiah and his father, of course, encountered concepts of the "world" in their own part of it, in Asante, and we must note the existence of what might be called comparative cosmopolitanisms, the development of concepts like worldliness, universality, and internationalism apart from or prior to Europe's. I am thinking in particular of Amitav Ghosh's *In an Antique Land*, which tells of commercial relations, friendships, and rivalries from the twelfth century among South Asians and Egyptians, Jews, and North Africans, among others in the Indian Ocean trade—until the early sixteenth century when the Portuguese arrived and "declared a proprietorial right over the Indian Ocean: since none of the peoples who lived around it had thought to claim ownership of it before their arrival"(288). Many of these people surely must have been, in a variety of ways, cosmopolitans before Europe.

And I am thinking of Barry O'Connell's sense "that indigenous peoples in North America might very likely have developed their own forms of the cosmopolitan." O'Connell cites the "extensive trading networks . . . that connected many different cultures not only within geographic regions but across vast distances." He adds that

In at least some parts of the country affiliation to a political entity was by choice so that people at least sometimes seem to have moved from one political unit to another. . . . Crossing cultural lines had to have happened and even though the number of "cosmopolitans" may have been small, they surely existed as mediators, traders, translators, etc. (personal communication, 4/4/01)

A great deal of further work is needed on this subject, work that is necessary to contextualize what I roughly present here, an account—lengthy enough and yet sketchy nonetheless[18]—of cosmopolitanism's history in Europe and the United States.

The Classical origins of cosmopolitanism derive not from Aristotle's chauvinist ethnocentrism but from Cynics and Stoics—from Diogenes, for example, who claimed that his true *polis* was the *cosmos*, making him *cosmou polites*, a citizen of the world. Thomas Schlereth's observation that "Stoicism . . . became a response to an immense world in which the insulation of the small city-state was stripped away and individuals had to come to terms with and find a place in an enormously enlarged environment" (xviii) seems applicable to the situation of individuals in many of the nation-states of the world today. Cosmopolitanism in the ancient world, however, also derives from Alexander the Great (said to have visited Diogenes), thus linking world citizenship to world conquest or imperialism, a linkage which we shall note also persists today in what Michael Geyer calls "corporate globalism" (525) and Richard Falk terms "globalization-from-above" (59) or "negative cosmopolitanism" (60). In the Christian tradition, Augustine's cosmopolitanism bases itself on the recognition that all are citizens of the "City of God"; we are all brothers and sisters in Adam, and we may be brothers and sisters in Christ.

It is in part the discovery of the "new world" in the fifteenth century that provokes or enables a revival of cosmopolitanism. As in the time of Rome (and in our own day), sudden and substantially increased local awarenesses that the world is very large and nearer at hand than one had thought tends to lead, on the one hand, to defending the primacy of Us (cf. *The Tempest* and today, in another register, the Ku Klux Klan), and, on the other, to great curiosity about Them. Important figures in Renaissance cosmopolitanism are Pico della Mirandola, Erasmus, Francis Bacon —Benjamin Franklin's idol in envisioning a worldwide brotherhood of science—and Montaigne, one of the "fathers" of anthropological cultural relativism (cf. his essay "On the Cannibals"). Eighteenth-century cosmopolitans thus were, as Schlereth has noted, already a third generation. Perhaps there already was a tradition of cosmopolitanism in America as well; Scott Lyons speaks of "the Haudenosaunee or Iroquois League" as a "more cosmopolitan example of a nation-people," quoting Oren Lyons, who writes that the "Haudenosaunee were—and remain—a multicultural nation-people" (Lyons 455).

As the nineteenth century approaches, Rousseau will champion love of country as a virtue against a cosmopolitanism already fading as "an overly intellectualized and philosophically abstract political norm" (Schlereth 111)—as, of course, some still regard it today. In the nineteenth century, European nationalisms overwhelm the cosmopolitan ideal (as twentieth-century nationalisms would as well), urging a movement, in David Hollinger's phrase, "from species to ethnos" (51) and, significantly, from culture to race. The racialization of the nation (*natio*, to be born) as a filiative entity of blood-brothers and -sisters, is a major development of nineteenth- century Europe and America, whose legacy retains potency in the present. (We will examine some of the workings of "Indian blood" in *Cogewea* in Chapter 4, and of "race" in *Indian Killer* in Chapter 5.)

But the United States has always been a civic not a *volkisch* nation; to speak of "my fellow Americans" is to speak of an affiliative aggregation of (to borrow the terms of the French Revolution) *citoyens* and *citoyennes*. Even in the United States, however, the nineteenth century was not especially hospitable to cosmopolitanism. Noah Webster's dictionary, published in 1828 (the year of Andrew Jackson's election to the presidency as champion of the "West" and conqueror of "savage" Indians), defines "cosmopolitan" in negatives only: "the cosmopolitan 'has no fixed residence' and is 'nowhere a stranger'" (in Bryant 280). Nonetheless, in the writing of Thoreau, in that of Herman Melville, and, it should be noted, in the work of the Pequot preacher William Apess on behalf of an anti-racist union of Christian fellowship, a universalist or cosmopolitan light still shines.

Cosmopolitanism was kept alive in mid-nineteenth-century Europe in Marx's appeal to the workers of the world, and—to select one important instance—it makes a return, later in the century, under the sign of the *intellectual*. The intellectual, Ross Posnock notes, was an "offense" to the nationalist. Intellectual was the name given in France, in 1898, to "those like Zola, who dared speak for universal rather than French values during the hysterical chauvinism unleashed by the Dreyfus trial" (1997: 324). The long-standing charge against the cosmopolitan, that she was rootless and so potentially a betrayer of the nation, was now leveled at intellectuals like Zola, who understood their loyalties to be to the republic of justice first, and to the French or any other nation only afterward. Suspicion about the cosmopolitan's relation to a nation-state, or, indeed, a nation-*people* and its claim to sovereignty, persists today.

Here I want briefly to return to Anthony Appiah's construction, "cosmopolitan patriotism," which I called an apparent oxymoron above. This is because Appiah's understanding of patriotism separates it from nationalism. For him, patriotism is a "*sentiment*" that, unlike nationalism, "can be made consistent with different political ideologies" (1997:619, my emphasis). He writes that his father, Joe Appiah, believed that "there was no point to roots if you couldn't take them with you" (618). And Joe Appiah's son, Kwame Anthony Appiah, believes that one *can* "be cosmopolitan—celebrating the variety of human cultures; [*and*] rooted—loyal to one society (or a few) that you count as home" (633). Again, this loyalty is patriotic but it is not nationalistic.

Appiah's particular loyalty or patriotism is to a society that encourages us "to love our country as the embodiment of principles, as a means to the attainment of moral ends," that might "enable a certain kind of human freedom" (1997: 628), in particular, the "form of freedom" invented by the French and American revolutions. But similar social principles, says Appiah, have "roots in Asante" (636), the society that he and his father "count as home" (633). Yet if patriotism is tied to place only as place is committed to *principle*, then "patriotism" hardly needs to be reconciled with cosmopolitanism because it has already been defined *as* cosmopolitanism—even the intellectual cosmopolitanism of Zola, as I have construed his position. Appiah's cosmopolitan patriot is loyal to the principle first and to the "home place" only as it embodies or adheres to that principle. This sort of love of country is not what one usually means by "patriotism"—although it is exactly what one has to mean by it if one is, in fact, to see it as consistent with a cosmopolitan position. Appiah's father— and Appiah himself?—can only be a "rooted cosmopolitan," or a "cosmopolitan patriot" because he believes the place or places to which he is loyal are places that "enable . . . certain kind[s] of human freedom." Would Native persons loyal to other principles embodied or adhered to in other places also qualify as cosmopolitan patriots? Would it be better to call them simply cosmopolitans? Might they not also be indigenists? If they are loyal to their nation right or wrong, then they are obviously nationalists—or patriots in the narrow sense of the term.

Patriots and nationalists who are loyal to their country even when its principles do not "enable . . . certain kind[s] of human freedom," may tend to be scornful of cosmopolitans who can only be selectively patriotic. And yet, in my view, cosmopolitans will probably find themselves supporting not only nationalitarian forms of nationalism, but also—if warily— most nationalisms directed against an oppressive colonial order. Being on the left, as Albert Memmi has described it, like being cosmopolitan as I have described it, "means not only accepting and assisting the national liberation of the peoples, but also includes political democracy and freedom, economic democracy and justice, rejection of racist xenophobia and universality, material and spiritual progress" (34).

In supporting nationalist movements, Memmi continues, leftists, like cosmopolitans, must understand that we are "perhaps aiding the birth of a social order in which there is no room for a leftist as such, at least in the near future"(34).[19] Nonetheless, I believe leftists and cosmopolitans must choose what Richard Rorty has called the principle of solidarity, a political morality, over the epistemological morality of objectivity. As Tobin Siebers glosses these terms, "we can support the truth"—or what we believe to be the truth—"or we can support our neighbor. To choose the first is to be objective; to choose the second is to support solidarity" (47). Cosmopolitans will choose solidarity knowing full well that those whom we have chosen to support may not always be overjoyed to find us marching with them.

But this is because cosmopolitans also understand, as Richard Falk makes clear, that to believe there can be a simple distinction between nationalism and cosmopolitanism today "inevitably overlooks the originality of our political circumstances in the late twentieth century—an originality that makes both poles problematic" (Falk 54) In the early twenty-first century, the "original" or special condition of "our political circumstances" is the predominance of "regional and global market forces" operating as "a structural and defining attribute of the current phase of international history" (55). Thus, as Falk unsentimentally acknowledges,

To project a visionary cosmopolitanism as an alternative to nationalist patriotism without addressing the subversive challenge of the market-driven globalism currently being promoted by transnational corporations and banks, as well as currency dealers and casino capitalists [!?!] is to risk indulging a contemporary form of fuzzy innocence. (57)

But surely the nationalist patriot must also not indulge in innocent visions either.

In much the same way, Immanuel Wallerstein comments that

What is needed . . . is not to learn that we are citizens of the world, but that we occupy particular niches in an unequal world, and that being disinterested and global [cosmopolitan?] on one hand and defending one's narrow interests [national?] on the other are not opposites but positions combined in complicated ways. Some combinations are desirable [to "help create a more democratic, egalitarian world"], others are not. Some are desirable here but not there, now but not then. Once we have learned this we can begin to cope intelligently with our social reality. (124)

In these regards, Falk continues,

extensions of cosmopolitan democracy suggest a possible reconciliation of nationalism and cosmopolitanism. If global economic governance structures are reoriented to express a kind of equilibrium between market-oriented (globalization-from-above) and people-oriented (globalization-from-below), then it is possible that political space will be recreated to enable the reemergence of the humane state. (Falk 59)

Or, as in the Native American struggle for sovereignty, some Other polity expressive of the nation-people rather than the nation-state. This once more seems to mean that cosmopolitans and nationalists will have to make common cause. For, as Neil Lazarus has written, "it is only on the terrain of the nation that an articulation between cosmopolitan intellectualism and popular consciousness can be forged" (91). Cosmopolitans and nationalists will—it must be repeated—thus join with indigenists: because it is only through local knowledges that "popular consciousness" can express itself. Cosmopolitan techniques of anti-imperial translation are necessary to engage with "popular consciousness," and cosmopolitanism, in this reading, is the critical perspective that is foremost concerned with fulfilling the "potentialities of both nationalism and radical intellectualism" (Lazarus 92).

*   *   *

At the most basic level, cosmopolitan perspectives on Native American literatures read them in relation to other minority or subaltern literatures elsewhere in the late-colonial or postcolonial world; cosmopolitan criticism must always in some degree be comparative. With traditional oral performance, for example, the cosmopolitan critic, like the rigorous nationalist, will insist upon the need to develop competence in the particular language from which the text of the original performance derives and the culture that formed and received that performance. The cosmopolitan critic, thus, would not dispute Craig Womack's observation that Creek literature derives from a "geographically specific Creek landscape and the language and stories that are born out of that landscape" (20). But the cosmopolitan critic might also wish to understand things about Creek (or Ho-Chunk or Tuscarora or Wendat) literature that could only be answered by *informed* comparison with other texts or traditional performances—in particular, those of tribal neighbors (to whom the landscape, as we have noted, may tell other stories) or of tribal peoples in a variety of landscapes (and with similar and different histories). For the earliest Native American written literature—autobiographies, novels, poetry—the cosmopolitan critic will attempt to allow the text to stand, in Barry O'Connell's title for his fine edition of the writings of William Apess, on its "own ground," without failing to consider relevant texts that are similarly and differently grounded.

The postcolonial perspective seems especially promising for the written literature of some indigenous peoples over the last thirty-some years. It might prove fruitful, for example, to examine the ways in which Native nationalism—a nationalism, as we have noted, that does not seek to express itself in the form of a state but that does link specific land claims and a people's experience to principles of sovereignty—operates differently or perhaps in some regards similarly in resisting colonial force to other anticolonial nationalisms elsewhere.

The cosmopolitan critic, as I have noted, can agree with Womack in believing that criticism of Native literatures "should be a study of the *primary* culture that produces them" (20, my emphasis), without, however, sharing his separatist conclusion that studying the effect of the meeting between that "primary culture" and other cultures is of little concern. Womack's distinction between "*our* canon" and "*their* canon," I must repeat, is hardly clear after five hundred years of contact.

Gerald Vizenor has explored the possibilities of Native cosmopolitanism in his fiction and criticism, celebrating the once pitied, or despised "halfbreed" as the "mixedblood" or "crossblood," and transforming the lowly "mongrel" into a hero of comic invention.[20] In a similar spirit, Louis Owens writes that his own important study of contemporary Native American fiction, *Other Destinies*, is "For mixedbloods, the next generation." I might also cite W. S. Penn, who subtitled his recent collection of autobiographical essays, *As We Are Now*, "mixblood essays on race and identity." These Native writers—along with Patricia Penn Hilden, Diane Glancy, Wendy Rose, Leslie Marmon Silko (in *Almanac of the Dead* and, now, *Gardens in the Dunes*), and Sherman Alexie (on alternate days[21]), among others—are all exploring different constructions of (to take a term once more from Vizenor) "post-Indian"[22] culture and politics.

Might this post-Indianness be seen as a form of cosmopolitan patriotism in that post-Indians are loyal to the principle of the collective good of the people (rather than "human freedom"), and to the principles Vizenor has called "continuance" and "survivance" wherever they may be found or carried? Although Craig Womack is a Creek in Canada who insightfully discusses Joy Harjo as a Creek in Arizona, I think Womack would consider himself and Harjo as nationalists away from home rather than cosmopolitan patriots. But obviously the distinctions can get very fine at this level of inquiry.

Sherman Alexie, as I have noted, has mocked mixedblood identification as fussy and pretentious; an Indian is an Indian, Alexie has said—and an Indian, as we shall see further, is not a Native American. Louis Owens and Gerald Vizenor have more than once been Alexie's targets; and yet the mixedbloods in their books are nothing if not Indian. Womack sensibly wonders whether "identifying as mixedblood, rather than as a part of a tribal nation, diminishes sovereignty" (in Penn 32). But Alexie, as we shall see, is neither tribal nor, in the usual meanings of the term, nationalist.

Vizenor's post-Indian mixedbloods, however, have values that are tribal (indigenist?) but not national. This tribalism, we might say, is "traditional" rather than traditional, with the inverted commas signaling a self-consciousness in the former that the latter, by definition, does not possess. Womack has defined contemporary Native traditionalism—what I have written as "traditionalism"—as "anything that is useful to Indian people in retaining their values and worldviews no matter how much it deviates from what people did one or two hundred years ago" (42).

Womack is trying to shift the balance of opinion that once (but not for well over half a century!) took anything that deviated "from what people did one or two hundred years ago" as evidence of a tragic fall from the traditional. But, as Marshall Sahlins has pointed out, " 'tradition' often appears in modern history as a *culturally specific mode of change*" (1995: 380, my emphasis). After first encountering invaders from more complex societies, Sahlins writes, "The first commercial impulse of the people is not to become just like us but more like themselves" (388), and the indigenization of modernity on the part of small-scale societies around the globe has been well documented. Nonetheless, as Sahlins continues, the advent of the colonial state interrupts and alters the possibilities of experiencing change as continuity. In Antonio Gramsci's useful distinction, the question is whether *dominance* has also achieved *hegemony*, the internalization on the part of the colonized of the worldview of the colonizer. In a great many cases—many of them quite surprising cases—it has turned out that peoples suffering intensive dominance have still managed to keep "their values and worldviews," in Womack's phrase, remarkably intact.

And yet Womack's "no matter how much" is troublesome; past a certain point, deviations from what people did a hundred years ago are simply too great to be "useful" "in retaining [older] values and worldviews." One cannot say "no matter how much," for too much will no longer enrich "native self-conceptions" (Sahlins 1995: 386) or be consistent even with traditionalism-as-change. Meanwhile, it does seem to me that the mixed-blood Indian characters in the work of a number of authors (Vizenor, Penn, Hilden, Glancy, Alexie, Owens, and others I haven't mentioned) are still best spoken of as Indians—I am agreeing here with Womack, in spite of his "no matter how much"—rather than as figures of hybridity. We will return to this issue in Chapter 5.

Critics both Native and non-Native who work from the cosmopolitan perspective can, like the nationalists, fully acknowledge the importance of the issue of sovereignty in the political struggle of colonized peoples all over the world and at home. Anticolonial cosmopolitans, as I have several times indicated, will wholeheartedly support nationalitarian nationalists, and, although somewhat warily, they—we—will also, in the name of solidarity, likely support (most of) those who instantiate the nation as synonymous with the people, both of which are aligned against colonialism. In the same way, cosmopolitans both Native and non-Native will also support indigenists whose traditional, place-specific values and principles constitute the local knowledge, the epistemological basis for an Other discourse, to be used against "the entire system" of colonial knowledge. (I argue for the value of indigenous Native historiography in Chapter 3.) The cosmopolitan critic knows that a commitment to sovereignty, the home place, and the oral and written traditions of their tribal nations are "roots" that all or almost all Native American writers will choose to carry wherever they may travel, or indeed, wherever they may dwell.

Cosmopolitans wish to see Native American literatures not appropriated by but *included* in anthologies of American literature. Cosmopolitans would also site Native literatures in resistance anthologies which would add to the category of national resistance to colonialism writing expressive of the resistance of incarcerated persons, of gays and lesbians, or people in concentration or internment camps—any literature directed against oppression and dominance. (I have noted the legitimate concern of nationalists and indigenists that such expansion might obscure the very particular situation of colonized Native peoples around the world. They are wary—with good reason—of any universalizing of resistance.)

As for pedagogical location, cosmopolitans would disperse the instruction of Native American literatures widely among departments of English, American Literature, American Studies, Cultural Studies, American Indian Studies, and Native American Studies. Although anthropology's history as the handmaiden of colonialism is well known, that history is not binding on the present, as it need not be on the future. Cosmopolitans, although fully aware of the animus against anthropology still expressed by any number of Native writers today, can nonetheless support the teaching of Native American literatures in departments of anthropology (at least in some departments of anthropology) in courses like "Representation and Self-Representation," "Ethnography and Literature," or "Postcolonial Literatures."[23]

Cosmopolitans of every sort can agree with indigenists on the importance of reading and teaching Native American texts—Black Elk and John Neihardt's *Black Elk Speaks*, N. Scott Momaday's *The Way to Rainy Mountain*, Leslie Marmon Silko's *Ceremony* and *Almanac of the Dead*, the poems of Simon Ortiz, Linda Hogan's *Solar Storms* and *Power*, among many others—which forcefully present non-Western worldviews. Cosmopolitans are interested in exploring how "seeing with the Native eye"[24] might relativize Western perspectives and whether or how that might alter aspects of Western epistemology and ethics. Cosmopolitan criticism is, in these many regards, what I have elsewhere called "ethnocriticism," and, as I have said here, it is importantly dependent on attempts at anti-imperial translation.

A cosmopolitan ethnocriticism will not rule out a priori any methodology because of its race, gender, or national origin. Recognizing the primary need to attend to the terms and categories Native people use for themselves, the cosmopolitan critic may nonetheless carefully draw upon "structuralism," or "deconstruction," Marx, Freud, Bakhtin, or feminism(s) for insights into a Native American text. Without doubt, the application—one might well say *imposition*—of these "Western" or foreign perspectives to Native texts can be yet one more instance of colonialism directed against the Native. This danger is very real. Several recent writers have noted the possibility of a second erasure of Native agency in this respect, in Julie Cruikshank's words, "first by colonial forces, then by post-colonial analyses" (2000:139), ostensibly sympathetic to Natives but quite careless of their actual desires. But this is only to say yet again that cosmopolitan criticism must be open to the work of indigenists as much as to the work of nationalists if it is genuinely to be responsible.

Chapter 2
On the Translation of Native American Song and Story

A Theorized History

For Brian Swann

This chapter reprints an essay published ten years ago in Brian Swann's edited volume *On the Translation of Native American Literatures.* After a good deal of reflection, I decided to leave it in its original form with only this prefatory note to serve as an explanation of that decision. As the preceding chapter should have made clear, translation in the figurative mode that I have called anti-imperial translation is of particular concern to the cosmopolitan critic. This concern brings the cosmopolitan critic into regular contact with the indigenist whose knowledge can relativize and even destabilize the knowledges that support imperialism, thus helping to clear a field for the liberatory efforts of the nationalitarian or nationalist critic.

In Chapter 3, I examine on their own terms and also offer some figurative translation of Native American histories into the "language" of Euramerican discourses of history. Here, however, the translation I historicize and theorize is literal translation in its work with literary material, "Native American song and story." Although written before this book was conceived, and so not as closely linked to the other chapters of this book as they are each to another, this chapter, it is my hope, nonetheless has useful work to do in regard to this book as a whole.

*   *   *

Any history of translations from the various Native American languages into English—a history also necessarily of transcription, of the transformation of oral literatures into textual literatures—must have some theoretical principle guiding its selection of examples. The most obvious principle (usually thought of by those who actually seek to apply it as the disinterested avoidance of aprioristic principle) is, of course, the principle of nonselectivity, or total inclusiveness: with world enough and time, one *might* produce the history of translations from Native languages by attempting to collect *every* translation extant. While such an encyclopedic project for most other subjects would, today, painfully recall the deluded efforts of George Eliot's Casaubon or Flaubert's Bouvard and Pecuchet, for our particular subject, it might, in point of fact, be almost manageable, the "facts" of the case, unfortunately, being so many fewer. But even were such a history to be produced—and it would, doubtless, be a valuable resource—it would still leave open the question, What to make of all these examples of various kinds?

My own attempt to sketch the history of translations of Native American literary expression will not even gesture in the direction of exhaustiveness. Instead, as a guiding principle for the examination of translations of Native American literatures from their earliest appearance until the present (and I don't pretend to know all of these), but also, potentially, for the examination as well of translations which do not as yet exist, I will suggest that all translations must situate themselves in relation to the principles of Identity and Difference (Sameness and Otherness, Likeness and Unlikeness, Ours and Theirs)—which principles, in any given translation, manifest themselves in terms of *accessibility* and *authenticity*, as these situate the particular translation in the disciplinary domain of art or of (social) science.

This is to say that Euramericans, to transcribe and translate Native American verbal expression, must assume that it is in some degree *like* Euramerican ("Western") literary expression (otherwise it would not be recognizable to "us" *as* literary art) but also that it is in some degree *unlike* Euramerican ("Western") literary expression (otherwise it would not take the obvious into account, that it is transmitted orally, in non-Indo-European languages, frequently in ritual or ceremonial performances, and so on). Western divisions of disciplinary labor have traditionally been such that the poets and novelists or literary critics are usually in charge of that which is *like* the literature we know, while the anthropologists and linguists have usually been in charge of that which is *unlike* what we know. In every case, it is my claim, all English translations from Native language performances cannot help but place themselves in relation to Western conceptions of art (literature) or of (social) science as they inevitably privilege *either* the Sameness of Native American verbal expression in forms aspiring to what is accessibly recognizable as literary, *or* its Difference, in forms committed to scientific authenticity and accuracy.

As James Clifford has written of musuem shows and collections of tribal art and artifacts, the decision to call certain "tribal" productions works of art or to call them artifacts is to place them in the context of aesthetics or of ethnography, emphasizing individual "genius" and its presumed capacity to transcend culture-specific determinations, or emphasizing exactly the force of cultural codes. But "Science," Clifford writes, "can be aestheticized, art made anthropological" (1988a:203), and something like this process has taken place in the history of translation from Native American literatures. When the literary people aestheticize science, accuracy and authenticity are inevitably lost in some degree; when the anthropologists scientize art, its charm, force, beauty are inevitably lost in some degree.

What must be noted, however, is that there is an imbalance here so far as the relation to original performances is concerned. Euramerican social scientists have regularly been able to operate apart from the concerns of Euramerican poets or literary critics; but the literary people, whether they were willing to admit it or not, have only rarely been able to work independently of the scientists. Simply put, the social scientists have been able to work directly with Native performers, or at least with Native language transcriptions, without worrying too much about any reductiveness in their procedures, for all that these confront highly complex and subtle esthetic acts. The poets and the literary critics, however, have very little been able to work directly with Native performers, or with Native language transcriptions because they have not, for the most part, developed competence in Native languages—for all that they may appreciate the aesthetics of Native expression.

As translators have become increasingly sensitive and sophisticated, they have, to be sure, attempted to see the relation between Identity and Difference, accessibility and authenticity, art and science as more nearly a dialectical than a purely oppositional relation.[1] Efforts to aestheticize science and to scientize aesthetics in these regards, are, I believe, wholly to be applauded—for all that, as I have tried to show elsewhere, it is unlikely that any fully satisfactory translation strategy—as accurate as it is accessible, as scientifically valid as it is aesthetically beautiful, etc.— can be produced.[2] Given the very different structure of Native American languages from Indo-European languages (and from one another as well), and given the different assumptions and possibilities of oral and textual performance, one cannot help but sacrifice, in some measure, closeness to the original for a sense of "literariness," or a sense of "literariness" for a sense of the actual structure and syntax of the original. All of this is to say, as Dennis Tedlock, in his seminal essay "On the Translation of Style in Oral Literature," quoted Herbert Spinden, that translators must work according to "the double standard of fidelity to the original source and artistic quality in the rendering" (Spinden in D. Tedlock 1983:32).[3]

Let me briefly mention two more matters before proceeding to the theorized history I have promised. First, it should be explicitly acknowledged that what follows is, indeed, an account of Indian to *English* literary translation. The work of Francophone persons in the Southeast and Northwest, or of Spanish speakers in Florida and the Southwest, important as these are, is not considered. And the work of even Anglophone scholars in what for five hundred years has been the Spanish-speaking world is barely alluded to. Clearly attention to both of these aspects of the subject is needed to supplement what I offer. Second, it will readily be noted that my account is exclusively concerned with the translation of what can generally be catalogued as Native American song and story, so that an important category of Indian discourse, that of oratory, is not considered.

I ask the reader to believe that this is not because I think Indian oratory uninteresting, unimportant, or irrelevant to the history of translation. Indeed, on the contrary, I think oratory raises so many questions of importance that it would extend this paper to unmanageable proportions to try to attend to it here. Donald Bahr's article on the subject and Andrew Wiget's discussion are the best brief overviews I know,[4] and I offer among the references at the end of this book work by Bahr, the Dauenhauers, Michael Foster, Miguel León-Portilla, and Joel Sherzer, which—along with the bibliographic references each of these provides—should enable the interested reader to pursue this subject in the detail it deserves.

*   *   *

Although Euramericans from the seventeenth century forward were quite certain that Indian peoples had need of Western texts—the Bible, most particularly, of course—in their languages, it took rather longer for them to decide that the textualization of Indian performances in English might be of interest and use to themselves.[5] Early European encounters with the possibility of an indigenous literature may be conveyed by a few lines from Lieutenant Henry Timberlake's eighteenth-century "Translation of the WAR-SONG, *Caw waw noo dee, &c*" from the Cherokee.

Where'er the earth's enlighten'd by the sun,
Moon shines by night, grass grows, or waters run,
Be't known that we are going, like men, afar,
In hostile fields to wage destructive war;
Like men we go, to meet our country's foes,
Who, woman-like, shall fly our dreaded blows.

However absurd Timberlake's couplets may look to us today as a rendering of anything Cherokee warriors might actually have sung—and Timberlake's "*Caw waw noo dee, &c*" indicates the limited extent of his interest in transcribing the Cherokee language original—it should be noted that his translation, in its adoption of the principle of Identity, its determination to present Cherokee song as recognizably literary, accessible to readers of, say, Dryden, is not lightly to be dismissed. If Timberlake is at all correct in his comment that "Both the ideas and verse are very loose in the original, and they are set to as loose a music," which, however, he finds "extremely pretty, and very like the Scotch" (83), his procedure certainly has a coherent logic to it. Still, it is obvious that we will never know, from Timberlake's rendering, what eighteenth-century Cherokee war songs were "really" like; all we can know from him is that they could be taken as sophisticatedly artful—no less so than Western literary art.

Moving forward to the mid-nineteenth century, I would cite Henry Rowe Schoolcraft's work as showing a certain awareness of the dialectic I have posited as inevitably operative. Schoolcraft's "Chant to the Firefly" offers a transcription of the Chippewa original, followed by what Schoolcraft calls a "literal" translation, and, finally, a "literary" translation. Here, first, is the Indian original, as quoted by Dell Hymes (1981:39):

CHANT TO THE FIRE-FLY

Chippewa (Ojibwa) (Schoolcraft's orthography is preserved):

Wau wau tay see!	Wau wau tay see!
Wau wau tay see!	Wau wau tay see!
E mow e shin	Was sa koon ain je gun.
Tahe bwau ne baun-e wee!	Was sa koon ain je gun.
Be eghaun—be eghaun—ewee!	

Schoolcraft's "literal" translation uses a kind of highly exclamatory prose:

Flitting-white-fire-insect! waving-white-fire-bug! give me light before I go to bed! give me light before I go to sleep. Come, little dancing white-fire-bug! Come, little flitting white-fire-beast! Light me with your bright white-flame-instrument—your little candle.

The "literary" translation, however, is versified. Here are the first four lines as reproduced by Hymes (40):

Fire-fly, fire-fly! bright little thing,
Light me to bed, and my song I will sing.
Give me your light, as you fly o'er my head,
That I may merrily go to my bed.

For an Indian "chant" to appear accessibly "literary," it would still seem that rhyme and meter are required; nonetheless, there is at least some recognition of the potential value of a more "literal" version. As the curious consequence of changing taste, Schoolcraft's "literal" version may, as Hymes has remarked, currently strike us as more "literary" than his "literary" version. That Schoolcraft has, at least, provided a rough transcription of the original is particularly fortunate—if only, as Hymes has acerbically remarked, because "thanks to Schoolcraft's scholarship, we can appreciate in depth how bad his translation is" (1981:40). Schoolcraft's "scholarship" importantly provides the basis for the possibility of "poetic retranslation" such as Hymes himself has offered.[6] Schoolcraft also translated—or, perhaps one should say offered "versions," or reinterpretations—of Native legend and story.[7]

In the last decades of the nineteenth century we find a substantial body of translations of Native American song and story that is quite remarkable for its solid linguistic data and its detailed ethnographic acquaintance with the cultures in question. For all that this work comes from "amateurs"—lawyers like Horatio Hale or medical men like Washington Matthews—not associated with the universities and only tangentially and irregularly to the government bureaus, it is not, as the conventionally received view would have it, vague and impressionistic. Indeed, this conventional view is badly in need of revision, reflecting as it does the triumph of Boasian standards for "scientific" translation (I shall briefly discuss these below). Horatio Hale's *Iroquois Book of Rites*, published in a volume of Daniel G. Brinton's Library of Aboriginal American Literature (1883), and Washington Matthews's translations of the Navajo *Mountain Chant* (1887), and of the *Night Chant* (1902) are two outstanding examples from this period, and there are translations worthy of contemporary attention to be found in the work of Major John Wesley Powell among "the Numic people of Western North America" and the Rev. H. R. Voth among the Hopi.[8]

I will cite the "First Song of the First Dancers" from Matthews's presentation of the *Mountain Chant*. There is, initially, a transcription of the original in the conventional orthography of the period (456):

Qaniè qaò yaè, qaniè qaò yaè
Qaniè iè oayè oayè.

1. Qadjinäia qaò yaè,
2. Kaç dsil çilhyíli qaò yaè,
3. 'Çaltsoï tsèë qaò yaè,
4. Cija cigèlgo qaò yaè.
   Náhi ìni èhi oayè, náhi ìni èhi oöhè.

9. Qadjinäia qaò yaè,
10. Kaç dsil litsòï qaò yaè,
11. Bitselitsòï qaò yaè,
12. Cija cigèlgo qaò yaè.
    Náhi ìni, etc.

5. Niqoyastcàdje qaò yaè,
6. Kaç dsil çolíji qaò yaè,
7. Kini bitsèë qaò yaè,
8. Cija cigèlgo qaò yaè.
　　Náhi ìni, etc.

13. Niqoyastcàdje qaò yaè,
14. Kaç dsil lakàie qaò yaè,
15. A 'a 'i tsèe qaò yaè,
16. Cija cigèlgo qaò yaè.
　　Náhi ìni, etc.

We next have something Matthews denotes simply "Translation." This, as the reader will note, includes not only linguistic but ethnographic information of a particularly important kind:

Translation.—1, 9. 'Qadjinàï, "Place-where-they-came-up," a locality in the San Juan Mountains where, according to their mythology, the Navajo emerged from the lower world to this. 5, 13. Niqoyastcàdje, another name for Qadjinàï. 2, 6, 10, 14. Kaç, now; dsil, mountain; ¢ilhyíli, black; çolíji, blue; litsòï, yellow; lakàie, white. These verses refer to four mountains surrounding Qadjinàï, which are designated by colors only to indicate their topographical positions. 3, 7, 11, 15. 'Çaltsoïaça litsòï, "yellow wing," a large bird of prey; kini, hen hawk; bitselitsòï, "yellow tail," a bird of undetermined species; a'a'i, magpie; tse, a tail; bitse, its tail. 4, 8, 12, 16. Cija, my treasure; cigèl, my desideratum, my ultimatum, the only thing I will accept. When supposed to be said by a god, as in this song, it means the particular sacrifice which is appropriate to him. In this case probably the feathers spoken of are "cigèl" and the mountains "eija." The refrain, "qaò yaè" is a poetic modification of qaa', it looms up, or sticks up, said of some lofty object visible in the distance, whose base cannot be seen.

Finally, there is a "free translation" (456–57):

Place-whence-they-came-up looms up,
Now the black mountain looms up,
The tail of the "yellow wing" looms up,
My treasure, my sacrifice, loom up.

Place-whence-they-came-up looms up,
Now the yellow mountain looms up,
The tail that is yellow looms up,
My treasure, my sacrifice, loom up.

Land-where-they moved-out looms up,
Now the blue mountain looms up,
The tail of the hen-hawk looms up,
My treasure, my sacrifice, loom up.

Land-where-they-moved out looms up,
Now the white mountain looms up,
The tail of the magpie looms up,
My treasure, my sacrifice, loom up.

I suppose it might be said that in addition to the advances made in linguistic and ethnographic information in the forty-some years separating the work of Schoolcraft and Matthews, the chief advantage the latter enjoys as a translator may be that he is not particularly interested in poetry as such. Matthews clearly is not indifferent to the matter of literary accessibility, and so he offers a loosely versified "free translation." But unlike Schoolcraft, Matthews does not find it necessary to push further toward a "literary" translation.

　　Matthews's procedure is worth comparing to that of another "amateur," one who is clearly more oriented toward the aesthetic/accessible axis of translation than—as in the case of Matthews—toward the scientific/accurate axis: Natalie Curtis Burlin. Burlin seems not to have been competent in any one of the several languages from which she offered translations, and, further, her pronouncements concerning the "primitive charm" of the art of a "child race" and her self-characterization as the "white friend" who "had come to be the pencil in the hand of the Indian[s]" (xxi) who "walked in the sunset hour of their native life . . . [with] the night . . . soon to come" (xxii) are deeply embarrassing to read today. Nonetheless, the translations from many Native languages of story and "legend" in her *Indians Book* of 1907, have much to recommend them, for she includes—albeit in a quite unsystematic manner—rough transcriptions of Native language originals with at least some of her "literal" and "literary" translations. Here is a Pawnee "Spirit-Dance" song as Burlin gives it (116) in Indian and in English in parallel columns:

Kehare Katzaru	**Song of the Spirit-Dance**

Ruwerera, ruwerera,
    Operit ruwerera,
    Operit ruwerera.
	Star of Evening, Star of Evening,
	    Look, where yonder she cometh,
	    Look, where yonder she cometh.

Rerawha-a, rerawha-a,
    Operit rerawha-a,
    Operit rerawha-a.
	Stars of heaven, stars of heaven,
	    Lo, the many are coming,
	    Lo, the many are coming.

Ruwerera, ruwerera,
    Atira ruwerera,
    Atira ruwerera.
	Mother-Moon, Mother-Moon,
	    Look, where yonder she cometh,
	    Look, where yonder she cometh.

Ruwerera, ruwerera,
    Operit ruwerera,
    Operit ruwerera.
	Star of Morning, Star of Morning,
	    Look, where yonder he cometh,
	    Look, where yonder he cometh.

Ruwerera, ruwerera,
    Atius ruwerera,
    Atius ruwerera.
	Father-Sun, Father-Sun,
	    Look, where yonder he cometh,
	    Look, where yonder he cometh.

There is no literal translation in this instance, and the "literary" translation, for all that it appeared in the twentieth century, takes as its model a pre-Whitmanian or -Dickinsonian aesthetic for poetry. For all of that, the juxtaposition of this translation to a (versified) "original" at least allows the general reader to wonder whether or how, for example, *ruwerera* and *rerawha-a* are related: are they singular and plural forms of the verb "to come," and, indeed, do they somehow include an inflection that would legitimate Burlin's shift from "Look" to "Lo"? In an appendix (544), Burlin offers at least some bits of inguistic information that might aid the reader concerned to know about these matters:

Ruwerera	operit	rerawha-a
it is coming yonder	*star (Evening Star understood in first verse, Morning Star in fourth)*	*they are coming yonder* (re, *yonder:* ra, *coming:* wha-a, *many*)
Atira	**Atius**	
Mother (Mother-Moon)	*Father (Father-Sun)*	

Even from this little, one can see that, indeed, there is no equivalent for either "look" or "lo" in the original, and that a "literal" translation of the first two stanzas might be something like, "It is coming yonder, Evening Star comes, Evening Star comes. / They are coming yonder, they come," and so forth. Burlin's procedure does not, to be sure, attend to linguistic or for that matter ethnographic data in anything like the detail of Matthews; indeed, her stated desire "that the *real* meaning [might] truthfully flash through the English words, and that the translation should retain the *fragrance* [!?], *the color, and, above all, the spirit* of the original" (xxv, my emphases) is such as to diminish the importance of such data; those translators after the "fragrance" and "spirit" of the original need not trouble overmuch with its actual words and phonemes. Still, it must be said for Burlin that she did take the trouble to consult both Native singers and storytellers as well as accredited linguistic experts.[9]

Further, Burlin's *Indians Book*, as in the example below, often tries to convey the melodic component of Native song, so that one may indeed recall that these particular compositions were sung, rather than recited. Schoolcraft, who offered a Chippewa "chant," and Matthews, who offered a Navajo "song," did not, to my knowledge, provide the reader with any guide to the musical content. Burlin (117), working with models established around the turn of the century by her contemporaries Alice Fletcher and Frances Densmore,[10] as in the example opposite, does offer such a guide.

Another important "artistic" contributor to translation in the first decades of the twentieth century is Mary Austin. To be sure, inasmuch as her work was, so far as I am aware, entirely uninformed by specific linguistic or ethnographic competences of any detail whatever, and explicitly offered not as translation but rather as "versions" or "interpretations" of Native American literary expression oriented toward the aesthetic dimension of charm and beauty, it could be argued that her work does not strictly belong in any history of translation practices. I am insufficiently dogmatic, however, to do more than note the logic of such an argument. Austin was quite influential in her time, and, for all the legitimacy of the subsequent criticism (of the 1970s and after) of her highly impressionistic manner, her efforts to bring to general attention the literary expression of Native American people is worthy of note.[11] This is most particularly the case because, in a manner very different from that of Natalie Burlin,

Tawi' Kuruks
Song of the Bear Society
Sung by Letakots-Lesa (Eagle Chief)

NOTE: Meter signature should properly read $\frac{2}{8}$ —Ed.

attention to Indian poetry for Austin was not an antiquarian occupation but rather a commitment to the present and future. It was Austin's unequivocal view that a relationship was "about to develop between Indian verse and the ultimate literary destiny of America" (1930:xv–xvi). Remarking on the similarities between the imagist and verslibriste manner of many of the poets of her period and the manner of at least some Indian songs, Austin insisted that "American poetry must inevitably take, at some period of its history, the mold of Amerind verse, which is the mold of the American experience shaped by the American environment" (1930:42). Perhaps to aid in this "inevitable" process, Austin, in her *American Rhythm* (1930:116), offered such texts as the following, from the Oglala Sioux:[12]

PERSONAL SONG OF DANIEL RED EAGLE

The fierce hawk of death is over me,
The fierce hawk of death.

Now and again
Its wing shadows
Brush my shoulders.

The fierce hawk of death,
When will it strike!

Here, Austin, to borrow a phrase from Michael Castro, "interprets the Indian"[13] in such a way as to align Native American literary expression with the dominant aesthetic principles for poetry in her own time. Insofar as she remakes Indian poetry according to the model of the imagists or verslibristes of her time, she is vulnerable to the criticism Karl Kroeber has recently made of Brian Swann's work and others have made of the work of Jerome Rothenberg (see below).

In varying degrees, then, there are a number of translations in the last decades of the nineteenth century and the first decades of the twentieth century that do indeed attempt to operate within the paradoxical or dialectical bounds of that "double standard of fidelity to the original source and artistic quality in the rendering," remarked by Spinden in the 1930s, with Hale, Matthews, and others more nearly emphasizing the former and Burlin, at least, if not quite Austin, more nearly emphasizing the latter. This dialectic, however, is largely undone by the work of Franz Boas and his students, the "double standard" somewhat crudely reduced to the single standard of anthropological scienticity.

That Boas *was* the founder of a genuinely "scientific" anthropology in this country has been the view militantly and persistently asserted by his students (e.g., Margaret Mead, Ruth Benedict, Alexander Lesser, Irving Goldman, and others). That assertion has been powerfully objected to by, among others, Leslie White and Marvin Harris; and I have myself published an interpretation of this debate.[14] For our present purposes, what needs to be considered is the nature of Boasian preferences in the presentation and translation of Native American literary performance. In what I take to be an oblique reference to Boas and his influence, John Bierhorst (1974:xii; my emphasis) remarks, "The school of literary anthropology D. G. Brinton might have founded in the 1880s failed to materialize in the tide of reaction that swept American Indian studies into the twentieth century (leaving the cult of myth and even *the comparative method*, the lifeblood of literary anthropology, far behind."[15]

In somewhat similar fashion, Dennis Tedlock (1983:31) has claimed that the Boasian advocacy of " 'a faithful rendering of the native tales' " for the most part produced "what professional translators would call a 'crib' or a 'trot'—not a true translation into literate English, but rather a running guide to the original text, written in an English that was decidedly awkward and foreign." This "awkward" English, which Tedlock refers to (38) as "informant English," I believe *might*—as I shall indicate in discussing the work of Anthony Mattina just below—have been exploited for literary rather than strictly literal effect. In this regard, that is, I disagree with both Tedlock and Dell Hymes insofar as they have asserted the necessity of the textual conventions of Western poetry for conveying the artfulness of Indian narrative. Nonetheless, Tedlock convincingly demonstrates that a good many of the literal prose translations of Boas and his students—among them those of Melville Jacobs, who did indeed wish to "enhance [the] enjoyment" (Jacobs in Tedlock 1983:40) of Clackamas narrative—are largely disastrous for perceiving let alone understanding the aesthetic strategies and effects of Native American literary expression.

Some sense of Boas's procedure may be gained from the example below, taken from his *Kutenai Tales* (1918:190–91):

64. COYOTE AND TREE CHIEF

Ho'ya's hutsqa`łanuxwa'te· k!a`k!łan·aq!o`x$_u$małe·'et.

(a) Coyote Becomes Tree Chief's Friend

Qao˘sa˘qa'$_a$ne·skı'n·ku·ts. nułpałnetı't$_i$ne· ka'qa·ps nıtsta'-
ha·łs ka'qa·ps nıtsta'ha·łs ksao˘ˇsa'qa·ps. qałwi'yne·: "hułts!-
ına'm·i·ł. ktsxa'ł·e·n ka'swu ne$_i$ nıtsta'hał pał kqa'kyam
kqasts!o'mqa'qa." ta'xa ne$_i$ nıtsta'hał qał'atı'łne· k!a`k!ła-   5
n·aq!o`x$_u$małe·'et. ts!ına'xe· skı'n·ku·ts. qo$_u$s qana'xe·. n'ıtkı'ne·
k$_u$wı'łq$_u$wa't!e·'s. n'u'pste· skı'n·ku·ts yu·hanqa'me·k. pał k.łıt-
q!uxma'saq! tsuk^{u}a'te· a'ł·a·s. qanakı'n·e· a$_a$'ksa'q!e·s. ta'xas
wıłkı`sqłe·k!a'łne·. qa$_a$nmıtu'kse· yaqa$_a$net.ła'$_a$ke· k!a`k!łan·a-
q!o`x$_u$małe·'et. łe'$_i$ne·s qo$_u$s qa'qałxona'pse· kwı'łq$_u$wat!s   10
skı'n·ku·ts. k!u'pxa ma'e·s k!a`k!łan·aq!o`x$_u$małe·'et, qake'$_i$ne·
ne$_i$ tłna'mu: "a: kse'$_i$łso$_u$k qo ha'mke· łe'ins swu'e·s
kanxa'łe·." nułpałnitı't$_i$ne· qo$_u$s ktsxana'me·s skı'n·ku·ts.
qayaqana'xe·. ma'te· ne$_i$s xałtsı'n'e·s k$_u$wı'łq$_u$wat!s. łaxa'xe·
ne$_i$s tłna'mu·'s. tınaxa'mne·. qakı'łne·: "ka$_a$ kı'nskił'a$_a$qa'ke·   15
qo$_u$ ku˘q^{u}a'ham łe'$_i$ne·." n'u'px$_a$ne· ne$_i$ tłna'mu ne$_i$s pał
n'ı'nse· ne$_i$s nıtsta'hałs. ma ksktłyıłna'$_a$ntstaps. qakı'łne·
skı'n·ku·ts·: "a: ma koq^{u}a'ke· łe'e·ns swu'e·s kanxa'łe·."
qao'$_u$ne· ne$_i$s ke'e·ns skı'n·ku·ts·. ta'xas sła˘qa˘qa'pse·
ktso'$_u$k^{u}at ktsxa'ł·e·ns swuı'se·s xałe''e·s. n'u'px$_a$ne· ne$_i$s   20
xałe''e·s ktsxa'ł·e·ns naso'$_u$kwe·ns. qao˘sa˘qa'$_a$ne· skı'n·ku·ts
a$_a$'kıt.ła.ı'se·s swu'e·s.

64. COYOTE AND TREE CHIEF

Well, I will tell you about Tree Chief. |

(a) Coyote Becomes Tree Chief's Friend

There was Coyote. He heard about a youth. | There was a youth.
He thought: "I'll go, | and the youth shall be my friend, because it is
said || that he is clever." The name of this youth was Tree Chief. | 5
Coyote started. He went along. He met | a mule. Coyote took him
and rode him. Because his legs were lean, | he took moss and stuffed

his legs. Then | he had big calves. Tree Chief's tent was on a river. ‖
Coyote came riding along on the mule | opposite (the tent). When   10
Tree Chief's mother saw him, the old woman said: | "Oh, I wish the
passer-by would be my son's friend!" | Coyote heard her talking. |
He went past. He left his mule and came ‖ to the old woman. He   15
entered, and said to her: "What did you say | when I passed there
on the other side?" The old woman saw that | he was a youth.
She was pleased with him. She said | to Coyote: "I said this: 'I
wish you would be my son's friend.'" | She did not know that it
was Coyote. Therefore ‖ she took him to be her son's friend. She   20
knew that | her son was to be a chief. There was Coyote | in his
friend's tent. |

Here, special phonetic symbols are employed to render the sounds of the
Indian original as exactly as possible (but, of course, only for the scientifically trained reader able to decode those symbols), and the original is
printed facing a sentence by sentence translation into English—a translation which attempts to achieve approximately word for word literality.
It should be fairly apparent, however—and I have not gone out of my
way to choose some particularly dreadful example—that, whatever the
gain in literal accuracy, it is purchased at a fairly considerable price in
the loss of literariness, a sense that these tales do indeed have the beauty
and power of sophisticated verbal art. Yet, to repeat, Boas's influence in
this area was enormous for much of the twentieth century.

   An extreme reaction against the apparently dead hand of this scientific
literality comes from the poet Jerome Rothenberg in the 1960s and '70s in
the practice of what he calls "total translation," a "means of delivery & of
bringing to life . . . words, sounds, voice, melody, gesture, event, etc., . . . a
full and total experience" (306). This is obviously something very far from
Boasian literal translation. The following lines are from Rothenberg's version of a Kwakiutl performance that he calls "Gift Event II" from his collection *Shaking the Pumpkin* (1972:1988):

GIFT EVENT II

Start by giving away different colored glass bowls.
Have everyone give everyone else a glass bowl.
Give away handkerchiefs & soap & things like that
Give away a sack of clams & a roll of toilet paper.
Give away teddybear candies, apples, suckers & oranges.
Give away pigs & geese & chickens, or pretend to do so.
Pretend to be different things.
Have the women pretend to be crows, have the men pretend to be something
    else.
Talk Chinese or something.
Make a narrow place at the entrance of a house & put a line at the end of it
    that you have to stoop under to get in.

Hang the line with all sorts of pots & pans to make a big noise.
Give away frying pans while saying things like "Here is this frying pan worth
    $100 & this one worth $200."
Give everyone a new name.
Give a name to a grandchild or think of something & go & get everything.

One does not suppose, of course, that any Kwakiutl performer actually ever said anything like "Talk Chinese or something." But Rothenberg's interest, like Burlin's or Austin's, is in the aesthetic feel of the thing, a rendering of the Indian performance in a manner that we can easily find, whatever its accuracy and authenticity, moving, powerful, and so on. Rothenberg has been extensively criticized for the liberties he takes with Native expression[16]—criticisms which, from a different quarter, have just recently been reiterated for some of the work of Brian Swann.

Swann's more recent attempt to privilege the charm and "literariness" of Native expression is much more sensitive to the sorts of issues just mentioned. What Swann offers in *Song of the Sky* do not claim to be "translations" but are, instead, readily acknowledged as poetic versions, "white man's poetry" (1985:4), but, nonetheless, a poetry based upon linguistically and ethnographically informed—but altogether literal and not very "poetic"—work of earlier anthropologists. I quote a lovely text based on material translated by John Swanton:

You
    where have you
            fallen
                from
                    fallen
                  You
              have been
          falling
       falling
   Have you
      fallen
         from the top
            of the salmon-
                 berry bushes
           falling
              falling[17]

As I have said, Swann is much more careful than his predecessors in the interpretive line ever were to admit that what he puts on the page does not closely conform to what any particular performance was "really" like. What he offers is, once again, an imaginative recreation for a Western audience of the feel or sense of what they said or sang. But, as Karl Kroeber (1989b:47) notes, "so far as *Song of the Sky* deserves and repays attention *as* modern [Euroamerican] poetry, its value for those interested in Indian poetry and song is principally in being so unlike the Indian songs it secondhandedly reshapes."[18]

I believe Kroeber is generally correct although insufficiently historical. The "interest," that is, that one may take in the work of Austin, Rothenberg, and Swann, is, to be sure, an interest largely determined by the likeness of their work to what Euroamericans of the 1920s, 1960s, and 1980s have found attractive in (some of) the poetry of those periods. But it does not logically follow that the poetry of those periods—and so the poetic "versions" produced according to the aesthetics of those periods—is necessarily "unlike the Indians songs it secondhandedly reshapes." Timberlake's "version," that is to say, conforms to an aesthetic that is probably very decidedly "unlike" any Cherokee aesthetic; there is almost surely a very bad fit between iambic pentameter couplets and Cherokee war songs. But it may be that the distance between imagist poetics or those of "open" poetry and Indian song is less; it may be, I mean to suggest, that the fit, as I have called it, is indeed somewhat better. (For all that, it remains the case that we will not get any sense of the word-for-word meaning and the ethnographic import of that meaning from these translators' procedures.)

In my terms, the procedures of Austin, Rothenberg, and Swann, as also those of Henry Rowe Schoolcraft and Lt. Henry Timberlake emphatically privilege the Identity of Native performance with that of Western literary art, assuming the likeness not the unlikeness of the two—and, indeed, they thereby mask much of the strangeness and Difference of Indian expression, as the price paid for asserting the aesthetic power of Native American work. I am quite sure that Rothenberg and Swann would agree that the danger of such procedures resides in the fact that they might unintentionally seem to suggest that, to cite William Bevis, we might still be able to "get" Indian literature almost as cheaply as we got Manhattan:[19] to suggest, that is, that the translator need not take the trouble to study the indigenous languages of the Americas (the resources for some of which today—grammars, dictionaries, textbooks—are considerably more abundant than they were in an earlier time), need not bother to learn very much about traditional cultures and their continuance today.

To convey something of the feel of the thing without so great a loss in formal structure and literal meaning as there was in Rothenberg's work, has been, in different ways, the aim of the transcriptions and translations of the two most influential contemporary mythographers, Dell Hymes and Dennis Tedlock. Hymes, a formidable linguist, has focused predominantly on myth narratives of the Northwest, rearranging and retranslating earlier transcriptions and translations. Emphasizing the dramatic

quality of Native storytelling from a linguistic and narratological perspective, Hymes has devised a system involving divisions into acts and scenes
and a translation method which offers Indian narratives in "measured
verse,"[20] determining line breaks according to the recurrence of linguistic particles in the original transcriptions from which he works. Hymes
scrupulously includes transcriptions of the Native text with each of his
own translations. I will cite the first section of his 1977 translation of a
much discussed Clackamas text called "Seal and her younger brother
lived there."[21] Hymes first gives the versified translation (1981:310):

SEAL AND HER YOUNGER BROTHER LIVED THERE

[*i. The "wife" comes*]

(A)	(1)	They lived there, Seal, her daughter, her younger brother.	1
		After some time, now a woman got to Seal's younger brother	2
(B)	(2)	They lived there.	3
		They would "go out" outside in the evening.	4
	(3)	The girl would say,	5
		she would tell her mother:	6
		"Mother! Something is different about my uncle's wife.	7
		It sounds just like a man when she 'goes out.' "	8
	(4)	"Shush! Your uncle's wife!"	9
(C)	(5)	A long long time they lived there like that.	10
		In the evening they would each 'go out.'	11
	(6)	Now she would tell her:	12
		"Mother! Something is different about my uncle's wife.	13
		When she 'goes out' it sounds just like a man."	14
	(7)	"Shush!"	15

It is followed by a versified original language text (312):

WÁLXAYU ICÁMXIX GALXÍLAYT

[*i. The "wife" comes*]

(A)	(1)	GaLXílayt, Wálxayu, wagáxan, iCámxix.	1
		LHúxwan qánCixbÉt, aGa iLGagílak gaLigúqam Wálxayu iCámxix	2
(B)	(2)	GaLXílayt.	3
		ALúya tLáXnix xábixix.	4
	(3)	Wak'aSkaS alagíma,	5
		agulxáma wákaq:	6
		"Aqu! Dángi iXlúwidix wiCLm ayágikal.	7
		"TL'á wiLÉkala-díwi alubáya."	8
	(4)	"Ak'waSka! IwímiLm ayágikal!"	9
(C)	(5)	I yatLqdix k'wátLqi gaLXílayt.	10
		Xábixix aLubáywa.	11

(6) AGa agulxáma: 12
     "Áqu! Dáng(i) iXlúwida wiCLm ayágikal.   13
     "Alubáya tL'á wiLÉkala díwi."   14
(7) "Ák'waSka!"   15

Hymes's interest in "performance," is discursive (e.g., 79–86, 200–259, and passim) and concerned with such things as the "presentational" strategies (317 ff) of narrative: working predominantly from texts, he does not much discuss the dynamics of actual performances.

These dynamics, however, are exactly what interests Tedlock, who, unlike Hymes, works from his own tape recordings, which he then transcribes and translates. His practice, initiated with Zuni materials in the 1970s, has for the most part been to break lines according to pauses on the part of the narrator, and to print each line according to a typographical scheme which attempts to indicate such things as the tempo of the narration, the performer's pronunciation of phonemes, his volume, and, indeed, even the audience's (generally rule-governed, but occasionally spontaneous) reaction and response. Tedlock's techniques are oriented toward the production of what he has called a "performable translation" (1983:13), its performability being aided by Tedlock's provision of a "Guide to Reading Aloud" (1983:20–22). I offer a brief excerpt from near the end of the long story from the Zuni Tedlock calls "The Girl and the Protector" (1983:104):

> When he reached the top he made this
> Old Lady stand up, (*softly*) he tried it there
> he tried it
> and it was working. When it was working
> HE STARTED OFF, and when he'd gone a way the Protector began to call out
>   (*as if from a distance, very high*):
> "Grandmaaaaaaaaaaaaaaaaaaaaaaaa come help me, some one
>   is cha sing meeeeeeeeeeeeeeeeeeeeeeeeee."
> His grandmother was making porridge.
> AFTER A MOMENT HE CALLED AGAIN and his grandmother heard him.
>
> When she looked outside he called again:
> "Grandma come help me, some one is chasing meeeeeeeeeeeeeee," he said.
> "Dearie me! grandson, you big fool," she said.

There is no versified Zuni original provided; Tedlock to my knowledge has only printed one Zuni versified original, for the story translated as "Coyote and Junco."

*   *   *

I suspect that the enormous influence of Hymes and Tedlock[22] derives from the fact that they have been foremost among those committed to mediating the distance between Identity and Difference in transcription and translation. Competent in the languages from which they translate, and committed to high degrees of linguistic accuracy, both are also thoroughly sophisticated in their aesthetic awareness (they have, for example, written and published their own poetry). For all their (salutary) influence, however, their methods have not exhausted the possibilities of contemporary translation. And, moreover, their insistence on the presentation of Native performance, regardless of whether these are sung, chanted, or narrated, in lines and stanzas, as "poetry" on the page, that is, rather than in the sentences and paragraphs of a prose page format, has increasingly been called into question for making a necessity of what is perhaps better considered an option.

Thus, Anthony Mattina, a Salishan linguist, has opted for prose in his translation of a folktale narrated by the late Peter Seymour, one of the last Colville speakers of western Montana. Resisting all claims that versified format is necessary for conveying the literariness of Indian narrations, Mattina forcefully insists (1987:142–43) that

Mythography is the work of collecting and transcribing once-oral texts. Narratives on the printed page are museum artifacts, just as arrowheads in a museum case are spent projectiles. A transcript of a narrative has no more sound than a musical score. The understanding which readers gain from the script is in direct proportion to what they know about the tradition and the context of the text. . . . Let the texts come forth, in whatever typographic arrangement the editor deems appropriate.

Mattina's prose, it should be said, is not standard English, but, rather, that pan-Indian phenomenon he calls "Red English," the English actually spoken by many contemporary Native American persons—in this particular case, the "informant English" of his collaborator in the translation project, Peter Seymour's cousin Mary Madeline de Sautel. I will not attempt to summarize Mattina's persuasive defense of "Red English" translations as literarily valuable[23] except to note his claim that they are indeed capable of conveying all the expressive elements one could ask of any literature. As the examples cited below indicate, along with his easily readable Red English translations, Mattina offers (1985: 92) a "continuous" translation, a transcription of the tape-recorded Colville original, and an "interlinear" translation:

They all have night caps on, that's their mark, what they go by. She matches them together, the oldest one with your oldest brother, he'll get her to go to bed with; and the next one with the next woman, he'll sleep with her; and the middle one,

he'll have the middle woman; and you two youngest, you'll go to bed with her.
(1985:25)

72. yə-yʕà-t   c-qʷəc-qʷác-qn-əlx,   c-s-ən-qáp-qən,
72. They all   have caps on,   night caps,

    c-s-łq̇-əlx-áyaʔ-qən, uł ałì?   ixì?   iʔ
    caps,   that's what

    k-t̓ək-mín-s, uł axà? cəm̓   ʔíck-st-əm-s;   cəm̓
    they go by,   and   they play with them;

    axà? anwì?   waỳ ilì?   nixʷ
          (with) you   also

a-s-ənk̓ʷ-əs-t̓íw-t-x.
(will play) the youngest one.

72. They all have caps on, night caps, caps, that's what they go by, and they
    play with them; the youngest one will play with you.

To bring this theorized history to a close, let me mention the contri-
butions to Native American song sets of the Southwest in the work of
Donald Bahr with Pima and Papago materials, Larry Evers and Felipe
Molina with Yaqui deer and coyote songs, and Leanne Hinton with Havasupai songs. In 1983, Bahr published an essay on four Papago "Butterfly
songs" in which he offered (1983:180)

a format and a method [for translation]. The format consists of certain writing
procedures: the use of plain language words, of song language syllable transcription, of slashes to show a theoretically important zone within song lines, etc. . . .
The method gives primacy to textual analysis and assumes in effect that song is a
special way of telling stories. . . . [But] versification is also present and is controlled
for . . . through the method of defining and rendering lines.

Bahr notes (1983:181) that Leanne Hinton's work with Havasupai materials in a number of ways parallels his own:[24]

The key similarity between our formats is the inclusion of native ordinary language interpretations. These are often lacking in publications of American Indian
songs, and we [Bahr and Hinton] feel that they should not be. We differ in where
the process goes from there. Hinton moves next into English words and mor-
pheme glosses and free translation, I [Bahr] into plain English equivalents and
Papagoized literal translation. We differ also on whether to include a separate
musical transcription: she would include one, while I would not.

I give, below, Bahr's "Song language and literal translation" (1983:176)
and his "Ordinary language version" (177) of the first song of the set he
considers.

```
Song 1
A    –    –    –    –    –    –    –    –    –    –    –

B                                          ge   si   CU   ke   HO   KI   MA   LI
          iya    toi   ñei   yo    pa      bi   ig   BLA  ack  BU   U    TIER FLIES
          herewill      ju    ump   and

C                                                    GA   MU   we   YA   HA   jo   WA   WA   ÑE
          ga mai hyo    si    me    ko    na   mo    A    A    way  NA   A    rrow STREEA     EATCH
          a  a          way   fa    a     a    ar

D                                     SU   WU   DA   YA    KI   WI   HI   HI   ME
                                      WA   TO   gi   STREE ME   mo   GO   O    O
                                           A    ter        EAM  OW   ards
                                                                ards

E                                     GA   MU   WI   PI
          da de ma     no   da  dai  wa   ke   MU   WI   PI   NO
          o  o         on   si  i    it   and  A    WA   A    ASH
```

Ordinary language version
Song 1

```
              ge si    /s-cúk ho     /hókimal

              Big      /black but    /terflies:

í:ya at o wa ñéiyopak  /gám hu wa    á/j wáwañ
Here will jump out and /away nar     /row stretch

gámai hu si mé:kdam    /sú:dagi á    /kimel
        Away far       /water stre   /am:

                       /wúi am hí    /him
                       /Towards g    /o,

      dá:m dádiwak     /gn hú wa     wí/pino
       On sit and      /away wa      /sh.
```

Although Bahr refers to what he calls "free translation" as the sort of thing that would probably approximate to what our historical overview of the subject has called "literary" translation, he does not care to provide such a translation (as Washington Matthews, who, although he did offer a "free translation," still did not go very much beyond the literal). By 1987, in a paper on Pima "Heaven Songs," Bahr does provide "free translations," along with what he here calls "Pima Language and English Syllable Matching Translation" (1987:210, 223). I will cite both translations for the first song of the set:

Song 1 (1)

```
                         ku   ña   si   ya   hu   nu   ki   me
                         ı    ı    ı    ı    ı    ı    ı    ı
                         and  I    he   ere  de   e    e    scend
                         ku   ña   si   ya   hu   nu   ki   me
                         ı    ı    ı    ı    ı    ı    ı    ı
                         and  I    he   ere  de   e    e    scend
i  ne pi a pe ka me ñe   we        na   ma   ne   hu   nu   ki   me
ı  ı  ı  ı  ı  ı  ı  ı   ı         ı    ı    ı    ı    ı    ı    ı
heere ba s a  a  ad ea earth  u    po   on   de   e    e         scend
                              soi  ga   le   ñi   boi  nag
                              ı    ı    ı    ı    ı    ı
                              po   o    or   my   y    heart
                         wa   ñi        pi   ma   ma   ce
                         ı    ı    ı         ı    ı    ı
                         that I         don' tkno o    ow
```

1 (1). Jesus descends to bad earth.

Here I descend.
Here I descend,

On this bad earth descend.
My poor heart,
I don't know.[25]

In his work on Pima "Oriole" songs, Bahr continues his willingness—
albeit still with some reluctance—to accommodate the literary reader's
interest in the English language aesthetics of Native American songs,
while resisting accommodation in any degree that might obscure the
formal, word-for-word syntactic as well as semantic integrity of the songs
he has tape-recorded. With Bahr's permission, I next cite some examples
from his work:[26]

Nee, k i:d hab hahawa ep kaij mas g tas mu:. O hob kaij i:da mat am ha-wi'in.
Eda g u'uhig pi mai mat has e-a:ngew, may has masma wo da:, "flai awai." Ne:, k
i:d hab ep hi kaij mas g tas mu:. "Tas mu:, tas mu:. Eda g we:s ha'icu u'uhig e-
kukui dagito," b hen kaij, b hen ha'icu hab kaij, "Jewed ka:cim ab t am hu i pi
sa:mun," "kwait" g jewed, wesko. "As g su:g u'uhig as so'ig kaij, c as g hejel an a'i
niok," b o ep kaidag.

			Ta		sai	waha	mu		mu	ki		m
			Ta		sai	waha	mu		mu	ki		m
	Je	wene	we	si	co	cu	ka	ke	n			
Ke	da	ke	we		sai	cu	yu	hine	kuk	uiwe	da	ni to
	Je	wene	ka		cim		ga	mu	pi	sa	mu ne	m
Su	hu	ga	yu	u	hi		ne	soi	newe	kai		ce
He	je	li	ga		mu	we	ne	no	ke.			

Look, and then this [song] says that the sun died. The other [previous song]
said that it flooded them [ancient creatures]. At that time the birds didn't know
[forgot] their flapping, how to fly, "fly away [as said in English]." Look, and this
[song] on the other hand says that the sun died. "Sun dies, sun dies. Just then
every kind of bird dropped its cooing," it seems to say, [and] it [next] seems to say,
"The laying land nowhere echoes," "quiet [in English]" is the land everywhere.
"Merely the mocking bird pitifully speaks, but it merely talks to itself," as it [song]
also sounds.

			Su		u	uun	Di		i	ie	s	
			Su		u	uun	Di		i	ie	s	
	La	aand	All	O	ver	Da	a	ar	k			
Just	The	en	All		Kind	Of	Bi	iird	Coo	iing	Dro op	Off
	La	aand	La		ying		A	way	No	E	cho in	g
	Mo	oc	king	Bi	i	i		ird	Pit	iful	Spe	eaks
	A	lo	one	A		wa	ay	Ta	a	alks.		

Sun dies,
Sun dies.
Earth everywhere dark,
Then every bird stops cooing.

Earth doesn't echo,
A mocking bird speaks pitifully.
Distant and isolated it talks.

From the literary end of the spectrum (Bahr and Hinton are trained primarily in anthropology and linguistics), Larry Evers and Felipe Molina have remarked that "From our perspective, the *sine qua non* . . . is an accurate transcription of a native language text along with an English translation faithful to it" (1987:25). They consider the Yaqui deer songs they have translated, and more recently, Yaqui coyote songs (1989) to be "a native American poetry" (1987:25; 1989:9), one whose ongoing production has been somewhat overlooked by literary critics excited by the so-called Native American Renaissance in writing.[27] Evers and Molina, on the page, look somewhat like Schoolcraft; the difference, an enormous one, is that their collaboration has produced both what seems to be sound "scholarship" and also sound translation. I offer one brief example (Evers and Molina 1987:51):

MAISO YOLEME

Ala inikun maiso yoleme
    hunu kun maiso yoleme
        ini kun tua maiso yolemeee

Ala inikun maiso yoleme
    hunu kun maiso yoleme
        ini kun tua maiso yolemeee

Ala inikun maiso yoleme
    hunu kun maiso yoleme
        ini kun tua maiso yolemeee

Ayaman ne seyewailo
    fayaliata naisukuni
        weyekai
        im ne yo siali vata paku
        weyekai
Hunu kun maiso yoleme
    hunu kun tua maiso yolemeee

DEER PERSON

So now this is the deer person,
    so he is the deer person,
        so he is the real deer person.

So now this is the deer person,
    so he is the deer person,
        so he is the real deer person.

So now this is the deer person,
    so he is the deer person,
        so he is the real deer person.

Over there, I, in the center
    of the flower-covered opening,
        as I was walking,
        here in the open green water,
        as I was walking,
So he is the deer person,
    so he is the real deer person.

Many others, of course, are also currently working to reconcile the principles of accessibility and authenticity, of Identity and Difference in the translation of Native American song and story—so many others, indeed, that to mention all of their work would soon expand my theorized history almost to the dimensions of that would-be comprehensive history I prefer to leave unattempted. I will therefore conclude by repeating my belief that it is not possible to imagine the discovery or invention of any ultimately and absolutely correct or fully adequate way to translate from oral

performance to page of text. Spinden's "double standard" will always p[...]
vide a tension, as I have called it a dialectic, with which translators m[...]
work. But this is not to say that each age must, in an outmoded vernacular,
simply "do its thing." To the contrary, what I believe this theorized history
of translation should demonstrate is that for the foreseeable future, the
conditions for any approximation to translational adequacy will be, first,
competence, command, or in a phrase Dell Hymes has stated, varied, and
repeated, a basic philological *control* of the language of the original; second, competence—in the sense of detailed knowledge—of the culture of
the original, an ethnographic control; and, third, some developed sense
of the strategies of literary expression both oral and textual in general. Although I am wary of both inadvertent and intentional shifts to the mode
of prophecy in criticism, I would nonetheless venture to predict that the
current conditions of possibility for the translation of Native American
song and story are decidedly hopeful.

Chapter 3
America's Histories

For Eric Cheyfitz and Michael Elliott

This chapter's title means to point to the fact that the history of America most of us know is not the only history of America. The indigenous oral tradition, for example, abounds with narratives that the contemporary Wyandot historian Clifford Trafzer calls, "the *first* history of the Americas" (474). This is "history," Trafzer notes, "in the *native* sense of the word," but not only in the "native sense," for Trafzer claims that these narratives of monster slayers, women falling from the sky, and emergences from deep within the earth "reflect *actual incidents* that occurred in world history" (486 n.2, my emphasis). These events are history, period.

I will try to show that Trafzer is right: these events are history. And I will also try to show that Trafzer's claim for Native history does not need to insist upon the factuality or literal accuracy—that's how I understand his phrase, "actual incidents that occurred"—of these incidents as a condition for their historicity. This is not to say that traditional Native historiography—history "in the native sense of the word"—cannot or does not produce factually accurate accounts of events in time—history in Our sense of the word. Euramerican history of a variety of kinds occasionally, perhaps even often, overlaps, complements, or dovetails with Native American history of a variety of kinds. My concern, however, is with types of Native American historical narrative that Our history calls myth because We can show them to be factually inaccurate, or, simply, not historical. My contention will be that Native historiography's accounts of events in time can and should be called both true and historical apart from their factual accuracy. I argue this position not as a matter of solidarity but as one of objectivity. I am not, that is, simply choosing to be on the side of the Natives, right or wrong, but, rather, I am saying that they are right:

what they traditionally take to be their true history is, indeed, historical even when it is not factually accurate.

I hardly mean to fault Trafzer for taking the tack that he does. As Greg Dening has noted, "It would be difficult to exaggerate . . . Euro-American culture's preoccupation with the past as historical fact" (55). And this "preoccupation," ethnocentric and itself historically determined, in the ongoing colonial context in which Native nations exist, exerts immense pressure on spokespersons for Native history to make their case on the field of fact, so determinedly (Dening says fetishistically) committed to accuracy and literal factuality is the dominant view. Trafzer is unwilling to yield the terrain of fact lest Native peoples' narratives of the past be consigned, as I have noted, to the subordinate status of myth, or, indeed, as has happened before, lest Native peoples themselves once more be considered "peoples *without* history."[1]

For a statement of the dominant view of history, let me turn to the eminent historian William Cronon. Writing in the *Journal of American History* in 1992, Cronon recognizes the postmodern contention that "history" may just be "an endless struggle among competing narratives and values" (1375), but nonetheless specifies criteria he believes must be met by narratives if they are to be considered historical. Historical narratives, Cronon writes, "cannot contravene known facts about the past" and they must conform to "the biological and geological processes of the earth [which] set fundamental limits to what constitutes a plausible narrative" (1347–48), plausible, of course, to us as factual history. These criteria will, obviously enough, be compelled to deny historical status to narratives of battling giants, warriors temporarily turned into buffalo, or to some of the other examples of Native "history"—I will drop the quotation marks for the rest of the way—that we will examine. But Cronon's view, which I cite as an admirable and generous version of mainstream views of history, need not—that is what I will argue—exclude other views.

Before going further, it needs to be said that traditional Native people also make a distinction between history and myth, although that distinction does not depend upon a judgment as to the greater factual accuracy of one of the two types of story. For traditional people, historical narratives tell of events nearer to the present in time, while mythical narratives relate an eventfulness very far distant from the present in time, when the world was young and "soft," or not fully formed. But both mythical and historical stories are true, and both are history in the sense that Dening—very differently from Cronon—defines the term. History, Dening writes, "is public knowledge of the past . . . public in the sense of being culturally shared" (36). "Histories are ways of knowing what happened in the past" (48) and, conversely, those ways of knowing the past that are culturally and communally confirmed are history.

Clearly, then, the Stone Boy stories discussed by Elaine Jahner (cf. Chapter 1) are mythical histories, a phrase that I do not here mean to be oxymoronic. For the Lakota, tales of long, long ago (myth) and tales of more recent times (history) are equivalently *true*: they conform to what is publicly and culturally agreed upon as knowledge about what happened in the past, and it is that agreement rather than their factuality (or possible lack of factuality) that confirms their truth.

In much the same way, Leonard Bloomfield remarks that Menomini stories "dealing with a far-off time when the world as we know it was in process of formation . . . are considered as true; they are told to inform and instruct" (xii), just as Stone Boy and other stories are told "to inform and instruct." When Bloomfield related the story of Gulliver and the Lilliputians to a Menomini woman and informed her that it "had merely been invented for pastime by a certain Englishman," her comment was, "So it is no more than a tale" (xii)—that is, a story that took place in nearer, historical time. But "no more than a tale" is not dismissive of the story's truth. What is dismissed is the aspect of "invent[ion] for pastime" or fictionality. This is how I understand the distinction Mrs. Kitty Smith intends when she tells Julie Cruikshank, midway through a traditional Tutchone narrative of a boy on a journey aided by an "invisible helper," "This is a *story*, you know, not 'story.' It's *true* story" (1998: 124). "Inventing stories," Bloomfield notes, "is not the Menomini way" (xii), nor does inventing stories seem to be the way of tribal people in general.[2]

I can think of two possible reasons for this; there may, of course, be others. (Or it may be that this is the sort of matter too complex for any specification of "reasons.") The first is, simply, that stories are traditionally told, heard, and passed down orally, mouth to ear, by persons who are or once were living, that is, who were themselves historically known. For traditional people, as the Brulé Sioux historian Clyde Dollar explains, "the idea of an historical fact . . . from the Indian side . . . is something one has been told by his elders and therefore is not to be questioned" (1). This already cuts against the grain of the dominant view of history that inheres in the etymology of the word, from the Greek *historia*, which means to learn or know by inquiry, that is, by *questioning*. Dollar continues,

Indeed, among the High Plains people, there is little interest in the subject matter of history per se beyond the repeating of its stories, and a deeply searching pursuit of data and facts on which to build veracity in history is frequently considered rather pointless, perhaps ludicrous, decidedly nosy, and an occupation closely associated with eccentric white men. (1)

One repeats what one has been told by one's elders—who are repeating what they were told by their elders; the authority of what the elders say derives from a continuous series of tellings; that is, after all, how the oral tradition reproduces the cultural knowledge necessary to sustain the community across the generations. What is said is what is so; why would anyone pass on what was not collectively accepted as truth? The regularly recurring feature of oral narratives, phrases like "so it is said," "thus they say," and so on, are indications on the part of the teller of the tale that he or she does not know the things related from personal experience. But the disclaimer is not in the least meant to suggest that what has been "said" is not true; to the contrary, that these things have over and over again been said is what confirms them as true. (And, as we have noted, even if objectively there have been changes to what has been said over and over, those changes are not perceived as such; the changed same is still the same.)

Here we might briefly note that Socrates's insistence that truth be arrived at only by persistent questioning of what was culturally accepted as true marks the end of the oral tradition in Athens and introduces a new mode, not only of philosophy but of history, that would triumph with the spread of writing. Socrates, of course, did not write; his student, Plato, would do the writing. But there should be no surprise that Socrates was condemned to die: he was the enemy of the transmitted oral tradition, of philosophy and history as communally-agreed-upon truth. Socrates called upon his students to question the elders.[3] We shall note further the ways in which persistent inquiry and alphabetic writing conjoin to produce a modernity hostile to the traditional, transmissional, and oral sense of truth.

The truth of traditional stories, myths, and histories is also borne out by what might be called the spatio-temporality of events in indigenous cultures. That is, traditional people tend to link events in time to specific places. Thus, for Western Apache people, history is a matter of what Keith Basso calls "narrated place-worlds," and "all narrated place-worlds, provided they seem plausible, are considered equally valid" (1996: 32) The "place-worlds" involved are either *still* present for anyone to see, or were once there and seen by the earliest narrators of the stories. This sort of plausibility is obviously very different from what William Cronon understands by the plausible. (Again, I hope it is clear that I in no way wish to treat Cronon's plausibility lightly; his plausibility is my plausibility. It's hard to give it up as determining, but that's just what I'm trying to do here.)

Consider, for example, these lines from a story called "The Battle of the Giants," told by Elizabeth Nyman, a Tlingit woman:

These mountains used to be fine;
they were nice and neat [regularly formed and spaced]
But when [those giants] fought [they rolled over them],

so some of them are [squashed in places] like that,
and like that,
those mountains. (Nabokov 31)

"These mountains" function as what Peter Nabokov has called a "topo-
graphic mnemonic" (32) where current features of the landscape—
mountains, as Elizabeth Nyman points out, that are not now "nice and
neat"—serve to recall a story associated with that particular place. Nyman
has been told by someone (who had been told by someone, who in turn
had been told by someone, who heard it from someone long ago who
may or may not have actually seen the events take place) that the mountains once were "nice and neat," and that it was battling giants that caused
them to be the way they are now. Mouth-to-ear personal transmission
of the tale and the concrete evidence of the landscape conjoin to affirm
the truth of "what is said," even about ancient, mythic time. Whether
this or other historically true narratives accurately conform "to the biological and geological processes of the earth," does *not*, here, "set fundamental limits to what constitutes a plausible"—or historical—"narrative"
(Cronon 1377–78) Instead, it is more nearly what Julie Cruikshank calls
"the social life of stories" that determines the link between "narrative,"
as it passes between storytellers and their audiences, and "knowledge,"
establishing which stories about the past are communally accepted as
what Kitty Smith calls "a *story*, not 'story.' . . . *true* story"; that is, as history.

Europe also has stories of the earliest times, and, once, they too were
passed down orally and considered historically true. But with writing,
things changed. Exact chronology became possible, and present accounts
could be carefully checked against past accounts. Increasingly complex
tabulations and calculations could be made; history modeled itself as a
science, and "scientific history," to cite Dening once more, "by definition,
was accurate." Then "being accurate became equated with being true,"
which meant that "history became equated with historical *facts*" (54–55,
my emphasis). As Marshall Sahlins sums up, an "epistemological union"
developed in the modern, Enlightenment West, "of the empirical with
the instrumental, which together make up the rational, also known as the
real or objective, in contrast to the fictionality of the irrational" (1995:
153). On Our side: writing, fact, reason, rationality, objectivity, history.
On Theirs: orality, fiction, irrationality, consensus, myth. Comparing the
terms in this list, we find left to us today only perhaps an advantage in
accumulated yet alterable (e.g., by further *inquiry*) fact—to which we cling
as the exclusive determinant of history. But, to return to Dening, "being
accurate [i.e., relying on the facts of the matter] is a fetish of a very special sort of history" (Dening 41). It is high time for us to abandon this

particular fetishism, and to withdraw the insistence that those who do not share this particular fetishism are somehow lacking, that they are a "people without history." It would perhaps make it easier for us to abandon that idea if we could recognize that people who do not share our particular fetish of the historical fact are not only *not* "without history," but that they are not without writing either.

Before going on to discuss some further examples of Native history and the kinds of writing sometimes used to help store historical information, I want to acknowledge my ethnocritical sense that the West's "special sort of history," deriving from a tradition of writing and Enlightenment modernity, however fetishistic or ethnocentric it may be, nonetheless continues to have important uses. What I am attempting to do here is to situate it, not to deny it. It's easy enough, after all, to understand why, for example, one might want to know *accurately* what the population of pre-Columbian North America was, or how many Africans died in the Middle Passage, or whether the Holocaust did or did not kill millions of Jews, and whether gay people and Gypsies also suffered. Literal accuracy and factuality, in these instances, is extremely important in determining the truth of history; and the alphabetic kind of writing we have, along with our Arabic (!) number system, is very efficient for establishing this sort of fact.

But what has been hard for us to see is that the truth of history does not always depend on determinations of fact. In 1973, Hayden White masterfully demonstrated the ways Western historians might agree upon the facts of the matter while disagreeing on what, with reference to Helen Blish (see below), I will call the truth of the matter. This, White showed, is because the historian's precognitive tropological preferences will cause him or her to narrativize the facts in such a way as to yield very different truths, what we are currently more comfortable in calling *interpretations*. Native historiography is different in that communal, cultural agreement on the interpretive truth of the narrative is what determines its historicity, apart from any disagreement that might (or, to be sure, might not) exist as to the facts of the matter.

The rest of this chapter looks at several examples of Indian history from the late nineteenth century to the 1970s, dealing with events from about 1820 or so to 1876. No one of these deals with such things as monster slayers or battling giants; our history, this is to say, has also recorded these events as "actual incidents that occurred." But in each case the Native account is very different from what Euramericans consider history (in general, Cronon's criteria). I will be arguing that this difference does not amount to an incommensurability between Our understandings and Theirs; that the two different languages for history are not, therefore, mutually untranslatable. I will also claim that they have already made great strides toward translating us, presenting a challenge to which we have yet to respond.

We will begin with some stories Native people told in answer to the question, Who killed Custer? We will then look at the Cheyenne explanation of how a band of men led by Stone Forehead, in 1875, managed to elude the U.S. troops pursuing them. Finally, we will consider a negative answer to the question, Did Sequoyah invent the Cherokee syllabary?

It will be noted that my choice of examples does not include the "hottest" current issues of historical contention between Euramericans and Native Americans, the issue of whether North America was or was not settled primarily by successive migrations across the Bering Strait, and the issue of the degree to which the Constitution of the United States was influenced by what the Founders knew of the Iroquois Confederacy. Nor have I chosen to discuss the historical authenticity of the Lenni Lenape text called the Walum Olum, and that of the speech said to have been delivered by the Dwamish chief, Seathl, in 1853 or 1854. In all four of these cases (as also in the cases I will shortly consider) a certain body of factual evidence exists, and, for the record, I will say that those facts incline me to believe that North America *was* primarily but not exclusively settled by migrations across the Bering Strait; that some but probably not a very substantial awareness of the Iroquois Confederacy informed the drafters of the Constitution; that the Walum Olum is a fraud perpetrated by Constantine Rafinesque; and that the speech attributed to Seathl as it currently circulates was for the most part composed by Dr. H. A. Smith around 1887.[4]

But the facts as presently constituted have left many Native persons skeptical of such conclusions. On occasion, they question the accuracy of those facts, but they also sometimes question whether the facts, even if accurate, adequately convey the historical truth of the matter. Meanwhile, the Native presentation of the historical truth of the matter—because that truth is sometimes not factually accurate—has left a great many mainstream scholars unable to accept that Native truth is indeed historical. Unfortunately, as Gail Landsman discovered in specific regard to the issue of Iroquois influence on the Constitution, the dispute cannot be resolved by shifting it away from matters of fact (or truth) to matters of "the politics of representation," the question of "who should rightfully control the representation of Iroquois history." This is because, as Landsman found, the political question of control itself always returned to the issue of who had "unique access to, and willingness to put forth, the 'truth' of Iroquois history" (170). As I will now attempt to show, I believe the only sensible way to reconcile the difference between traditional Native history and modern Euramerican history is for us to reconsider the place of factual accuracy in the determination of history. That attempt also has its politics. This means that I have come to accept Iroquois influence on the Constitution, the genuineness of Seathl's speech, and alternative versions of the peopling of the Americas as historically true although factually inaccurate. To the extent that writing such a sentence is troubling to me; to the extent, that is, that I cannot undo my own obsession with factual accuracy in the determination of historical truth, I believe I can—more on this below—translate what the Natives are saying so that any factual inaccuracy in what they are saying does not invalidate its historicity.

As an example, David Oestreicher's work entirely convinces me that the Walum Olum is a fraud. Some Lenni Lenape agree (not necessarily on the basis of Oestreicher's researches), and do not see it as part of their nation's authentic history; other Lenape people feel differently. I will probably not live long enough to see a time—which may or may not ever come—when the Walam Olum is generally and consensually accepted by the Lenape as true history or generally and consensually rejected. Were the Lenape to agree on the historical truth of the Walum Olum, and were I still around to be aware of that agreement, I would have to attempt some cosmopolitan translation. I—or someone better qualified—would have to find a language in which it were possible both to believe factually that the Walum Olum was constructed by Rafinesque and also to believe truthfully that Rafinesque's construction had become Lenape history.

*   *   *

In 1909, with support from the Philadelphia merchant and philanthropist John Wanamaker, Joseph K. Dixon convened what he called the Last Great Indian Council. One thing Dixon wanted to know from the Plains warriors in attendance was the identity of the man who had actually dispatched Pahuska, Son of the Morning Star, Longhair George. And he offered a cash payment for the information. But Custer had shorn his trademark blond tresses just before the Battle of the Greasy Grass on June 25, 1876, and the Lakota and Cheyenne who had participated in wiping out his Seventh Cavalry could not distinguish him from any of the other horse soldiers during the fight.[5] They said they did not know for certain who had (f)actually killed Custer.

But the whites were persistent; so the warriors met and, either as a joke as some have claimed, or in full seriousness according to others, they selected Brave Bear, a Southern Cheyenne, as the killer of Custer.[6] Whether in jest or in earnest, for them the matter was now settled. In answer to the question, Who killed Custer? from this time forward, the historical truth passed on by the community of elders attributed the deed to Brave Bear. Dixon refused to accept this truth—the culturally and socially determined consensus as to what happened in the past—as answering the historical question he had posed.

Later, in 1926, an older and much smaller group of Native survivors gathered on the Little Bighorn battlefield to commemorate the fiftieth anniversary of the Custer fight. Asked yet again, Who killed Custer? the aged warriors once more convened, deliberated, and this time agreed upon the Minneconjou chief, White Bull, a nephew of Sitting Bull, as Custer's killer. When White Bull was persuaded to write his autobiography in 1931, he not only wrote (in the Dakota language) about killing Custer, but also made four color drawings of the deed—which, by agreement of those authorized to confirm or deny it, was his to claim—at least from 1926 on.[7]

Obviously there are two different languages of history being spoken here, the one, as Clyde Dollar has described it, offering as history the agreed upon past as determined by the elders; the other, a realist language, as William Cronon has described it, insisting upon empirical evidence, and the accurate, scientific facts of the matter. This instance differs from the others we shall look at in that the historical truth at issue was of no particular concern to the Sioux and Cheyenne except as they were pressed by the whites. As we shall see below, there is no Winter Count for the year 1875–76 that takes the Custer fight as chief marker for that year, and even the Lakota, Amos Bad Heart Bull who made, as we shall note further, 59 drawings of the Little Big Horn Battle was much more interested in Major Reno's troop than in Custer. But when asked "to put forth . . . the 'truth' " (Landsman 170) of this particular incident in Plains history, the answer to Who killed Custer? was provided by the consensus of the battlefield survivors, elders with the authority to speak the publicly agreed upon and culturally shared knowledge of the past.

Let us next consider an event first described by George Bird Grinnell in 1910, and then included in Father Peter Powell's *People of the Sacred Mountain: A History of the Northern Cheyenne Chiefs and Warrior Societies, 1830–1879*. . . .[8] Grinnell writes that "In 1875, thirty-three Cheyenne young men left the Southern Cheyenne agency at Darlington, I.T. [Indian Territory] to go north and join the hostile camp" (573). But, as Powell picks up the story, "while they were crossing the flat prairie lands in central Kansas, they saw dust rising behind them. Soon they could make out the forms of soldiers moving in on them" (2: 895) Realizing that his men's weak and hungry horses could not outrun the soldiers, their leader, Stone Forehead, stopped the party. Powell continues, "He told those who had robes to turn their robes with the woolly side out, as a buffalo wears his robe. Then he instructed all the men to sit down on the prairie, cover their heads with their robes or blankets, and look at the earth" (895).

At this point Stone Forehead, keeper of the Sacred Arrow bundle of the Cheyenne (Maahotse), walked around his men and their horses four times, bearing the bundle, praying, and singing a holy song. "The soldiers kept coming," Powell writes, "They were so near that it should have been easy for them to see the many-colored horses of the young men." But "All they saw were some buffalo lying down or grazing upon the prairie. The young men sat still . . . to all appearances they were a group of buffalo. . . . Stone Forehead had transformed them into buffalo" (896).

Powell's phrasing—"it should have been easy" for the soldiers to see the Indian horses, and "to all appearances [the Cheyenne] were a group of buffalo"—might seem to hedge the matter; and Grinnell, earlier, had written, "it is believed, while the soldiers were passing the arrow man had transformed the Indians into buffalo" (574). So perhaps the soldiers were bleary-eyed, or drunk, or just not very good at distinguishing buffalo *robes* (and blankets?) from "real" buffalo; maybe that might even factually explain why they didn't notice the apparently obvious group of horses. But there is no ambiguity in Powell's one sentence paragraph, "Stone Forehead had transformed them into buffalo," as there was no ambiguity on the part of Stacey Riggs, one of Stone Forehead's party, who was Grinnell's source for this story. Riggs (not identified by name in Grinnell) concluded his story saying, "I am educated and I am a Christian, but I must believe what I myself saw" (Grinnell 574, Powell 2: 1355 n.1). Powell notes that "Baldwin Twins, a former Keeper of Maahotse, recounted this same episode to [the] author [to Powell] in 1960" (2: 1355 n.1). For nearly a century, then, the public knowledge of the past culturally shared by the Cheyenne—Cheyenne history—records that Stone Forehead saved his men by transforming them into buffalo.

The historian, John Moore, in a review of Powell's work responds to this—and other similar reportage by Powell—with the observation that "One looks in vain in these volumes for a more common-sense evaluation of military tactics" (in DeMallie 1993: 535 n.10). But we know from Clifford Geertz among others that common sense is culturally constructed. Powell in his Preface noted that "Whenever possible, [he] used Cheyenne accounts of the events and people portrayed" (1: xvii–xx). But these "accounts," although consistent with traditional Cheyenne notions of common sense—and of history—are not consistent with Euramerican notions of common or historical sense. Cheyenne historical truth does not accord well with Western factual plausibility.

I will offer only one more instance of a Native history that is not consonant with mainstream American history. In *Tell Them They Lie: The Sequoyah Myth*, a book published in 1971 by a Cherokee descendant of Sequoyah, Traveler Bird, the author insists that all the histories of Sequoyah's life and achievements published so far are a "myth." To take only the central issue, all the earlier histories recount Sequoyah's extraordinary invention, in about 1821, of a 92-symbol syllabary in which the Cherokee language could be written. A lie, says Traveler Bird. According to him, Sequoyah was not the inventor of Cherokee writing. Rather, Bird writes, "this symbol system had been used . . . for nine summers before European invasion on Gvanahani [sic] (San Salvador Island)" (19), that is, since 1483. The symbol system came to the Cherokee when "The remnant Taliwa Tribe incorporated with the Cherokees during the fifteenth century, and brought their symbol writings with them" (20 n.). The Taliwa came from "the Southwest, . . . Their lands were the plateau country of the Great Plains," and they had suffered much. There were only twenty-five surviving Taliwa, but they brought "the thin gold plates of their written language" (32).

Various agents of the United States knew of the Cherokee syllabary by 1791, but concealed its existence from the public until 1821 (13–14), at which time they realized it could be kept secret no longer. George Guess was actually a white man whom Sequoyah killed in 1786, taking his name at the suggestion of the great Dragging Canoe, a fierce resister of the whites (45). But the whites promoted the Indian now called George Guess

as the bastard Cadmus of a white man. He must have the stain of white blood in order to have the ability to use his brains. They dared not reveal to the American public that this Indian man was a fullblood of the Seven Clan Scribe Society—an ancient society which excluded mixed-bloods and traitors. (115)

Although George Guess and George Gist have generally been used almost interchangeably as "white" names for Sequoyah, according to Bird, George Gist was not George Guess but a separate individual. George Gist was a "fullblood Cherokee . . . of the Paint Clan [who] could neither write, nor read in his native syllabary" (115). The traitorous Cherokee progressives, together with American missionaries, turned this fullblood, too, into a "mixed-blood—the bastard son of a German peddler" (116), and used him for ceremonial occasions celebrating the apparently new literacy of the Cherokee. Finally, the famous "painting [of Sequoyah] that hangs in the Library of Congress" portrays neither Sequoyah-George Guess "nor the scapegoat, George Gist, but . . . Thomas Maw" (118). In addition to a number of cited sources, Bird refers also to family oral tradition and a large number of documents in the Cherokee syllabary which he has not, to my knowledge, made available.

In a disparaging review of Bird's book, the American historian John White simply dismisses it as an "elaborate fabrication." And it has been suggested to me that Bird may be an eccentric with some curious agenda of his own. My inclination, however, is more nearly to agree with Raymond Fogelson, who in a review of the book makes the case that to dismiss it outright comes at a price in historical knowledge (109). I will return to Fogelson's reasons for this conclusion; in terms of the argument I am developing, one way not to dismiss it as history is to loosen our hold on history as a matter only of fact, and/or to engage in some translative labor.

These few examples—a great many could be added—illustrate some of the ways in which Native people think and speak about history, and it is obvious that their conception and their language differ considerably from that of the modern West. This difference, as I noted at the outset, has all too often been considered a lack. The reasons for this lack may be proposed independently of one another or relationally, and I want to look at some of them here.

It has been proposed, for example, that traditional people, in Claude Lévi-Strauss's well-known thermometric metaphor, live in "cold," that is to say, timeless or static societies, as opposed to our own "hot" or rapidly changing societies. And where there is no change, there can be no history. In a late interview (1991), Lévi-Strauss expanded on this point, acknowledging that "cold" societies are not, of course, timeless in fact—although they do wish to be. Their ideal "is to remain in the state in which the gods or ancestors created them at the origin of time." Of course, "they no more escape history than other societies," for all that "they mistrust and dislike" this history, which is "something they undergo" (Lévi-Strauss and Eribon 125). Here is an unfortunate perpetuation of the notion of "the timeless primitive" (Rosaldo 24), tied to a late colonial denial of agency to the Native when time and change do obtrude. We shall see similar notions in the thought of Lévi-Strauss's countryman, Jean-François Lyotard. And yet both Lévi-Strauss and even more emphatically Lyotard propose their notions with an anticolonial intentionality. Where does such error come from? I think it comes from an unfortunate exaggeration of two more or less accurate perceptions.

It seems reasonable, that is, to assume that all historical moments, on the one hand, bear some resemblance to other historical moments, while, on the other hand, they are also different from other historical moments. Every historical moment of which we know and speak is both like and unlike all others. Modern Western cultures tend to privilege historical difference; for Us, it is the uniqueness of the moment, its qualitative difference from the past out of which it comes and the future to which it leads, that gives it its particular historicity. Traditional Native cultures, however, tend to privilege historical identity or sameness. (As, indeed, other traditional societies did in the past and as religious cultures or subcultures also do in the present.) Obviously each new moment does not exactly replicate moments in the past, but each new moment, in Jack Goody's term, is "homeostatic" with the past; its qualitative sameness is the essence of its historicity. What was, is—and will be, with whatever differences. Traditional people, however, tend to deemphasize, and sometimes even deny the differences. Misunderstanding the processes at work here, the Western observer may exaggerate this insistence on sameness to the point of concluding that traditional societies are, indeed, timeless and changeless.

But this is certainly not the case. Indeed, as I have quoted Marshall Sahlins in Chapter 1, tradition may be a name for a culturally specific modality of change; tradition is the means by which changes are integrated into what has been known before. This requires what Goody and Ian Watt have referred to as "structural amnesia" (57), a kind of selective forgetting, or unconscious adjustment of past detail to consist with present reality, which is, of course, more readily carried out in a predominantly oral society than in a literate one (although it does seem that Stalin's Soviet Union made a powerful effort in these regards). As Goody and Watt note of the Tiv people of Niger, there is no "contradiction between what they say now and what they said fifty years ago, since no enduring records exist for them to set beside their present views" (34).

Accurately noting the general absence of alphabetic or phonetic writing (but, as we shall see further, there are other kinds of writing) and the paucity of "enduring records" that would allow indigenous people to make *literal* comparisons "between what they say now and what they said fifty years ago," Western observers exaggerate the consequences of such absence. Goody and Watt put the case quite plainly: "add writing," they write, "and history *proper* begins." If writing is necessary for history, and Native peoples have no writing, then it is easy to say they have no history. But this requires a very specific nonrecognition or undervaluation of the forms of writing Native people most certainly do have, and the forms of history—however different from ours—that writing complements and/or enables.

Thus, in the nineteenth century, we find the noted historian Francis Parkman asserting that "Indian traditions are very rarely of any value as historical evidence" (in Jennings 22). In the twentieth century Robert Lowie emphatically stated, "I cannot attach to oral traditions any historical value whatsoever under any conditions whatever," affirming this extreme view two years later in his Presidential Address to the American Folklore Society. "Indian tradition," said Lowie, "is historically worthless" (in Nabokov 43). In 1952 we find the British anthropologist A. R. Radcliffe-Brown affirming that "In the primitive societies studied by social anthropology there are no historical records" (in Rosaldo 25). And this is only a very small sampling of remarks of this sort. I will, therefore, repeat my contention that, although Their history and Ours are obviously different, that difference is not a lack (e.g., Lévi-Strauss), nor—we turn now to Lyotard—is that difference absolute, so that Their historical knowledge and Our historical knowledge are incommensurable and mutually untranslatable.

The case for the epistemological incommensurability and untranslat-ability between the knowledge of the modern West and that of tradi-tional indigenous societies is today associated foremost with the work of Lyotard and his conception of the *différend*, "a case of a conflict between (at least) two parties that cannot be equitably resolved for lack of a rule of judgment applicable to both arguments" (1968: xi) In Lyotard's view, the difference between the "narrative knowledge" of traditional societies and the "scientific knowledge" (he doesn't use "science" as carrying any con-notation of superiority) of modern societies constitute just such a "dif-ferend" because "It is . . . impossible to judge the existence or validity of narrative knowledge on the basis of scientific knowledge and vice versa: the relevant criteria are different" (1984: 18ff). Our historical narratives and theirs have nothing in common.

I want to disagree with Lyotard on this matter generally and in re-gard to historical knowledge particularly. But first it may be useful to place his thought in historical context. Lyotard's conception, that is to say, of a radical discontinuity between discourses of knowledge is, as David Murray has pointed out, a contemporary restatement of Johann Gottfried von Herder's and Wilhelm von Humboldt's nineteenth-century concept of the radical discontinuity or mutual untranslatability of lan-guages. While their view avoided, as Murray has shown, the unfortunate consequence of the evolutionary view of language that ranked different languages as "higher" or "lower," it also—perhaps more unfortunately— avoided the evolutionists' sense at least of the "*continuity* between lan-guages" (Murray 1991: 8). Herder and Humboldt, to the contrary, urged a view that emphasized "the organic unity and separateness of each lan-guage, constituting a whole 'thoughtworld.'" To "stress [the] difference rather than [the] continuity of cultures and languages," Murray notes, "and the development of a Romantic and organic view of culture which saw each culture as a separate entity . . . meant that the ground was laid for individual languages to be seen as unique" (1991: 9)—unique and conse-quently mutually incomprehensible or untranslatable.

This has also been taken as the necessary consequence of the usual understanding of the linguistic theories of Benjamin Lee Whorf, for ex-ample, Whorf's analysis of examples from Hopi that seem to "prove" that the Hopi have no sense of time.[9] This may be connected to that form of radical relativism in anthropology that Dan Sperber (critically) sum-marizes as the notion "That people of different cultures live in different worlds" (36). Sperber writes, "In prerelativist anthropology, Westerners thought of themselves as superior to all other people. Relativism replaced this despicable hierarchical gap by a kind of cognitive apartheid. If we cannot be superior in the same world, let each people live in its own world" (62). But, as Amanda Anderson remarks, "The assumption of incommensurability among cultures, communities, and histories does not logically entail (or necessarily even tend to promote) indifference: it can just as easily issue in wonder, awe, or distant respect (13–14).

This latter, as David Murray describes it, leads to a "modern version of the sublime" (1991: 10), the consequence of which has been either " 'the horror of helplessness' " (Fishman in Murray 10) "at being trapped in our language, or an excitement at the idea of a genuine otherness beyond our capacity to understand." (10) This sort of excitement, as many have noted, is what seems typical of Lyotard's work. In the face of the differend, "All we can do," Lyotard writes, "is gaze in wonderment at the diversity of discursive species as we do at the diversity of plant or animal species" (1984: 26).

Indeed, Bill Readings, one of the leading interpreters of Lyotard in the Anglophone world, in an essay called "Pagans, Perverts, Or Primitives? Experimental Justice in the Empire of Capital," thinks that in fact it is a good idea to consider an Aboriginal community as very nearly a type of "plant or animal species," so different are they from us. I take time with this because we are invited to this view in the interest of "justice." Consistent with the quote from Sperber above, the dilemma of how to treat a presumed absolute epistemological difference entails an ethical choice. Rather than resolve epistemological difference by force alone, might making right, Lyotard and Readings wish to act in the interest of justice—but they are barred from doing justice according to the principle of objectivity (because Their truth and Our truth are simply incommensurable) and they are barred from doing justice according to the principle of solidarity because the principle of solidarity is ours not theirs. (We shall return to this odd logic in a moment.)

Discussing a Werner Herzog film about a conflict between an Aboriginal group (never identified in Readings's essay) and the Ayers Mining Company that comes before an Australian court, Readings details the many ways in which, as he finds, "the language of the Aboriginal is untranslatable into the language of the Court" (183). In legal discourse, and in general, he finds, "*our* modernity . . . silences any argument structured on other principles" (170). Whenever "the rules of evidence of western rationality and the temporality of western historicism prevail," the result, Readings writes, is "victimization and terror" (171).[10]

Yet his Lyotardian solution to this problem is, to my mind, bizarre. The only solution, says Readings on the basis of his reading of Lyotard, is to abandon the search for a solution. We must avoid repeating the error of representing them as "an other to western modernity that haunts its margins" (172). Indeed, "ethical responsibility demands a quasi-esthetic experimentation if justice is to be done to an Aboriginal claim that can only be evoked as irrepresentable" (173).[11] Quasi-esthetically, all we can do in the interest of justice is to "keep difference in question," for "no translation is possible" (185) between their language and ours. To avoid violence, Readings concludes, we must "relinquish the concept of the human, to separate liberty from fraternity" (186). I can only gasp at this! No epistemological objectivity can ally us; Their truth plus Our truth equals a differend. And no solidarity can ally us; we must "separate liberty from fraternity!" Not only is this strange, but it is dangerous as well for any one concerned with justice.

I take so much time with Readings and Lyotard because I agree with them as to how much is at stake in the debate about epistemological commensurability and epistemological, cultural, and linguistic translatability, while disagreeing as strongly as possible with their conclusions and the consequences of those conclusions. If one adopts an attitude of indifference or of awe toward those who speak different languages, deciding that the difference in language is so great that the possibility of "fraternity" is an illusion, the result, it seems to me, is not liberty and justice. Rather, the result is Auschwitz, Dachau, and Buchenwald;[12] the result is the Middle Passage, the Constitutional conception of "three fifths of a man," and lynch law, along with the Trail of Tears, the Long Walk, Sand Creek, and Wounded Knee. The list can be expanded all too easily.

As we shall see further, it is only by extending the cosmopolitan commitment to fraternity as a structure of feeling beyond the nation (I have joined a term from Raymond Williams and a title from Bruce Robbins and Pheng Cheah), and by choosing solidarity even when it sometimes conflicts with objectivity as we know it, that differentials of power can be confronted in a commitment to justice. But this requires that we put no speaker beyond the pale of nonviolent translation.

Curiously, Readings, contrary to his claim that the unnamed Aboriginal group is untranslatable, translates them regularly (perhaps violently, too). Take, for example, his assertion that "the force of their silent accusation is to make us ask, 'Who are we to speak?' " (186). This is obviously a translation of their silence: their silence is an accusation; it provokes a particular question. Or, discussing an occasion on which the Aboriginal people buried sacred objects, Reading states unequivocally that the burial was performed "in a time that is not historical in any sense we might recognize" (181). How does he know that? Is it that he has tried to translate their sense of time and history and failed? Or is it rather that he has simply determined a priori that their sense of time and history just must be—whatever it is—something beyond our powers of recognition? Then, in a translation I suspect is thoroughly mistaken, Readings announces that the Aboriginals are not a "we," that is, they are "a community that is not modern, that doesn't think of itself as a people" (184). As Tobin Siebers has said of "the notion of symbolic violence," "This position has no political viability, and it is ethically incoherent" (68).

Perhaps it might accurately be said of many contemporary Native communities that they both are and also are not "modern"—although to place them in relation to modernity is already to translate them, for good or ill. Unless you have heard more than a community's silence; unless you have heard what they think of anything you may have tried to say, how can you confidently say what an entire community is or is not? There is no contemporary Native American community "that doesn't think of itself as a people." That Native communities do so think of themselves, as nationalist critics have forcefully insisted, is something we can and must understand, and I suspect this might be the case with Aboriginal groups as well. Readings' willingness to state that these indigenous Australians do not think of themselves as a people, is once again not to leave them untranslated (because untranslatable) but to translate them very badly. Deciding that they are not a people is, indeed, as Readings bizarrely recommends, to withdraw fraternity, to the point virtually of denying them humanity. Granted, Lyotard and Readings make this move in the interest of ending the violent history of—here—discursive imperialism. But their tactic for doing so opens the door to even greater violence.

Humans do not live in different worlds; they do not speak private languages, or operate according to knowledge systems that other humans can never hope to recognize, let alone understand—at least in some measure, at least in part. Translation, therefore, is possible. But from at least the moment when Columbus took six Natives from the island of Guanahani to Spain, "in order that they may learn to speak"[13] (69), European translation of the indigenous peoples of the Americas has most certainly been a violent and destructive colonial practice.

Eric Cheyfitz has provided the most detailed and intensive account of the links between property and "proper" speech, "defined inescapably as the *national,* the *domestic,* the *familiar,* the *authoritative,* the *legitimate,*" (90) all of which were ours and none of which belonged to them.[14] "The European process of translation," Cheyfitz writes, "displaced or attempted to displace . . . Native Americans into the realm of the proper . . . not so these Americans could possess the proper but so that having been translated into it they could be dispossessed of it . . . and relegated to the territory of the figurative" (59). Survival for Native people, Cheyfitz argues, has depended on resistance to the *translatio* imposed by Europeans.

Is nonviolent translation, what I have several times called anti-imperial translation, possible? Cheyfitz himself notes that "While the *translatio* dreamt and dreams of empire, the struggle for voice, *the assertion of the necessity and difficulty of translation,* persisted and persists in various

forms from Native American resistance to physical and cultural obliteration"(124) to the struggles of African Americans and other peoples. This
necessary and difficult translation, it may be said, is a translation against
empire. At this point, I will briefly turn to postcolonial anthropology
(which has faced problems of translation now for nearly fifty years) for
some further thoughts on this matter.

Peter Whiteley offers what he calls four "simple truisms" (1998:14)
which, "were it not for the madness of the postmodern moment . . . would
be needless to state" (14–15). I will quote Whiteley at some length. His
first "truism"

> is an existential realism about human social life. The second is a belief that lan-
> guage can indeed describe experience, both individual and collective. . . . Third,
> cultural ideas are intersubjective in Wittgenstein's sense and they get expressed
> and acted upon in objectively describable social practices. Fourth, this intersub-
> jectivity must—because of irrefutable species conditions of Homo sapiens sapi-
> ens—be potentially extensible across linguistic barriers; in short, just as there can
> be no private language, . . . there can be no private culture, whose key saliences
> and engagements are de jure incommunicable to others. (15)

Anthropologists, Whiteley later continues, need "to show, through an
absolute dependency on ethnography as translation, the instrumental
necessity of treating language as referential" (45). "In privileging difference," as we have of late tended to do (and properly), Whiteley writes,

> anthropologists tend to obfuscate cross-cultural commonalities—in such areas
> as production, reproduction, and organization—that are readily commensurable
> and translatable. . . . In short, a cross-cultural intersubjectivity of the experienced
> phenomenal world strongly suggests parallel systems of referentiality in many
> conceptual domains; indeed, this is the sine qua non for much intertranslatability,
> and the precondition for more fine-grained, context-sensitive translations. (45)

This account recognizes that not all "conceptual domains" will have "parallel systems of referentiality," thus making "intertranslatability" difficult
in some instances. But it insists on the commensurability of all varieties of
human experience in some important degree; there are no private languages and no private cultures; we do not quite live in different worlds.

But, again, can we represent Other cultures and translate them without
reproducing the history of imperial translative violence? The only answer
I can offer is that, given the deeply unsatisfactory alternatives, the effort
seems worth making. There is no work in the world, after all, without,
in the phrase of Jean-Paul Sartre, dirty hands. If one does not choose,
with Lyotard and Readings, to be an apparently innocent spectator in
the garden or zoo of difference, absurdly claiming that we can't learn
from them "because the notion of common humanity is *ours*" (Readings
171) not theirs, then, yes, the intransigent fact of existing power differ-

entials will come into play, and harm might be done. I certainly believe that sometimes one must stay out, keep silent, admit to being at a loss for words. In any case, the decision *not* to translate them is a decision only those in power can make.

We know well, for example, that, however strange the actions of the invading Euramericans might have seemed to indigenous persons, however unlike any known speech the sounds they made may have been, still, because these strangers had powerful weapons and increasingly great numbers, there was no choice but for Native people to try to understand their ways and their words, even, sometimes, to "learn from them," regardless whose idea that was. Native people began to translate Europe as a necessity and an opportunity from the first moments of contact.

One of the ways they did this was by incorporating Our writing into Their writing for the recording of history—a history Europeans and indigenous peoples began to have together as well as separately. Just as there is no people without history, so, too, is there no people without writing—by which I mean material or tangible means of information storage, or in I. J. Gelb's phrase, "A system of human intercommunication by means of conventional visible marks" (in Basso and Anderson 50–51).[15]

I differ here from those like Jack Goody who believe that the term "writing" ought only to be applied to writing systems whose "essential service is to objectify speech, to provide *language* with a material correlative, a set of visible signs" (1968: 1 my emphasis) productive of what John DeFrancis calls "visible speech." DeFrancis believes that "no sets of symbols not based on the representation of sounds have been shown capable of conveying anything more than a limited range of thought" (248), and J. T. Hooker agrees. These views would disqualify Native American "picture writing" as writing, to be sure.

But others, like Albertine Gaur, take writing strictly as a means of information storage. Its purpose is to preserve knowledge and not only knowledge-in-speech. Gaur sensibly suggests that writing developed "when the sum total of available knowledge had become too large to be stored in human memory." In the same way, it has presently "become increasingly obvious that information can once again be stored, quite effectively, without writing" (210).

What I will, therefore, call Native *writing* included such things as the "string balls" of various materials constructed by Yakima girls from their early childhood and the birchbark scrolls of the Chippewa *mite* priests.[16] There are the Iroquois wampum strings which, as Sir William Johnson wrote in 1753, "they look upon as we our letters, or rather bonds"[17] (264). There are Plains pictographs painted on tipis, robes, and shirts, and Lakota winter counts which we shall consider further.

The first detailed accounts of the "Pictographs of the North American

Indians" and "Picture-Writing of the American Indians" are by Garrick Mallery, whose studies by those names appeared as a "Preliminary Paper" for the Fourth Annual Report of the Bureau of American Ethnology (1882–83; published 1886) and as the Tenth Annual Report of the Bureau of American Ethnology (1888–89; published 1893). Mallery's researches revealed written means for announcing visits and departures, along with directions traveled. "Conditions" (such as "I am starving" 1893: 347) could be conveyed in writing, along with the warning (Ojibwa) that a murderer is at large (1893: 353). There are Ojibwa and Cheyenne letters, some of the former actually coming to be sent through the mails. And there are Iroquoian and Algonkian tribal designations (1893: 377ff). Mallery also "reads" the tattoos used in many tribes, along with property markings, decorated clothing and tipis, inscribed grave posts, illustrated pipe stems, personal names, and pictographic representation of stories. He shows that Native people "wrote" biography and autobiography,[18] and, in a chapter called "Ideography," demonstrates that indeed "abstract ideas [were] expressed pictorially" (1893: 584) as well, perhaps—for those who knew how to read—conveying a fuller range of thought than DeFrancis allows for. Mallery also comments on the Sequoyah syllabary (1893 665). A good deal of his work, however, concentrates on the by-now well-known Lakota winter counts. These are Native American traditional, written histories.

Lakota winter counts date the beginning of a year from the first snowfall; thus each "winter," as Raymond DeMallie explains, spans "parts of two years on the western calendar" (1992: 3).[19] The keeper of the winter count chooses an important event of each winter for which he names it. Thus there is, for example, the winter called "many died of smallpox," or "the stars fell," or "many flags were given," or "thirty Sioux were killed by Crow Indians." (We have already noted that there is no winter count extant that chooses the Custer fight as the important event to mark the year 1876–77.) DeMallie cites an 1877 letter written by James Bradley, a military officer serving in the Dakota territory, in which Bradley wrote of an old man of the Crazy Horse band who rode into the Indian Agency with "a stick about six feet long, covered with notches, thousands of them. . . . he said it was the history of the world from the beginning, handed down by his fathers" (1992: 2). Although this old man never seems to have made his winter count available to Bradley or to any other of the whites, the first winter count to be published also dates from 1877. Kept by Lone Dog, a Yanktonai, and painted on hide, it was brought to public attention also by Garrick Mallery, in his "A Calendar of the Dakota Nation." Lone Dog's winter count covers the years from 1799 to 1870, has been much studied, and has inspired at least one volume of contemporary Native American poetry.[20]

DeMallie discusses in detail the winter count of the Brulé Sioux, Brown Hat, or Battiste Good, which is composed of "pictographs representing each winter from 1700–1701 to 1879–80" (1992: 4), along with twelve more "composite pictographs" that "take the count back by generations" to the beginning of the Lakota as a people. English words are written into Good's winter count, as well as dates—July 4, for example—assumed to be historically important to the U.S. Americans. Good's winter count was continued by a man named High Hawk who brought it forward to 1921–22. DeMallie calls the Good winter count "a hybrid document," for it employs traditional mnemonic devices important to cultures that preserved and transmitted knowledge orally while "appropriating the numerical chronology" (1992: 7) as well as some of the alphabetic writing of the whites. In the same way that both oral and literate technologies are present, so, too, as noted above, are Native and Euramerican conceptualizations of "history" present, the Good winter count once more representing as history what Euramericans would typically call myth but also what we would admit as history.[21]

Helen Blish, the editor of the extraordinary corpus of drawings done by the Oglala Dakota, Amos Bad Heart Bull, between 1890 and 1913, opens her work with a careful consideration of Native pictographic historiography that builds substantially upon Mallery's account. Blish finds the winter counts to be aimed at portraying the history of a particular group (Oglala, Yanktonai, Brulé, etc.), rather than as a history of the Plains in general or of the world. In her reading, the winter counts do not "aim at narrative" (24), serving instead to provide "effective calendric milestones" (24) and "a trustworthy supplement to the memory" (26). Along with Lone Dog's winter count, she mentions others by the Flame, whose count stretches from 1786–87 to 1876–77, and by Short Man, whose count runs from 1821 up to 1923.

Amos Bad Heart Bull's extraordinary body of work consists of 415 drawings and paintings.[22] For Blish, these amount to no less than "the complete history of the Oglala Dakotas for the last half at least of the nineteenth century and the beginning of the twentieth" (27), and she finds "that the record is fairly accurate historically, there is no doubt" (28). Unlike the winter counts, Bad Heart Bull's "manuscript," as Blish terms it, does provide a "chronological and coherent sequence" of events that is "*narrative* rather than calendric" (27, my emphasis).

In her third chapter, "The Bad Heart Bull Manuscript as History," Blish compares Bad Heart Bull to Herodotus, judging him superior to the Greek "Father of History" (29), in that he "does not preserve *merely* the record of exploits of arms," but also gives "a complete cross section of the life of his people—social, economic, ritualistic, political, and military—*as he knew it*." "Once it becomes evident that the record is historical in nature," she notes, "the important question is, 'Is the record a true one?'" At this point, Blish, who died in 1941, goes on to anticipate contemporary debates about the place of fact in history, commenting that "truth in the portrayal of history is of two kinds: truth to detail, accuracy in point of facts enumerated; and faithfulness to the spirit and atmosphere of the times, truth in the bodying forth of the character of a people and its life as a whole" (29). Her view is that "Both types of truth are of extreme importance, but for the moment the second will interest us more, for a worthy and dependable physical and spiritual panorama is more significant to sympathetic understanding than the detailed description of episode, institution, and object" (29).

Here we have an early and powerful defetishization (cf. Dening) of fact, accuracy, and scienticity as always of primary importance to historical narrative, and an acknowledgment (without, it should be noted, dismissing the value of factual accuracy) of the importance for history of "truth in the bodying forth of the character of a people and its life as a whole." This is also the conclusion to which I have come, a conclusion, let me note, representing a decided shift in my thinking since 1998, when a version of this chapter first appeared.

*   *   *

Here we may turn back to the question of who killed Custer, how Stone Forehead's band eluded the troops, and whether Sequoyah invented the syllabary in which the Cherokee language could be written. Any nonviolent, anti-imperial translation of the answers some Native people have given to these historical questions requires that we follow Helen Blish and those who have come after her, and abandon the ethnocentric insistence that there can be no history without fact, accuracy, and scientific rationality—which, also, with Blish and others, does not mean denying that fact, accuracy, and scientific rationality can also be of enormous importance to history.

Asked in 1909 to say who had killed General Custer in the Battle of the Little Big Horn, the survivors of that 1876 fight reached agreement that it was the Cheyenne warrior Brave Bear; asked again in 1926, a smaller group this time pronounced that the killer was the Minneconjou, White Bull. The 1909 decision may have been based on consideration of the facts as those in attendance at the gathering knew and understood them, and it is also possible that a review of the facts in 1926 led some of them later to conclude that, after all, White Bull was the man who killed Custer. It is also quite possible that not the facts of the matter but the truth of the matter was the old warriors' chief concern. Perhaps in this instance, as Loretta Fowler has remarked of the Arapaho, history "operates as a con-

ceptual framework for interpreting and shaping social action" (in Nabokov 6). This "framework," Fowler continues, need not "necessarily [be]
related to events as recorded by observers" in order for it to have real
historical force, or, quite simply, for it to be fully entitled to the name of
history.

In these regards, perhaps a detailed analysis of the situation of the various Lakota and Cheyenne divisions in 1909 and 1926, of Indian-white
relations on the Plains and in the United States generally, and of the position and status of Brave Bear and White Bull among the Cheyenne and
Lakota in each period, would make clear that the warriors were offering
an analysis, in Fowler's sense of an interpretation of events, intended to
shape social action: an analysis that can only be called historical even if
it did not necessarily (but we can't be sure of that) establish the factual
identity of the warrior who killed Custer.

To much the same point, Peter Nabokov cites Richard Dorson's study
of Ojibwa and Potawatomi stories about relations with white people, in
which Dorson found that, even when the "face-value factuality" (in Nabokov 92) of the stories might be doubtful by Western standards, the stories
were nonetheless essential as "documenting [the] attitude" of the narrators. In this regard, as Dorson notes, the stories "served as tribal history and provide[d] the emotional bases for subsequent relations between Indians and white men" (in Nabokov 92). Reviewing a wide range of
stories preserving tribal history, Nabokov concludes that from the Western historical perspective, "Indian 'memories' about . . . distant times are
bound to be more interesting as commentary than documentation" (49).
More "interesting," to be sure, so far as "documentation" or "face-value
factuality" are our foremost concerns. But I am claiming, as strongly as I
can, with Helen Blish and Greg Dening, that "face-value factuality" need
not be our foremost concern, nor should Our translation of Their history
relegate it to "commentary" as a historical category of lesser worth than
the category of "documentation."

Discussing John G. Neihardt's later interviews with Black Elk, in which
Black Elk offered a history of his Lakota people, Raymond DeMallie
notes, "Although from a white man's perspective this history is really
myth—a series of non-chronological anecdotes full of mystical happenings—from the Lakotas' perspective it is the only true history because
it explains the moral framework within which Lakota culture developed
and flourished" (1984: 69). Much as I respect and admire DeMallie's
work, it nonetheless seems to me that if, "from a white man's perspective
this history is really myth," then it is time for the "white man's perspective" to broaden and for us to learn from it. It is time to recognize that
the Stone Boy stories Jahner discusses, the Custer battle survivors' pronouncements, and Black Elk's "non-chronological anecdotes full of mys-

tical happenings" are also "true history"—although they are not always "plausible," in William Cronon's terms, as factual and accurate history.

Apart from religious conversions, or whatever we call radical episte-mological shifts such as that of Calvin Martin in his work since *Keepers of the Game*, of course it is unlikely that anyone trained in Western modes of thought will accept accounts of "mystical happenings" as factual and accurate. But that is not necessary. What is necessary is that we stop using terms like "myth," "anecdotes," and "mystical happenings," as standing in simple and subordinate opposition to "history"—a category that We think cannot exist apart from empirical, factual accuracy. (Let me once again confirm my wholehearted appreciation of factual accuracy and my commitment to showing certain histories—those of "the Holocaust never happened," "the slaves were really happy," or "the Indians attacked us unprovoked" variety—to be without any foundation in fact and thus, to those playing by the cultural rules of facticity, to be largely unhistorical.) We need to recognize that there are times when, as Blish so eloquently put it, "a worthy and dependable physical and spiritual panorama is more significant to sympathetic understanding than the detailed description of episode, institution, and object" (29), and that the significance of that sort of "panorama" is *historical*.

It is in this spirit that Paul A.W. Wallace writes of his conflation of "the three main versions" of the legend "of Deganawidah and the founding of the Iroquois Confederacy" (vii). Wallace makes clear that he has not attempted the

task of disentangling fact from folklore in the story of these heroes. . . . No effort is made to distinguish between what the Iroquois actually received from Degana-widah and Hiawatha while they lived and what the popular imagination after their death gave back by way of tribute to their memory. (5)

Rather, he continues,

The purpose in these pages is to show the legend in its dynamic unity: to let it appear as the constructive force it actually was, one that seized on the minds of the Iroquois, directed their moral energies to the preservation of the Peace, and so gave them an influence on history out of all proportion to their numbers.

In similar fashion, when the Cheyenne tell Father Powell that the rea-son Stone Forehead's warriors could elude the pursuing soldiers was that he turned them into buffalo, we need not assume that the Cheyenne are insisting factually, literally, empirically that the warriors became four-legged creatures with tails, horns, and so on. If that is the only way we can understand "turned into buffalo," then we confront the need for trans-lation that is indeed a mediation between Our language for history and Theirs, an anti-imperial translation that is not an obliteration of their speech. What, then, might such a translation look like? I am not expert in Cheyenne language or culture, but some responsible effort must here be proffered. So I will try.

One possible translation of the Cheyenne view—and Father Powell makes the point that something like this was the view of the matter recounted to him, in 1960, by Baldwin Twins, a Cheyenne who had himself twice served as Keeper of Mahootse—is that Stone Forehead, leading his men north in 1875, made the decision that the only chance they had to escape the soldiers was to rely on the power of a more- or other-than-natural sort, the only power in regard to which they believed themselves to be superior to the whites. Stone Forehead, also known as Sacred Arrows for his role as Keeper of Mahootse, the Sacred Medicine Arrows of the Cheyenne, was a man who had such power, and he used it in a manner consistent with Cheyenne belief. To think of "turned into buffalo" this way, rather than fixating literally on the proposal that two-legged persons became four-legged persons and so on, is to take the Cheyenne narrative as opening questions which may be of exemplary historical usefulness both to the Cheyenne and to academic historians, conveying as it does the "moral framework" within which these people shaped their lives.

Not to translate in this way is, in fact, to *create* a Lyotardian differend, a situation in which two incommensurable languages are being spoken, where one need not exist. I recall, in these regards, an episode from one of Carlos Castaneda's "Don Juan" fictions in which "Castaneda" responds to "Don Juan"'s telling him that he had become a crow the night before by asking whether that meant he had grown a beak, wings, and feathers. "Don Juan"—and I think Castaneda scripted the invented dialogue very skillfully, here—simply does not understand what these questions have to do with his having become a crow. The two men really are talking at cross purposes, and there is not much possibility of mutual translation. So, too, would we be talking at cross purposes to the Cheyenne if we pursued their claim that Stone Forehead had turned his men into buffalo by insisting that "being turned into buffalo" either means having grown four legs, horns, and so on, or else it means nothing, certainly nothing historical. It has been my contention throughout this chapter that one can both believe in the importance of fact and accuracy for history and also believe—with Blish, Dening, and others I have cited—that there are true histories that may not be factual and accurate.

Let us return now to Traveler Bird. His account of Cherokee history and of Sequoyah in particular is at many points at odds with histories that have preceded and followed his own, and it is probably not to much point for me to compile a detailed list of these discrepancies much beyond those I have already noted in my brief summary of his book. I do, however, want to note one particular point at which Bird differs from a (somewhat) more mainstream account. I think it is illustrative of what is at issue in his book's claim to historical truth.

Late in his book, Bird briefly discusses one John Hunter or John D. Hunter. John Dunn Hunter was the white author of the *Memoirs of a Captivity Among the Indians of North America*, first published in London, in 1824. Bird has Hunter scheming with the Texan Stephen Austin and only "pretending to be the friend of the Indian" (126). Hunter and a Cherokee named Richard Field, according to Bird, "were killed by orders from [Cherokee] Chief John Bowl in January, 1827" (128).

In his Introduction to a reprint of Hunter's *Memoirs*, Richard Drinnon, Hunter's radical (hence my parenthetical "somewhat" above, as a qualifier to "mainstream") editor, writes that not only were Austin and Hunter violently opposed to one another's Indian policies, but it was Austin who "bought off the Indians . . . and arranged to have the Cherokees" kill Hunter along with Field. (xxviii). It is Drinnon's contention that "Hunter was killed by the same American nationalism and racism which made so many of his red friends 'vanish' " (xxix).

Now I cannot imagine that Traveler Bird doubts the violence of "American nationalism and racism"; what is important to note is that that is not his concern here. Whatever the Americans may be or do, Bird's history focuses on the Cherokee and the case to be made for their national, historical, political, and cultural sovereignty and autonomy as revealed by the "true" story of Cherokee literacy. This, I believe, is what makes his account of Sequoyah far more interesting as history than an "elaborate fabrication," the fantasy of a single eccentric, could possibly be.

I want to develop this point a bit further. Let's return to a passage I quoted in part above, in which Bird explains the decision of the traitorous Cherokee leaders and the vicious American missionaries to "play up the discovery of the syllabary." Bird writes,

They would pretend to the United States Government and the American public that the Cherokee Nation was indeed becoming civilized, and had produced a genius. But they would make certain that the Cherokee Indian who "caused it" was known to the public as the bastard Cadmus of a white man. He must have that stain of white blood in order to have the ability to use his brains. They dared not reveal to the American public that this Indian man was a fullblood of the Seven Clan Scribe Society—an ancient society which excluded mixed bloods and traitors. (114–15)

Thus Bird attempts to present Sequoyah, in Raymond Fogelson's words, as "the last link to traditional knowledge and autochthonous wisdom" (109). Bird produces Sequoyah as "an appropriate culture hero for modern Indian militancy" (Fogelson 109). His commentary has historical force apart from its factual accuracy because it conveys a truth shared by many Cherokee people—again, regardless whether they would defend this truth by way of a point by point defense of Bird's "facts."

Let me offer but a single illustration of this. At the very end of their 1964 volume, *Folktales of the Oklahoma Cherokees*, the Cherokee scholars Jack and Anna Kilpatrick offer a brief interview about Sequoyah with a man named Asudi. Asudi is ninety-two years old; his first language is Cherokee and his English, according to the Kilpatricks, is "fair" (xi). Anna Kilpatrick asks Asudi whether Sequoyah was "a full-blood Cherokee?" Asudi answers, "Yes." Kilpatrick follows up: "He didn't have any white blood? . . . he was not part-white, was he?" Asudi affirms, "All Cherokee" (181). In an endnote, the Kilpatricks remark that, while "Without hesitancy the Cherokees admit that their greatest political leader, John Ross, was but one-eighth Cherokee; . . . they insist that Sequoyah was a full blood, *all the literature to the contrary notwith-standing.*" [23]

In his "Bibliographical Note," Traveler Bird claims to speak for a substantial number of people, and my example above may well bear him out on this. Bird writes,

> I have re-created my ancestor in his own image through words and thoughts of a foreign language—not from the books in libraries, nor government records. In so doing, I have sought the *truth* as it exists in the hearts and minds of some 13,000 fullblood kinsmen living in the hills of Eastern Oklahoma, the Smoky Mountains of North Carolina and those of Mexico who still speak, read and write our native language, and who have managed to keep our culture, values and sane life-ways. Whether this is your truth, I don't know, nor does it matter—it is mine, and that of the minority faction of my people, whose ancestors refused to yield. (143–44)

The bibliography that follows will not please academic historians, just as the documentation throughout the book (some of it decidedly from "books in libraries" and in "government records") is easily called into question. But there is a truth here that must be taken into account for any comprehensive view of Cherokee history then, and especially now. I do not say this as a sentimental or "politically correct" conclusion. Nor do I say it, let me once more state as explicitly and emphatically as I can, as part of a call to abandon fact and accuracy in history, that is, to abandon objectivity. It *is* important to know the facts as accurately as possible, but the facts do not always convey the truth of history, as the truth of history does not always require factual accuracy.

The history of America must no longer be written without a recognition that there are histories of America. No "useful accounts of history can or should be fashioned without consulting those whose history it is," as Keith Basso has written (1996: 34) Moreover, if "we are to understand history as lived reality," as Raymond DeMallie said in his 1992 Presidential Address to the American Society for Ethnohistory, "it is essential to understand the perspective . . . of the actors involved" (1993: 526). Not merely the perspective, but the worldview as well. In this regard, to cite Bernard Fontana, "It is veracity in their terms which counts" (370)—or which most certainly must be taken into account. As Abraham Wolf Robe, a Kutenai elder, assured the ethnographer Harry Turney-High in 1939, as Kitty Smith insisted to Julie Cruikshank in 1990, "this is not one of the fairy stories I am telling you, but a fact. It is real history" (in Nabokov 15). What I have tried to show is that, regardless of the presence or absence of factual accuracy in some Native histories, these narratives nonetheless have every legitimate claim to be taken as "real history."

Chapter 4
From "Half-Blood" to "Mixedblood": *Cogewea* and the "Discourse of Indian Blood"

For Louis Owens

> Dismantling the intricate edifice of racism embodied in "Indian blood" is not simply a matter of exposing its essentialism and discarding its associated policies, but a more delicate and complicated task: that is, acknowledging "Indian blood" as a discourse of conquest with manifold and contradictory effects, but without invalidating rights and resistances that have been couched in terms of that very discourse.
> —Pauline Turner Strong and Barrik van Winkle[1]

Published in 1927, and until recently thought the "first" novel by a Native American woman,[2] Mourning Dove's *Cogewea: The Half-Blood* was paid little critical attention until 1978, when Charles Larson commented upon it in an appendix to his *American Indian Fiction* in regard to the issue of dual authorship. Mourning Dove—or Hum-ishu-ma, also known as Christine Haines and Christine or Chrystal Quintasket—this is to say, had completed a first draft of the novel in the years 1912–14, but, after meeting Lucullus Virgil McWhorter, a white businessman with a keen interest in Native American culture and in federal Indian policy, worked with him in the winter of 1915–16 to revise the text. Finding a publisher in the years of the First World War and immediately after proved difficult, and, in 1922, McWhorter undertook his own independent revision, expanding the text by adding passages critical of the government's Indian policy and "elevating" Cogewea's diction in many places. Although *Cogewea* bears a copyright date of 1927, it appears that books were not available until June 1928, and it was only then that Mourning Dove herself saw the changes made by McWhorter.

Cogewea was for years out of print until the University of Nebraska Press reissued it in 1981 with an introduction by Dexter Fisher (Alice Poindexter Fisher), a revised version of part of her 1979 dissertation on Mourning Dove and Zitkala Sa (Gertrude Simmons Bonnin). Since that time, Jay Miller has done important editing work on Mourning Dove's autobiographical manuscripts, and Alanna Kathleen Brown—who has substantial disagreements with Miller[3]—has provided much of the major criticism.

Of the two epigraphs Louis Owens chose for his study of the Native American novel, *Other Destinies* (1992), one is a quotation from Mourning Dove's *Cogewea: The Half-Blood* and one is from Gerald Vizenor's "Crows Written on the Poplars," an autobiographical text published in 1987. Both refer to "Indian blood," and taken together the two passages may be read as marking a shift in Native American literature from *Cogewea*'s view of the constraints on the "half-blood" early in the twentieth century to Vizenor's very different sense of more open possibilities for the "mixed-blood" nearer the century's end. The two epigraphs also serve to contextualize and historicize Owens's dedication of his book, "For mixedbloods, the next generation." This chapter, dedicated to Louis Owens, attempts to elaborate and expand on his insights into *Cogewea*'s depiction of the situation of the "half-blood" in the period just before and after the First World War. My cosmopolitan commitment to comparativism will place "the discourse of Indian blood"[4] in the broader context of what F. H. Matthews has called " '20's Americanism," and a racism directed at blacks and other immigrants perceived as not-quite-white, as well as against Native American people.

* * *

The epigraph Owens chose from Cogewea quotes her on the plight of Native persons of mixed parentage or "blood" as follows: "Yes, we are between two fires, the Red and the White. Our Caucasian brothers criticize us as a shiftless class, while the Indians disown us as abandoning our own race. We are maligned and traduced as no one but we of the despised 'breeds' can know." Owens's quotation from Gerald Vizenor, who wrote some sixty years later, offers a very different view of the "mixed-blood." Rather than passive subjects, "mixedbloods," Vizenor tells us, actively "loosen the seams in the shrouds of identities."[5] Now, just past the turn of the twenty-first century, it is apparent that Vizenor was at once both accurate and prophetic.

By 1987, Native mixedbloods, along with a range of biracial, inter-racial, and multiracial persons, had already complicated the most com-mon American racial categories, in particular the dominant category, white, or as Mourning Dove put it, "Caucasian." For all that race in America remains, as it always has been, a matter foremost of black and white, nonetheless, looking back on the century just past, we can see, as Strong and van Winkle write, "that race is not at base only about black and white, though it is indeed a product of European colonialism" (1996: 565), of which the invasion of America is a particular type.

Lise Funderberg notes that "Some population experts and multiracial support networks estimate that there are currently [1994] at least one million mixed-race people in this country (*of all mixes, not just black and white*)" (11, my emphasis). Maria P. P. Root adds that "The rate of multi-racial births have [sic] increased at an even faster rate" than the "al-most fourfold" increase in "the past two decades [1970s and '80s] [of] interracial marriage rates" (1995: 231) while "More children of Japanese-Americans are born to interracial couples than same-race couples" (231). It is presently the case that "The highest intermarriage rates are those of American Indians. Majorities of American Indian men (52.9 percent) and American Indian women (53.9 percent) married whites rather than American Indians" (Lind 38). This fact gives rise to bitter jokes about the diminishing quanta of "Indian blood," as in Marie Annharte Baker's lines, quoted by Strong and van Winkle, "I might terminate/if I get nose-bleed" (1996: 552) To "get the joke," they note, it is necessary "to under-stand both the blood reckoning that defines Indian identity and the his-tory of governmental efforts to 'terminate' the official [federal] status of Indian tribes" (1996: 552–53).

It is no joke, however, that Article 1, Section 2, Clause 3 of the Consti-tution of the United States does not count Indians as part of the Ameri-can population "because [they were] not taxed," and, further, as Vine Deloria, Jr., writes, "the Constitution clearly excludes American Indians" (1992: 301). Milner Ball, a professor of constitutional law, states that "The American story of origins fundamentally excludes tribes and denies them voice" (2300).

Formal racial classification, however, was not operative on the census until 1850, and it was then left to white census enumerators to decide whether or not to accept the classification offered by those who were counted. At that time, one of the possible classifications was "mulatto," and mulattos, as Anne Fleischmann writes, were "Once defined as a third race and counted as such in the 1850 census" (247). (The category mu-latto, as we shall note further, was dropped from the census in 1920.) Racial self-identification for the census did not begin until 1970, and we may note that the recent sharp increase in the number of persons self-identifying as American Indian (an increase of 259 percent between 1960 and 1990!) almost certainly exceeds what might be attributable exclusively to a rise in birthrate among Native people. Instead, it seems reasonable to assume that persons who did not identity themselves as Native in the past are currently choosing to do so, while others are doing so on the basis of a recent "discovery" of an indigenous ancestor.[6]

Reflecting these developments is the substantial increase in the number of books with titles like *American Mixed Race: The Culture of Microdiversity*; *Racially Mixed People in America*; *Black, White, Other: Biracial Americans Talk About Race and Identity*; *As We Are Now: Mixblood Essays on Race and Identity*; and *Half and Half: Writers on Growing Up Biracial and Bicultural*.[7] This suggests that the "seams in the shrouds of identities" will certainly continue to "loosen," as what Maria P. P. Root has called "the psychological browning of America" proceeds apace. (This particular development is marked by the increase in books devoted to the study of "whiteness.")

But this is hardly to instantiate a linear narrative of progress for those of us who wish, as George Hutchinson writes of Nella Larsen's project in *Quicksand*, to undo "the violence of racialization as such . . . in the attempt to make it ethically insupportable, an affront to humanity" (345). The task is to undo white privilege, maintained by "racialization" with all its confusions and contradictions—confusions and contradictions that have not yet led to the destruction of the discourse of race, a particularly complex and "flexible" discourse. Gail Bederman, citing Foucault, observes the way in which the very "contradictions [in discourses] frequently give them a tenacious power over people's thoughts and actions [and] allow people to bend them to their own purposes" (24). Thus, as Michael Elliott soberly concludes his study of racial discourse in the narrative of law in the nineteenth century,

The ability of the hegemonic order . . . to incorporate ideas and traditions that are inconsistent with one another has made race into more than a simple definition of group identity. Race has come to comprise a set of social beliefs so flexible that they are capable of surviving the most withering intellectual attacks. (1999: 633)

But this should not dissuade us (Hutchinson, Elliott, Bederman, myself, and many others) from mounting "the most withering intellectual attacks" we can on race and blood discourse as it impedes "rights and resistances" to white privilege.[8]

The passage from *Cogewea* Owens chose for his epigraph continues in the novel (Owens quotes this continuation later) with Cogewea stating explicitly that, "If permitted, I would prefer living the white man's way to that of the reservation Indian, but he hampers me" (41). All the same, Cogewea insists she "will *never* disown my mother's blood. Why should I do so? Though my skin is of tawny hue, I am not ashamed." Although, as I have noted, formal racial definitions first appeared in the census for 1850, it was not until the 1880 census, as David Theo Goldberg writes, that, "the request for information about 'Indians' had become more specific" (240), with white enumerators being "instructed not to accept answers they 'know or have reason to believe are false." Full-bloods were listed by tribal affiliation, but, curiously, at this time the children of Indian and white parents were marked " 'W' . . . reflecting the presupposed closeness . . . between 'Europeans' and 'Indians'."

With the tremendous influx of immigrants in the decades between 1880 (5.2 million in the 1880s alone) and 1924 (at which time immigration was severely curtailed, while American Indians were granted citizenship by law), American preoccupation with racial purity developed acutely. Thus, as Anne Fleischmann writes, with reference to the work of Joel Williamson, "Between 1850 and 1915, . . . this third race [mulattos] virtually disappeared from America's racial landscape" (247), legally to be vanished, as I have noted, in the 1920 census. F. James Davis calculates that "passing" on the part of people who formerly would have moved between the worlds of whites and blacks "probably reached an all-time peak between 1880 and 1925," so that even by conservative estimates "at least 90,000 blacks began passing as white during those forty-five years alone" (in Spencer 138). Fleischmann makes clear that *Plessy v. Ferguson*, the infamous "separate but equal" ruling in 1896, whatever else it did, "gave official sanction to the 'one drop' rule," holding "that individual states could decide whether and how to classify citizens by race" (244). In many southern states, apparently, legislation was hardly necessary. Michael Elliott writes that "Tennessee was the only state to have codified [the 'one-drop' rule] into law as of 1910; Virginia did not adopt its more famous one-drop law until the 1920s" (1999: 617)

By 1930, the census also counted any person " 'of mixed white and Negro blood', irrespective of how small 'the percentage of Negro blood' " as "Negro," while a person part Indian and part Negro "was to be listed as 'Negro *unless the Indian blood predominated and the person is generally accepted as Indian in the community*' " (Goldberg 241, my emphasis) By 1930 as well, someone whose parentage was Indian and white "was to be counted as 'Indian, except where the percentage of Indian blood' was deemed very small or"—again—" 'the person was generally considered white in the community' " (241–42). Thus the rule of "hypodescent" applied: any person with only one white parent "was to be designated according to the race of the parent not white" (242).

In the brief passage I have quoted from *Cogewea*, Mourning Dove invokes the categories of "blood" and skin color as the visible indicators of race, while also agreeing with the directions to census enumerators that racial categories are not only biological but sociocultural as well.

In this context, I will cite two key passages—at least one of them very well known—from the work of two important writers of the first two decades of the twentieth century, Charles Alexander Eastman and W. E. B. Du Bois, on the subject of blood, race, and identity in the America of roughly the 1890s to the late 1920s. Both Eastman and Du Bois are trying to understand how the Native American and the African American can live a life in which they are both one and the other as well rather than a life in which an enforced either/or choice limits their human possibilities.

Eastman, the best-known Native intellectual and activist of his time,[9] moves to the conclusion of his 1916 autobiography, *From the Deep Woods to Civilization,* by writing, "Yet even in deep jungles God's own sunlight penetrates, and I stand before my own people still as an advocate of civilization" (194–95). At this time, "civilization" was still a noun that tended to appear only in the singular, a time, that is, before culture as a noun that would readily take the plural form came into common use. Eastman's "deep jungles" seem a metonym for Africa, the "heart of darkness," as it were, and thus presumably the place of *least* "civilization." Eastman's "own people" are likely, here, to mean Indian people generally rather than Dakota or Sioux people specifically, and the choice for them is not between darkness and light but between "savagery" and "civilization." Insofar as Indian lifeways were perceived to be "savage" in comparison to "civilization," they were clearly doomed to "vanish" or become extinct. Eastman, therefore, stands as "an advocate of civilization."

Nonetheless, Eastman's final paragraph affirms,

I am an Indian; and while I have learned much from civilization, for which I am grateful, I have never lost my Indian sense of right and justice. I am for development and progress along social and spiritual lines rather than those of commerce, nationalism, or material efficiency. Nevertheless, so long as I live, I am an American. (195)

It is the "Indian sense of right and justice" that encourages "development and progress along social and spiritual lines." Eastman here affirms the strong sense of collectivity and community—long perceived as dangerously communistic by many Americans—at every point underpinned by religious or spiritual meaning as the genius, as it were, of the Indian way, while nonetheless accepting the American way, one that, as Eastman fully understands, tends toward "commerce, nationalism, or material efficiency." However difficult it may be to reconcile the very different strengths of Indians and Americans, Eastman's testimony makes clear that it is not only the "half-blood" but the "fullblood" as well who may have the desire to be both an Indian and an American. Eastman, in these regards, is, as our current terminology has it, a "hybrid" person of a more conscious and intellectual type than Cogewea. But hybrids who wished to live a hybrid life—both/and rather than either/or—faced profound dilemmas in this period.

As alternatives to the dominant "melting pot" ideology committed to nativism and the reservation of the term "American" effectively to white, bourgeois Christians, what F. H. Matthews calls a "revolt against Americanism" was undertaken by writers and intellectuals like William Carlos Williams. As I have quoted him in the Preface, Williams is first and foremost in revolt against the legacy of Puritanism. Others, like Randolph Bourne, turn this into a revolt against acculturation/assimilation for the immigrant; rather than melting down the foreign qualities newcomers bring with them, America must foster them, becoming a land in which "cultural pluralism" or "ethnic particularism"—what in our own time has reappeared as multiculturalism and the celebration of "diversity"—comes to define our particular kind of nationhood. Yet another sort of opposition to melting pot, monocultural "Americanism" in the 1920s, proposed a version of the cosmopolitan ideal in one or another of the forms we have examined in Chapter 1.[10]

Educated Indians like the historical Charles Alexander Eastman and the fictional Cogewea would have found it difficult to feel comfortable with any of these options. The melting pot ideal, as we have seen and shall see further, would require the relinquishment of Native traditions entirely, as, indeed, would the cosmopolitan ideal as it presented itself in that period.[11] And the Dawes Act of 1887 along with the Indian education policies of the period, both of which we shall discuss just below, committed as they were to disallowing Indians an ethnic (and, of course, a sovereign tribal existence), left little room for being an Indian—as racial prejudice "hampered" even those Indians who would be Americans.

This same dilemma, the desire and the difficulty, that is to say, of being both a Negro and an American had been described earlier in the century by W. E. B. Du Bois in his powerful and by now well-known description of what he called the phenomenon of "double-consciousness":

It is a peculiar sensation, this double-consciousness, this sense of always looking at one's self through the eyes of others, of measuring one's soul by the tape of a world that looks on in amused contempt and pity. One ever feels his twoness,—an American, a Negro; two souls, two thoughts, two unreconciled strivings; two warring ideals in one dark body,[12] whose dogged strength alone keeps it from being torn asunder. (3)

DuBois continues, in some degree foreshadowing Eastman's commentary, that the Negro

would not Africanize America, for America has too much to teach the world and Africa. He would not bleach his Negro soul in a flood of white Americanism, for he knows that Negro blood has a message for the world. He simply wishes to make it possible for a man to be both a Negro and an American, without being cursed and spit upon by his fellows, without having the doors of Opportunity closed roughly in his face. (3)

Du Bois's understanding of "blood" is generally consistent with the term as used by other African American, Native American, "ethnic," and, indeed most mainstream intellectuals of this period. "Blood" in most of these usages is synonymous with race which is itself loosely and variously synonymous with culture, nationality or nation, and even language.[13]

As I have noted above, it was regularly possible to argue on the basis of race as either a biological fact or a social construct, but also as both a biological fact and a social construct. The confusions here—or, following Bederman and Elliott, the discursive "complexity" and "flexibility"— are illustrated in the following comment of Henry Roe Cloud. Although he had earlier taken a master's degree in anthropology from Yale, Roe Cloud, as late as 1934, during his tenure as Superintendent of Haskell Institute, could still write, "Haskell Institute is definitely committed to the preservation of Indian race culture" (Crum 179; Pfister 27). Alain Locke, less than a decade earlier, in his Introduction to the influential anthology he edited called *The New Negro* (1925), also can speak of African American writing as both an expression of racial essence and also of cultural/historical formation. Locke concludes his foreword to the anthology writing that

Negro life is not only establishing new contacts and finding new centers, it is finding a new soul. . . . There is a renewed race-spirit that consciously and proudly sets itself apart. Justifiably then, we speak of the offerings of this book embodying these ripening forces as culled from the first fruits of the Negro Renaissance. (xvii)

Soul, race, and organic or "natural" imagery ("ripening forces," "first fruits") are used to describe a *renaissance*—surely, one would think, a cultural development. But Locke may well see this cultural development as indeed stemming from a new *race* spirit. My point is simply that Locke, Eastman, Du Bois, and, as we shall see further, in particular Arthur C. Parker, along with Mourning Dove all conflate the languages of culture with those of race.

It was exactly this synonymity between race and culture that the work of Franz Boas sought to contest. Boas has been the subject of a good deal of recent work,[14] so I will simply use a sort of shorthand here. Just as Freud's dictum was (another shorthand, to be sure!), "Where id was, there shall ego be!," so, too, did Boas in effect say, "Where race was, there shall culture be!" Although Walter Benn Michaels has argued that Boas's culture concept and indeed the culture concept generally rest on an implied appeal to some sort of racial essence; although Vernon J. Williams has argued that Boas had not indeed resolved the conflict "between the values of cultural determinism and the values of racial determinism" (10) and thus still reflected what George Stocking has called the "Lamarckian assumption" that "social innovations and traditions could be transmitted across generations through biology" (in Elliott 2002: 87); nonetheless, I believe along with Michael Elliott that Boas's 1911 "Summary" to his *The Mind of Primitive Man,* addressing "Race Problems in the United States," is properly read to affirm the fact that "there is no scientific basis for excluding immigrants on the basis of their race or for continuing to discriminate against African Americans because of their presumed inferiority" (Elliott 2002: 63).

It has not been usual to consider Du Bois and Eastman together,[15] although we may note a contemporary linkage of the two on the part of Mrs. Mary Roe in a letter to Henry Roe Cloud, the first fullblood[16] Native American (Winnebago) to graduate from Yale (1910). Mrs. Roe wrote that she did not think Eastman's *Soul of the Indian* (1911) nearly so good as Du Bois's *Souls of Black Folk* (1903), adding her hope that Henry would be the one to do the best Indian "soul" book. Although Roe Cloud did not write such a "soul" book, he did, in 1916, the year Eastman's *From the Deep Woods to Civilization* appeared, compose a brief autobiography of his own called "From Wigwam to Pulpit: a Red Man's Story of His Progress from Darkness to Light." So far as I am aware, this remains unpublished (see Crum 172).[17]

Joel Pfister, to whose research I am indebted for information on Roe Cloud, notes that "Mary saw Henry as the W. E. B. Du Bois of the Indians" (46). Other Native activists of the period seem to have been more aware of Booker T. Washington, Superintendent of the Hampton Institute[18] for Freedmen in Virginia, as a type of the "race leader."

The references here to Du Bois, the earlier reference to Nella Larsen, the further references below to some few other African American writers, and, as will be apparent, the way in which I contextualize Sherman Alexie's novel, *Indian Killer* in relation to African American writers in the chapter that follows is the result of that cosmopolitan interest in comparativism I outlined in Chapter 1. Here with *Cogewea,* and in the next chapter with *Indian Killer,* the hope is to avoid what Alan Wald has called "One of the weaknesses" of criticism from the perspective of "internal colonialism,"[19] the "tendency to focus on one colonized group at a time, rather than in comparative perspective" (23). I strongly agree with Wald that the particular situation of one colonized group, in this case Native Americans, is sometimes more fully understood when set in relation to the situation of other colonized groups, specifically for my purposes in these chapters, African Americans. This having been said, I want also to reaffirm here in practice what I proposed in theory in Chapter 1, that it may also be important—*not*, that is, necessarily always a "weakness"—to keep one's focus quite intensively "on one colonized group" (as in the assertion of nationalism, as we have noted, as a liberatory force).

*   *   *

A "Negro and an American"; an "Indian and an American." Once more we may ask what it might mean to try to be both in a period when the dominant society was more and more strongly pressing an either/or agenda, and the alternatives—a cultural pluralism modeled on immigrant ethnicities and a cosmopolitanism modeled on the "postethnic"[20] ideals of a decided minority of intellectuals—were not especially attractive to African Americans and to Native Americans. Specifically, what might it mean in Mourning Dove's *Cogewea*? One thing it might mean is for Cogewea to have been welcomed rather than "cursed" for her entrance as a contestant in both the "ladies" horse race and the "squaw" race. I am referring to an important scene in the seventh chapter of the novel, which is prepared for in Chapter VI, called "The Fourth of July." Horse races are part of the Fourth of July celebrations in the time and place of *Cogewea*, and for the women there were two races, the "ladies race" and the "squaw race." Cogewea, it seems, had initially planned to enter only the "ladies race." This decision prompted Jim, her half-blood would-be suitor, to say (sparing the pronouns), "Am only anxious for you to win the ladies race today. Want to see you put it over them there high toned white gals who think they can beat the Injun gals a ridin" (58)[21]. It's then that Cogewea decides she will *also* ride in the "squaw" race. In "elation" she says, "I'm part Injun and can participate in that as well as in the ladies race. They can't stop me from riding in both races, can they? If there's any difference between a *squaw* and a *lady*, I want to know it" (58–59).

In a curious choice of words—"I am going *to pose* as both for this day" (59, my emphasis)—Cogewea for a brief moment suggests that identity may be a matter of performance, a suggestion which runs against the grain of the discourse of blood that otherwise dominates the novel. As readers of the book will know, Cogewea is not "stopped" from riding in both races; nonetheless, although she has good enough mounts and is a good enough rider actually to win in both, she is welcome in neither race, as the events of Chapter VII make clear.

The desire to enter both races—and both meanings of "race" obviously resonate here—is further testimony to the fact that there are "two war-ring ideals" in Cogewea's "tawny skin." Mixed race person that she is, it is extremely difficult for her at this historical juncture, as I have tried to show, to be both an Indian and an American. Whites "hamper" her in her attempt to be "American," and any desire she might have to live as an Indian-identified person seems to be thwarted by her feeling of being "disowned" and "abandoned" by those of her "own race." If "maligned and traduced" by both Americans and Indians, allowed to be neither an American nor an Indian, how, might she live? [22]

Cogewea is understandably conflicted and confused. In Chapter XV, ironically titled "The Superior Race," Cogewea engages in conversation with her soon-to-be-proven-evil, smugly "superior" white suitor, Alfred Densmore. Their talk initially engages the question of the value of oral narrative as history, perhaps in a manner not so very different from the issue as we have considered it in Chapter 3. Cogewea's traditional grand-mother, the Stemteema, has told a story about a Jesuit who arrived in Okanogan country prior to the visit of Lewis and Clark. Densmore finds this difficult to credit inasmuch as none of the history texts he knows mention such an incursion. In the absurdly lofty diction ("Are oral im-partations of mind-stored truths to be reckoned as naught?" (129), for which McWhorter must be held responsible, Cogewea defends her grand-mother's account. "I am confident," she says, "that the first white man to come among my primitive [sic] people, was a priest from the Hud-son Bay outfit in Canada" (130). She and Densmore next discuss religion, and then the "Discovery by Columbus" (133) and "the coming of the Mayflower"—these last, in Cogewea's opinion, "tainting with death the source of our very existence" (133). The two return to the subject of reli-gion, which leads Cogewea to "wondering if there will any place for us in the hereafter. As a half-blood, I suppose that I will be left entirely out in the cold" (134).

Densmore asks Cogewea why she usually speaks of " 'our' people, or 'my' people, when referring to the red side of your house," reminding her that "you are as much Caucasian as Indian. Your sympathies should be equally divided" (134). In response, Cogewea offers the "passionate reply," "It is because I prefer the Indian!. . . I have no more occasion to feel debased on account of my native blood than pride for my heritage of foreign shame" (135). When Densmore objects, Cogewea offers another diatribe against the whites, once more in the "elevated" language almost certainly the result of McWhorter's independent editing of the text in 1922. Cogewea "fiercely" refers to Native people as a "race" and a "nation" on whom has been "entailed . . . the cursed taint of an hitherto unheard of blood pollution" by the "Caucasian" (135–36). Although Densmore, for his own purposes, suggests that she and he "relegate all racial differ-ences to the discard of forgetfulness" (136), Cogewea cuts the conversa-tion short. Just a moment later she conveys to him her sense that her "field of conquest is . . . limited" to her "own kind: the breed" (149).

Later still in the novel, in Chapter XXII, Cogewea repeats to Jim LaGrinder, a "breed" like herself, "I like the Injun breed best" (201). It is unclear whether Cogewea means mixed race Indians in particular or Indians generally. In any case, she still keeps Jim at a distance. Jim, for his purposes, reminds Cogewea, "You're a breed, same as myself," and ap-peals to racialist "common sense," with the words, "You know the callin' of the blood" (202). This chapter ends with Cogewea dashing off, "leaving her dusky lover pondering in doubt" (203).

Cogewea's traditional grandmother, the Stemteema, hates the whites ("I hate the pale-faced race" 217) for the wrongs they have done to Indi-ans and to Indian women most particularly. She desires her granddaugh-ter "to marry some one of her own kind and class" (216). She warns Cogewea, by means of story, ceremony, and dreams of the dangers that await the Indian wife of a white man. When Cogewea seems likely to go off with Densmore, the Stemteema appeals to Jim, "a stranger. But the blood-tie was there, strengthened by a mutual knowledge of [their native] language" (216).

Nonetheless, Cogewea does agree to become Densmore's wife and to go east with him, and this decision is also put in terms of blood discourse. "My Indian Spirit," Cogewea says, "tells me that I am stepping wrong; that I am leaving the trail marked for me by inevitable decree"—by her "Indian blood," it would seem. In any case, she will rebel against the in-evitable, appealing explicitly, now, to the power of her other "blood." She will go with Densmore because her "white blood calls to see the world— to do—to live" (253). The villain exults at her acquiescence and thinks how easy it will be to do away with Cogewea and thus obtain the money he believes is hers! The chapter ends with an explicit return to race as Dens-more plans out his next day "with the breed girl," and "With supreme ela-tion . . . contemplate[s] the discomfiture of his haughty, copper-skinned rival [Jim]" (255).

Beaten, robbed, and abandoned by the treacherous "Caucasian" when he learns that she does not have the money the ranch-hands in jest had told him she did, Cogewea returns to the Flathead, and, after a two-year period of melancholic soul-searching,[23] in the end marries Jim, and even comes into a substantial inheritance. This arrives as unexpectedly as it was unintentional: Mr. McDonald, Cogewea's white father, whom she had presumed to have died long ago, we are told, had intended to leave his second, white wife all his substantial fortune, with a mere twenty dollars going to each of his three half-blood daughters. But, "owing to a technical flaw" in the will, the girls actually will receive "a quarter million dollars each" (284).

Thus the novel has a "happy" ending; its plot is of a "comic" type, similar to the endings found in plays like Shakespeare's *All's Well That Ends Well, The Taming of the Shrew,* and *The Tempest,* or novels like *Tom Jones* and *Pride and Prejudice,* in which marriage and prosperity mark the conclusion. In Mourning Dove's novel, the comic ending is even doubled, as Cogewea's younger sister, Mary, the "shy girl," blue-eyed, yet most traditional of the three sisters and closest to the Stemteema, herself an heir to a third of the McDonald fortune, marries Eugene LaFleur, Frenchy, a French aristocrat.[24]

Louis Owens writes that "the novel concludes ambiguously with the prospect of a wealthy Cogewea and Jim living happily ever after, a matched pair of mixedbloods in the lap of luxury" (47). For him, this ending leaves

the dilemma of the mixedblood poised between worlds . . . unsolved. Very literally allowed a place in neither the Indian nor white races, Cogewea will marry Jim LaGrinder and produce children who will, like the parents, be halfbloods. The novel ends on a note of stasis, with nothing resolved, none of the many questions answered. (48)

I think Owens is right. Yet we know that Mourning Dove insisted on a happy ending for her story, holding firm against the advice of her collaborator/mentor, L. V. McWhorter, who recommended a tragic ending for the tale. Their difference of opinion here may reflect Mourning Dove's belief in Indian "survivance," in Gerald Vizenor's term, as against McWhorter's belief that Indians would, regrettably, vanish. What, then, might Mourning Dove have imagined as the social possibilities for Cogewea? If Jim and Cogewea are to live "happily ever after," what identities and social locations might be available to them in the period after World War I?

*   *   *

We know that the "boarding school experience" for Native Americans from 1875 to 1928 was, as David Adams has called it, an "education for extinction." In these years, Adams writes, the new form of Indian War would be "ideological and psychological, and it would be waged against children" (27). The victory for tribal sovereignty represented by the ruling in *Ex Parte Crow Dog* (1883) was quickly undone by the passage of the Major Crimes Act (1885),[25] to be followed by the now infamous Dawes Allotment Act (1887), which sought to break up the tribally held landbase.[26]

General Richard Pratt, founder and long-time superintendent of Carlisle, left the school in 1904, after which the policies that were to achieve the objective of his much-quoted slogan, "Kill the Indian and save the man!" were somewhat modified at Carlisle and in Indian policy generally. But no American Indian contribution to American culture and society was seriously envisioned. Even anthropologists like James Mooney, the government "amateur," and Franz Boas, the university professional, scrupulously devoted to the preservation of Indian material and discursive culture in museums, government publications, and universities, still could not see Native lifeways as having an ongoing, functionally operative existence.

If one looks at the careers of those two very different physicians Dr. Charles Alexander Eastman (Santee Sioux) and Dr. Carlos Montezuma (Yavapai/Apache); of the orator, prose writer, community service worker, and musician Zitkala Sa (Yankton Sioux); or of the museum anthropologist Arthur C. Parker (Seneca), among others, one finds, as Philip J. Deloria has put it, "all the crucial and contradictory markers one might expect . . . when the figure of the Indian was used to make claims about identity" (126) — both Indian and American identity, each identity usually associated with the possession of closely related but differentially valued types of "blood."

Cogewea's older sister, Julia, in marrying John Carter, the atypically "good" white man, illustrates one possible choice available in the period, the decision not to use the "figure of the Indian" as a "marker" of identity, or, rather, however regrettably, to reject it. We are told that Julia "had favored Cogewea's marriage to the fair stranger [Densmore], rather than with her own mixed or Indian blood," not because "she was ashamed of the Red race, but since civilization was the only hope for the Indian, it would, she reasoned be better to draw from the more favored and stronger, rather than to fall back to the unfortunate class so dependent on their conquerors for their very existence" (274). Julia's position, whatever one thinks of it today, must be understood in the context of the period,[27] indeed, of a long history in which Indian-white intermarriage was discussible, and generally, if uneasily, acceptable. If Julia chose "civilization," largely abandoning her Native background, some of the "Red Progressives" of this era,[28] even in their choice of "civilization," may still have imagined themselves as mediators or bridge builders between Indian and white identities. Thus Philip Deloria says of Charles Eastman that "He lived out a hybrid life, distinct in its Indianness but also cross-cultural and assimilatory [sic]. By channeling both a Dakota past and American-constructed Indian Other through his material body . . . Eastman made it ever more difficult to pinpoint the cultural locations of Dakotas and Americans" (123–24).

As I have discussed the matter above, it does seem clear that Eastman attempted to live as *both* "an Indian and an American." But Deloria's statement of the issue here seems to me somewhat unhistorical. I am wondering, that is, in what ways Eastman's life might indeed be "distinct in its Indianness" in the decades just before and after the First World War, as well as "cross-cultural and assimilatory." Eastman certainly had lived "a Dakota past" in his youth, and, as an older man, he did, indeed, leave "civilization," as it were, for a cabin in "the deep woods." And, too, he surely could not escape being known to Indians and Americans in some degree through the image of the "American-constructed Indian Other." But I am less sanguine than Deloria about any likelihood that the unquestionably "hybrid" Eastman could serve as an exemplary type to make "it ever more difficult," in a *positive* way, "to pinpoint the cultural locations of Dakotas and Americans." *Looking back*, we can see that that *should have been* the effect of Eastman's complex example. But I think it could not have been the effect then. Whatever fascination hybridity rightly has for us now, as I have more than once tried to make the point, the period we are considering was not particularly open to the complex possibilities of a hybrid "cultural location" as represented by someone like Eastman. Ideologically, Indians had to assimilate—become "civilized"—or vanish, no matter what alternatives to assimilating entirely or disappearing entirely persons like Eastman might present.

Because it was believed that Indians could indeed become "civilized," they might also, to return to a matter raised briefly above, intermarry with whites—something which had not only not been prohibited in this country, but in some quarters positively regarded (even before Thomas Jefferson) as a possible solution to America's "Indian problem." For individual Native persons, this would require that they first leave their tribal nations and immerse themselves in white civilization, as in Carlisle's "outing" system.[29] Or, of course, their tribal nations might just wither away, the hoped-for consequence, all in all, of the Dawes Act. Or Native persons might, it seems, even come from tribal nations that were not, paradoxically, Indians at all. The odd logic here is based upon a performative understanding of ethnicity or identity rather than the more usual blood logic. (We have already seen Cogewea take this tack accidentally or unconsciously on one solitary occasion.) Thus New Mexico Chief Justice John Watts, in his decision in the case of *United States v. Lucero* (1869), as Michael Elliott discusses it, ruled that the people of Cochiti Pueblo "and indeed all Pueblo Indians were not actually 'Indians' " (Elliott 1999: 627). This was because, as Watts asserted, Indians were not settled people, but, rather savages "given to war and the chase for a living" (in Elliott 627). Inasmuch as this was not the Pueblo Indians' manner of living, it would necessarily follow that they could not be Indians! Whatever the particular argument, what is being allowed here is that Indians—like the Jews or Irish or other European immigrants over time—could somehow become "white,"[30] making intermarriage not really miscegenation. (But, as always, blacks, whether they wished to or not, were not allowed to become "white," and miscegenation rules remained in effect, as we have noted, until the last third of the twentieth century.)

In spite of the history and the court rulings I have cited, any Native person who might wish to live in the white world even as an American citizen—Indians only became citizens by act of Congress in 1924—might still find him- or herself "hampered," in Cogewea's term. I want to look at some of the writing of the mixedblood Seneca scholar and "museum man," Arthur C. Parker, for examples of what Strong and van Winkle have so well described, the way the discourse of Indian blood, although it is "a discourse of conquest with manifold and contradictory effects," can attempt nonetheless to validate "rights and resistances . . . couched in terms of that very discourse" (1996: 565), in this instance to remove the bars to assimilation on the ethnicity-immigrant model. Parker, I am saying, wants to make a case for "civilized" Native persons as Americans and to reduce the degree to which they are "hampered" by the whites. His invocation of "blood" in the discourse of race, however, is troubling in a manner common even to what may be called anti-racist racism in this period.[31]

Parker seems to have come to the fairly widespread conclusion that Native people would have to choose "civilization" and become Americans, or vanish. In Philip Deloria's account, Parker used "the dubious notion of eugenic science to claim a privileged status for Indians as true natural Americans" (125), that is, to nominate indigenous people as the most likely persons of color—persons other than European immigrants—to become "white" and assimilate successfully. Deloria makes a strong case for the positivity of Parker's position as "resistance" of the sort described by Strong and van Winkle, although Parker's 1916 "Problems of Race Assimilation in America with Special Reference to the American Indian," as I have said, is replete with all the uncomfortable confusions of racialist thought. Deloria recognizes this, I think, when he writes of Parker's "anxieties about immigration and racial (read national) declension and improvement" (125). But a parenthesis will not suffice to turn the "racial" into the "national" in Parker's work.

Parker claimed, for example, that "While much has been written concerning the low-grade half-breed it is found as a matter of actual observation that where healthy whites of good morals marry Indians, the children of the unions are not inferior, but most frequently possess the good traits of each parent" (299). Parker could not have known what was biologically involved in the passing of "traits" from parent to child, of course. To state what is now obvious, good "health" in children is partially attributable to genetically "healthy" parents; good "morals" have no genetic base whatever. He compares Indians to some immigrant groups in an attempt to argue for the former by disparaging the latter, claiming that "There is not the prejudice against good Indian blood that there is against some foreign bloods *because of race*" (in Hertzberg 163).

Parker here engages in the "strategy of triangulation," as Michael Elliott describes it, a strategy used in the nineteenth century to deny "rights to a particular racial group but also to affirm them" (1999: 625) for another group (as in the example of Justice Robert Taney, above, who triangulated whites, blacks, and Indians to deny the possibility of citizenship to the descendants of slaves while holding out it out as a possibility for those Indians who would leave their "savage" tribal condition). Elliott notes a similar tactic on the part of Justice John Marshall Harlan, in his dissent in *Plessy v. Ferguson* (1896): "Instead of arguing for the universal rights of humanity, Harlan's attempt at exposing the illogic of segregation denigrates the Chinese in order to elevate blacks" (1999: 625 n.21). Referring to "a race so different from our own that we do not permit those belonging to it to become citizens of the United States . . . the Chinese race," Harlan noted that nonetheless Chinese people might ride in the same rail car as "the white citizens of the United States," whereas blacks would be "declared . . . criminals, liable to imprisonment" for doing as the Chinese (in Elliott 1999: 625 n. 21).

Parker works in a similar fashion when he writes, "The Korean carries the stamp of his Mongolian origin forever and some deep instinct in our natures makes us dislike the Mongolian [!]" (286). It's not clear who is included in Parker's first-person plurals, "our" and "us": White American citizens? Indians and whites together? He goes on to note that what Americans dislike in "the Negro" is not so much "his natural servility and his imitativeness" (291), traits that, if "natural," must be inherited in the blood. Rather, "It is the 'darky' habits of the Negro and not his black skin that makes the white man look down upon him." Are these cultural "habits," like skin color, "servility," and "imitativeness," also inherited? Inherited and—here is the standard contradiction of racial discourse in this period—yet also socially produced? Learned—but only because of some racial predisposition to such learning? Native people, in Parker's view, are more fortunate; not skin color but only "backwardness" stands in the way of assimilating the Indian into the dominant society.[32] And at this point Parker turns inclusive and egalitarian, noting that "When by intermarriage *any one or all the racial elements in the country have fused their blood,* we may say that there has been an amalgamation" (302, my emphasis). Thus, it does seem that Parker believed, as Hazel Hertzberg writes, that as a consequence of intermarriage "Indian blood was diffusing 'through the veins of the white race' while at the same time the Indian was being absorbed" (163).

With reference to Du Bois, Parker might appear to be claiming that Native people are in some degree "Indianizing America" through inter-marriage, although "the white race," through those same intermarriages, is also Americanizing the Indian. In a talk some five years earlier, Parker had called for the Indian to "assimilate yet retain his Indian individu-ality" (in Hertzberg 63). Whatever Parker had understood then as the basis or content of "Indian individuality," by 1916 he makes clear that it cannot any longer be cultural individuality or distinctiveness. This is be-cause "The assimilation of the Indian means the blotting out of nearly all that was previously his in lines of culture." (300) The great question once more is just what, exactly, of "Indian individuality" might remain, once "nearly all . . . in lines of culture" has been "blotted out"? What, for example, might actually be "distinct in its Indianness," for Eastman, as Deloria has written, once he—or Cogewea, or any other Native person— had powerfully advanced in Americanness?

I don't want to be misunderstood here as somehow saying that people with strong Indian identities are deceiving themselves because Indian identities and American identities are ultimately "the same." Very early in this book, I specifically objected to such an argument on the part of Scott Michaelsen. My observations in these regards, first, are directed toward the first three decades of the twentieth century, not to the present. Sec-ond, even for that period I am *not* saying that, once a Native person has become "civilized"—more or less comfortable or mobile or accepted in the dominant society—he or she is no longer Indian. My point, rather, deals with what it might be, in or about any given person, that can actu-ally be specified as distinctively Indian (or Jewish or Irish), if it is not— as in these decades it apparently was not—culture; and if it is not—as in these decades it was, although it cannot be now—race or "blood"? Many Native intellectuals have provided a variety of answers to these questions today, some reverting to "blood logic," others instantiating cultural fea-tures (language, religion, indigenist worldview), commonalities of experi-ence ("growing up Indian" in all its variations, identification with the vic-tims and survivors of genocide), and, of course, nationalism. But—and this is particularly my point—no one, Native or non-Native, was very clear on these matters in 1927 (probably not even Franz Boas).

Perhaps—we return to Parker and to 1916—Parker believed in some essential moral, spiritual, or philosophical ground—Eastman's "soul of the Indian"?—on which the individuality of the Indian might rest; more likely, he is willing to beg the question, given his strong sense that assimi-lation is absolutely necessary—because otherwise, "well, you'll become extinct" (304).[33]

It would seem to be just this sort of assimilation (and "amalgamation") that Julia McDonald Carter has chosen—and, as we have noted, for the very reason given by Arthur Parker. So far as "culture" is a living and life-defining thing, Julia seems to have felt it necessary to allow it largely to be "blotted out." As I noted earlier, Julia's situation, if not her sisters', may, indeed, be understood according to the ethnicity-immigrant model. Julia's and John Carter's children will not hear Salish spoken at home (the novel does not make clear how well Julia—unlike Cogewea and Mary, who are fluent—understands or speaks her native tongue), and will likely retain only some words and phrases they will recall having heard from their grandmother, their aunts, and their uncle, Jim LaGrinder. They may remember seeing the sweat lodge built for the Stemteema when they were young, but they are unlikely to have a strong sense of what it meant or what it "was for." (And Julia's and John's children's children will very likely seek to find out all they can about their great-grandmother's language, people, culture.)

The novel's treatment of Mary McDonald, the youngest sister, blue-eyed, yet the most traditional of the three sisters, is interesting in these regards, for Mourning Dove has let Mary voice a criticism that certainly pertains to Julia and may serve as a warning to Cogewea. Praising the "good medicine of the sweat house Spirit," Mary decries "the fate of the average breed[s] of today" who are "encouraged to try to forget their Indian ancestry, after they once learn the white man's books and ways." She offers the comparative judgment that "Some of the Indian system is bad, much of it is good," and she therefore—this was more or less Eastman's position—can only protest that "it must all give place to that of the Shoyahpee" (242), the white man. But, again, how to actualize the "Indian system" in "civilized" life in that day and age?[34] And, what will become of Mary, as the wife of a rich Frenchman?

Finally, let us return to Cogewea and Jim. Cogewea is deeply bound up in the contradictions of her age—contradictions, it should be said, that were acutely exacerbated by a Carlisle (or similar boarding school) education.[35] She can speak her Salishan language, as she can speak "cowboy" and anachronistic "elevated" English with equal fluency. Jim, too, understands the Native tongue and is much impressed by the sweat lodge ritual—although, as he admits, he hadn't paid much attention to that sort of "Indian" thing before. On the other side of the matter, we may note that "His schooling was limited to indifferent reading and writing" (18–19).

Cogewea, Mrs. James LaGrinder, like her sister Mrs. John Carter, will probably preside as the homespun hostess of a great ranch. Unlike her sister, she will probably not allow her assimilated life to be purchased at the cost of a wholesale "blotting out" of her Indian culture. But she most certainly will not follow the Stemteema back to the reservation, to live in a tipi, or, as the condemnatory phrase for Carlisle backsliders had it, return "to the blanket." As for the identities and social locations of any children Cogewea and Jim might have, one can only note the range of possibilities historically available to them, from types of activism in favor of or opposed to the Indian Reorganization Act of 1934 and John Collier's reforms,[36] to forms of traditionalism, to further assimilation, to symbolic constructions of a variety of kinds of "Indianness" under extremely difficult conditions.

*   *   *

Owens, then, is correct; although *Cogewea* "is the first novel by an Indian writer to attempt to define the complex dilemma of the mixedblood" (45), it leaves that dilemma "unsolved" (48), with "none of the many questions answered." For those questions to begin to be answered and that dilemma in any degree to be solved, the allotment period would have to end and a great deal of history would have to be made. In this regard, it may fairly be said that *Cogewea*'s irresolution provides an extraordinarily accurate account of the betwixt-and-betweenness of mixedbloods of different blood types and quanta in the period.[37] Yet all this sounds as though the book's ending is bitter or sad—as, indeed, I believe that Larsen's *Quicksand* and Johnson's *Autobiography of an Ex-Colored Man* end bitterly and sadly. But *Cogewea*'s ending is comic, and it was Mourning Dove who insisted that her novel have a happy ending. Perhaps it may be said, then, that, although Mourning Dove could obviously not participate in the "structure of feeling" (in Raymond Williams's phrase) of Gerald Vizenor's—of our present—time toward the mixedblood, yet she could very nearly imagine it, if only for a moment.

In Chapter X, not lugubriously but humorously titled "Lo! The Poor Breed," Mourning Dove has Cogewea engage in a discussion of race, blood, and blood-mixing with both Densmore and Jim. She is quite agitated as a result of reading a novel called *The Brand*, which the narrator characterizes as "an unjust presentation of Indian sentiment and racial traits; *The Brand*—stigma of the blood" (89). *The Brand: A Tale of the Flathead* by Therese Broderick (Tin Schreiner) appeared in 1909, and, although Cogewea is quite correct in saying that "The thing does nothing but slam the breeds! . . . You are only an Injun! —a miserable breed!" (89), she is entirely mistaken in her interpretation of the title, which refers in large measure to the surprise ending of the novel (I won't give that away). Although Broderick does indeed have Henry West, the male lead in the novel, miserably lament that he is "only an Indian," she also makes him a Harvard graduate and a very rich and attractive man. *Cogewea*'s narrator is also mistaken in claiming that West "curses his own mother for [his Indian] heritage" (91)—he most certainly does not—although the fact that Broderick has this extraordinary young man "deem . . . himself beneath" the white heroine, "not good enough for her" is unfortunately true. To "cap the absurdity of the story," the narrator writes, the halfbreed Indian "weds the white 'princess' and slaves for her the rest of his life" (91). This, too, is in error. It is only on the very last page of the novel that the white "princess"—I think we can fairly call her that—decides that her love for this man is so great that she can "forget" he is an Indian. (The novel's last, melodramatic line is "*I have forgotten*"—but she also must forget something he has done that reveals the surprise meaning of the title.) And I think there is little chance of Henry West's slaving "for her [Bess Fletcher] the rest of his life."

Peter G. Beidler has suggested that Cogewea's errors in reading *The Brand* were intended by Mourning Dove. It is Beidler's view that "Cogewea fails as a literary critic because she cannot see past the assimilationist racism she has herself internalized and because she refuses to take seriously the messages that stories [traditional stories told by the Stemteema] can give" (62). I find this intriguing but too ingenious by far. Where else in *Cogewea* do we find such subtlety on Mourning Dove's part? Rather, I believe that Mourning Dove either never read all the way through *The Brand* or had forgotten a good deal of it by the time she composed the comments by Cogewea I have quoted.

Nonetheless, it must be said that *The Brand* has certainly influenced *Cogewea*: it contains a Fourth of July horse race won by Henry West, who nonetheless gives up his prize. There is a scene in which the "white princess" shoots a rattlesnake, and another in which a beloved horse must be shot—scenes that, with variations, we find in *Cogewea*. In *Mourning Dove, A Salishan Autobiography*, Jay Miller cites Mourning Dove describing her first draft of *Cogewea* as a story about a "young Indian agent who uses an Indian maiden's love lightly" (165). Obviously there is nothing of that in the published novel, but *The Brand* has as its villain an Indian agent who betrayed both a white maiden and an Indian maiden, Henry West's sister, Helen.

But let us return to *Cogewea*. Still furious at *The Brand*—and, as I have said, if Mourning Dove's novel gets a lot of Tin Schreiner's novel wrong, it does get the abject and obnoxious "only an Indian" strain entirely right—Cogewea offers yet another account of the difficult situation of the "breed," "half and half—American and Caucasion [sic]—and in a separate corral . . . despised by both of our relations" (95). And then, suddenly, her mood changes: "'But you wait and watch!'" exclaimed the girl with animation. 'The day will dawn when the desolate, exiled breed will come into his own; when our vaunting 'superior' will appreciate our

worth.' " Can this be a faint gleam of the day when the seams in the
shrouds of identity will indeed have been loosened? Even, perhaps, the
day when, as van Winkle and Strong conclude with reference again to
Vizenor, "white settlers" and "crossblood earth divers succeed in their
efforts to dredge up those 'few honest words' upon which to create a new
'turtle island' " (565).[38] I'd like to think that this is the farthest horizon
of *Cogewea*'s social imaginary, and that perhaps we are at least a little bit
closer to it today than Mourning Dove was in the first decades of the twentieth century.

Chapter 5
The "Rage Stage": Contextualizing Sherman Alexie's *Indian Killer*

For Pat Hilden and Shari Huhndorf

> "At times the poetic elan coincides with the revolutionary elan and at times they diverge."
> —Jean-Paul Sartre

Sherman Alexie's *Indian Killer* (1996) begins in the "winter" of 1968–69,[1] in the delivery room of "An Indian Health Service hospital," on "this reservation or that reservation. Any reservation, a particular reservation" (3). There a dark-skinned boy is born to a fourteen-year-old Indian[2] woman who has apparently agreed to give him up for adoption. The transfer of the infant to his adoptive parents is violent: "A man in a white jumpsuit" and a "white helmet" (6) arrives in a helicopter and seizes the boy. Then, as the helicopter lifts off, the "helicopter gunman locks and loads, strafes the reservation with explosive shells" (6). The narrator remarks, "Suddenly this is a war" (6). The war that immediately comes to mind, of course, is the war in Vietnam, then escalating. But, as I hope to show, the particular "war" that Alexie's novel dates from about 1968–69 is a war waged, not in the faraway jungles of Vietnam, called "Indian Country" by American troops, but, rather, nearer to home, in American Indian Country; and this is a war to end domestic colonialism rather than a war to preserve foreign colonialism.

After a flight of "hours, it could be days" (7)—as will already be clear ("this reservation, that reservation," etc.), here, as in his earlier fiction, Alexie works in the mode of postmodern play with realistic conventions—the helicopter brings the infant to Bellevue, just outside Seattle, where he is delivered into the hands of a "man and woman, both white and handsome" (7). They will name him John Smith (this John Smith or that John Smith? any Indian John Smith?).[3] This first of the novel's three sections is called "Owl Dancing" and its first chapter is called "Mythology."

By the time John is in high school, his experience has already been such that he "repeatedly promised himself he would never be angry. He didn't want to be angry." Nonetheless, he finds he must often "lock himself inside a [toilet] stall and fight against his anger" (18–19). The "rage he didn't like to feel" (41) persists, however, and that rage eventually tells John just "exactly what to do with his life": John "needed to kill a white man" (25). John will speculate throughout the book as to *which* white man is the one who most needs killing, finally deciding on a particular individual—whom he does not actually kill. Still, as late as five pages from the end of the novel, a police officer states, "John Smith was the Indian Killer. Case closed" (415), and it is no wonder that at least one reviewer of the novel[4] had no doubt whatever that John Smith was, indeed, the Indian killer of the title. But this is surely mistaken.

Although we are never told "exactly" what she plans to do with her life, Marie Polatkin, a young Spokane student at the University of Washington,[5] has feelings of anger and rage not dissimilar to John's. Marie is someone who "always wanted revenge" (34); she has "Hateful, powerful thoughts," indeed, she "wanted every white man to disappear. She wanted to burn them all down to ash and feast on their smoke" (85). Later, remembering that "Indian blood had often spilled on American soil," Marie "felt a beautiful kind of anger" (360). As she insists to her teacher, the despised anthropologist and Indian wannabe Dr. Clarence Mather, "if the Ghost Dance worked, there would be no exceptions. All you white people would disappear. If those dead Indians came back to life. . . . They'd kill you. They'd gut you and eat your heart" (314). Later, coming upon an attack on John by two white boys, Marie is "shocked by her anger. . . . Nearly blind with her own rage, she had wanted to tear out their [the two white boys'] blue eyes and blind them" (375).

Inasmuch as the killer has by this time actually eaten the heart of the second man he has killed, and earlier "tor[n] the white man's [the first victim's] eyes from his face and swallowed them whole" (54),[6] Marie's desires to eat Mather's heart or tear out the eyes of white boys might suggest that she herself might be the killer. But this, too, seems surely not the case.

Another person who might be the killer is Marie's cousin, Reggie Polatkin.[7] Reggie has blue eyes himself; and he has also beaten and nearly blinded a white boy. Reggie has more than enough anger and rage to lead to murder. It is Reggie who pointedly responds to Jack Wilson's[8] question whether "an Indian would do something like that" (kill white men) by noting, "Maybe the question should be something different. Maybe you should be wondering which Indian wouldn't do it. Lots of real Indian men out there have plenty enough reasons to kill a white man" (184). Reggie adds, with reference to himself and his friends, Ty and Harley, "Three at this table right now." Certainly Dr. Clarence Mather would agree, at least so far as Reggie is concerned. Indeed, Mather goes to the police to suggest that Reggie might be the killer. Mather says he "always worried that Reggie was going to hurt somebody," because Reggie "said he dreamed about killing people" (394). Not only Reggie worries Dr. Mather, but Marie does as well. Having dropped her from his class in Native American literature,[9] Mather also tells the police that Marie might be involved with the killings. When asked why he thinks so, he responds, " 'She said she'd eat my heart' " (394), not an exact quotation of Marie's words, but close enough.

If truth is to be found in dreams, then even Jack Wilson might be the killer. The twenty-third chapter ("Dreaming") of the novel's third section ("Last Call") finds Wilson dreaming about John Smith wielding the knife that killed the two white men. But then the dream shifts and "Wilson saw himself with that knife. Wilson saw himself pushing the knife into one white body, then another and another, until there were multitudes" (391). This is followed by a single sentence paragraph from the narrator, "Isn't that how it happened?" an interrogative that is repeated five times in the chapter's two-and-a-half pages. Is that how it happened? Probably not—for all that Alexie's point would seem to be that, well, yes, it could have happened that way. Wilson *could* have committed the murders, as John Smith *could* have committed the murders, as Marie and Reggie Polatkin *could* have; as maybe any Indian, this Indian, that Indian, a particular Indian could have. A "real Indian" (184), Jack Wilson says, would not do such a thing. But in his dream Wilson, who believes himself to be Indian—whether Wilson is a "real" Indian, or, indeed, what a "real" Indian is, is left open—sees himself stabbing "multitudes" of white men.

Mark Jones, the young white boy kidnaped, terrorized, but spared by the killer is the only living person actually to have seen the "real" killer, and, he tells the police, the killer wasn't a man *or* a woman, because the killer had lots of owl feathers, "On the wings . . . it was a bird." The boy adds, "It could fly, I bet." When the investigating officer attempts to pursue this, asking, "The bird could fly?" the boy rather enigmatically insists, "No, no. *It* could" (324, my emphasis). Mythology? Dream? Truth?

The chapter in which John Smith apparently commits suicide is called "Flying." But Marie, who is presented throughout as a fairly trustworthy character, insists that John "wasn't the Indian Killer" (415), as she also says she herself had nothing to do with the killings (416). She is less sure about Reggie, but, as I've noted, Reggie seems very unlikely to be the killer as "it" will appear in the last chapter of the novel; and Wilson almost surely could not be the killer. This is because in Chapter 27, John Smith — who by this time does indeed seem quite mad, not simply angry — has somehow "finally understood that Wilson was responsible for all that had gone wrong." John kidnaps Wilson, ties him up, and reaches "into his *pocket*" for "his knife. A *thin* blade" (404, my emphasis) — and so rather a different knife from the knife wielded by the killer earlier in the novel. In the chapter called "Flying," John slashes Wilson's face before stepping "off the last skyscraper in Seattle" (411) — falling or "flying" to his death, one would think. If so, it is apparently the death of John's body only, inasmuch as, after hitting the ground, "John" pushes himself up to stand "above the body embedded in the pavement" (412). Then, "John" walks off into the desert in search of an "Indian father. . . . And maybe an Indian mother" (413).[10]

Whatever "John" 's ontological status — is the "John" who is walking the "real," historical John Smith, 1968/69–96? a mythological (and so, a *differently* "real") "John Smith"? — and wherever "he" or "it" may be going, just as *Indian Killer* began with birth, so it ends with death. Or, because the final chapter is called "Creation Story," perhaps it is more accurate to say that the novel ends with the projection of a re-birth (for Indians only) that will come after death (the deaths, most particularly, of white men).

In 1996, the year of *Indian Killer*'s publication, at "A cemetery on an Indian reservation. On this reservation or that reservation. Any reservation, a particular reservation" (419), the killer ("the killer" is a phrase repeated some twenty times in barely a page!) sits alone on a grave. Then the killer dances a dance he/she/it "knows . . . is over five hundred years old" (420).

In the immediately preceding chapter, Marie Polatkin had said, "if some Indian is killing white guys, then it's a credit to us that it took over five hundred years for it to happen" (418), adding, "Indians are dancing now, and I don't think they're going to stop." The final chapter proves Marie to be right, for, as the killer dances, "a dozen Indians, then hundreds, and more" (420) arrive at the cemetery. The killer has a "beautiful knife, with three turquoise gems inlaid in the handle" (419).[11] We know that the killer has used that knife lethally at least twice and that the killer carries two scalps. (The killer has also used that knife to cut the pajamas of the boy, Mark Jones, he has kidnaped and returned.) The "killer can dance forever. The killer plans on dancing forever" (420); as Marie had predicted, "Indians *are* dancing now" (418, my emphasis), and they aren't going to stop. The Indians who come to join the killer quickly learn "the same song . . . the exact dance." Not only Indians but owls, "birds of prey, birds of prayer" (419) come to the cemetery. The last sentence of the novel is "The tree grows heavy with owls" (420). There are references to owls and owl feathers throughout the novel, and I will note in relation to this last chapter, Chapter 31, "A Creation Story," that Chapter 3 is called "Owl Dancing at the Beginning of the End of the World." We shall return to these matters at the end of this chapter.

The dance these Indians are dancing, we have remarked, is an owl dance, portending death, yet also a ghost dance of renewal and rebirth — but, again, only for Indians and only after the death or disappearance of the whites. Earlier, Marie had objected to Clarence Mather's statement that the "Ghost Dance was not about violence or murder. It was about peace and beauty" (313). Rather, "If Crazy Horse, or Geronimo, or Sitting Bull came back," Marie insisted, "they'd see what you white people have done to Indians, and they would start a war. . . . They'd read books by assholes like Wilson [whose "books are killing Indian books" (68)], and they would start killing themselves some white people, and then kill some asshole Indians, too" (314).

Earlier in the novel, that same homeless Indian man who commented to Daniel Smith on the odd choice of his son's name, had also said, "This Indian Killer, you see, he's got Crazy Horse's magic. He's got Chief Joseph's brains. He's got Geronimo's heart. He's got Wovoka's [not Jack Wilson's] visions. He's all those badass Indians rolled up into one" (219). Pointedly, he adds, "Killer's got himself two white guys? And that little white boy [Mark Jones], enit? That makes the score about ten million to three, in favor of the white guys, enit? *This Killer's got a long ways to go*" (220, my emphasis).

All this seems consistent with Leslie Marmon Silko's observation in *Almanac of the Dead* that "The Indian Wars have never ended in the Americas" (n.p.). And, in Alexie's recent and disturbing story, "The Sin Eaters" — we shall return to it briefly below — "war" is most certainly what is being waged against Indians in the United States. But *Indian Killer* does not imagine an end to war — or no end short of the deaths of all or a great many more white people. *If* (I want to be tentative here) Alexie's *Indian Killer* does indulge the fantasy of such a threat, it would be very different in its imaginary from Silko's *Almanac of the Dead*. For although Silko's novel insists that "The ancient prophecies . . . foretell the disappearance of all things European" from the Americas, *Almanac* does not insist on the disappearance or death of all those of European descent in the Americas. This is the case as well with another document of the 1990s — not a work of fiction — to which I want to turn for a moment, the Report of the Indian Nations at Risk Task Force (INARTF).

The INARTF Report, called "Toward True Native Education: A Treaty of 1992," also refers to the "war . . . over the continued existence of tribal societies of American Indians and Alaska Natives" (15). But the Report is a "treaty," and it offers itself as a document which, if accepted, might put an end to Indian war. The INARTF Treaty also proposes a "*new* Ghost

Dance," but the Ghost Dance it envisions "calls Native *and* non-Native people to join together and take action" (28). This appeal, like that of Silko's *Almanac,* has no equivalent in *Indian Killer,* whose own Ghost Dance is for Indians only, and for Indians who have "got a long ways to go" (220) killing whites before they can even the score.

Although there most certainly is anger and a considerable amount of violence in many earlier Native American novels—I will quickly review some of these below—*Indian Killer* is the first Native American novel I know to take a very particular sort of Indian rage, *murderous* rage, as its central subject—and, it would seem, to encourage its expression. This rage, according to the narrator, can be documented at least from the nineteenth century, when it could be seen in the eyes of the "defeated warriors" (341), and it continues to be present in the eyes of John Smith. In a photo, John Smith "stared into the camera with obvious anger. He had eyes like the eyes of all those old-time Indians who were forced to sit still for Army photographers. Those defeated warriors always had smooth faces and flat expressions, but their eyes were dark with a feral, kinetic hate" (341). No wonder Marie Polatkin has said, "If those dead Indians came back to life. . . . They'd kill you. They'd gut you and eat your heart" (314). This particular sort of red rage has an affinity to the black rage that, as I want to consider it now, was perhaps first expressed in African American fiction in 1940, continuing through the '50s, and escalating through the late '60s.

In Native American fiction of an earlier period, the sort of rage documented in *Indian Killer* is specifically *not* to be expressed in aggressive violence. I am thinking back to D'Arcy McNickle's *Wind from an Enemy Sky,* begun in the 1930s but not published until 1978, after McNickle's death. Like better known work of the late 1960s to the late '70s by N. Scott Momaday and Leslie Silko, which we shall examine below, McNickle's novel sees the sort of murderous rage felt by Bull, a traditional leader of the "Little Elk" people, as a temptation that must be overcome.[12] But *Indian Killer,* to the contrary, insists that continued violence directed by whites against Indians will be productive of anger, rage, and a desire for murderous revenge that must be expressed, not repressed or channeled into other possible action, and this, I think, is indeed something new, and also something frightening.

That Indians today might be angry should come as no surprise. Consider the following statistics. They would not have been available to Alexie at the time he was writing, but I have no doubt he would surely have suspected what they confirm. A study by the U.S. Justice Department released in February 1998 found that "Native Americans are far more likely to be the victims of violent crime than members of any other racial group" (SPLC June 1999: 3). In particular, the Report notes that, while "Some

70 percent of whites are attacked by whites, and more than 80 percent of blacks are victims of other blacks," for Native people "70 percent of violent crimes against Indians are committed by members of other racial groups, *mainly whites*" (3, my emphasis). Regardless whether Jack Wilson has any "Indian blood" or not, his experience as a police officer has taught him "that most of the monsters were white men" (161), and Justice Department statistics would seem to confirm that,[13] at least so far as Native persons are concerned. In this context, John Smith's "need . . . to kill a white man" or Marie's and Reggie's desire for "revenge" should not be hard to understand. As John had said to the elderly black man he knew as Paul Too,[14] "You'd kill white people if you could" (30).

*   *   *

What Indian wouldn't have reason to think of killing white people? What black person wouldn't? If the former question seems not to have been posed in quite so stark a manner in the Native American novel before *Indian Killer*, the latter question had been raised at least some sixty years ago by Richard Wright in his powerful novel *Native Son*, which warned America that continued violence against blacks by the dominant white society might lead at least some black people to kill whites if or when they could.[15] Wright's protagonist, Bigger Thomas, does indeed kill a white woman—accidentally, but also, as he comes to realize, inevitably. By the end of the novel, Bigger Thomas's murder of Mary Dalton, a terrible act to be sure, has nonetheless been presented as "an act of *creation*" (366); what Bigger "killed *for*," if not the killing itself, Bigger insists, must have been "*good*." (392, my emphasis). Are the murders of white people in *Indian Killer* also "good," part of "a creation story"?

In 1952 the protagonist of Ralph Waldo Ellison's *Invisible Man* prefaces his story by narrating an incident in which he "accidentally bumped into a man," a "tall blond man" who "looked insolently out of his blue eyes and cursed [him]" (8). The narrator attacks the man and is about to draw his knife when he realizes that "the man had not *seen* me," and so he had "almost been killed by a phantom," an "invisible man." A few years later, writing in 1955, a year after the Supreme Court's desegregation ruling in *Brown v. Board of Education*, James Baldwin, in an essay pointedly titled "Notes of a Native Son," concludes by affirming the necessity of balancing a noncomplacent acceptance of human imperfection with a refusal to accept injustice. Earlier in the essay, however, Baldwin too recounts an experience of rage at refusing to be served in a "whites only" diner and the expression of that rage in a violent act. In 1963, Baldwin would title his new book of essays with the warning, *The Fire Next Time*.

By 1968–69, the "winter" of John Smith's birth, two black psychiatrists,

William H. Grier and Price M. Cobbs, had published a book much noted at the time,[16] called *Black Rage*. The book's first chapter asked the question, "Who's angry?" The simple answer was, a very great many black Americans. African American writing by the late 1960s, I am saying, seems to have been expressing the same anger against oppression on its pages that African American activists were also expressing in the streets. Black political action and black writing, each in its own way, similarly reflected black anger and rage. Here it is also important to note that these are the years in which the work of another psychiatrist, the Martiniquais, Frantz Fanon, who worked with torture victims of the French in Algeria, first appeared in American editions. Fanon's 1952 text, *Black Skin, White Masks*, was published in the United States in 1967. Fanon's *The Wretched of the Earth*, with a lengthy Preface by Jean-Paul Sartre, appeared in the United States in 1968 and importantly theorized the therapeutic possibilities for the oppressed of violence against the colonial oppressor.

To offer only a few more examples, 1968 was the year in which Eldridge Cleaver's *Soul on Ice*, mostly written in prison, along with Etheridge Knight's *Poems from Prison* appeared. In that same year Leroi Jones (not yet Imamu Amiri Baraka) with Larry Neal published an anthology titled *Black Fire*. The following year Jones published *Four Black Revolutionary Plays*; he had already responded to the calls for black self-protection issued by Malcolm X (assassinated in 1965) and the Black Panther Party (Cleaver became its first leader) with *Arm Yrself or Harm Yrself*.

Of course, to a very nearly unprecedented degree, 1968–69, when *Indian Killer* begins, was a winter of extraordinary historical importance for all Americans. It was in 1968 that Robert Kennedy and Martin Luther King were assassinated,[17] and violent protests occurred at the Democratic Convention in Chicago as the Vietnam War expanded in scope. Early in 1968, when Sherman Alexie was about two years old, Seattle, the setting for *Indian Killer*, was, according to Vine Deloria, Jr., "the high point of the red power movement" (1990a: 182),[18] modeled on the black power movement then being developed by the Student Nonviolent Coordinating Committee (SNCC). It was in the winter of 1968–69 that the National Indian Youth Council[19] issued its statement of Indian "self-determination," and in the fall of 1969 a group of Indians of many nations (among them Grace Thorpe, daughter of the great athlete, Jim Thorpe) and led by Richard Oakes claimed the former federal prison island of Alcatraz under an old federal law, and succeeded in holding it for nineteen months. Paul Chaat Smith and Robert Warrior specifically note that "One of the groups directly inspired to action by Alcatraz was the Seattle Indian community" (89). It was around this time, too, that Dennis Banks and Russell Means of the American Indian Movement began to command "attention by leading demonstrations and issuing militant statements"

(Hagan 171). AIM "established a reputation for being able to generate headlines and to be an effective advocate for Indian people in various protests around the country" (Smith and Warrior 115).

It was also in 1969 that Vine Deloria, Jr. published a seminal text, *Custer Died for Your Sins*. Deloria's fourth chapter, a devastating attack on anthropology called "Anthropologists and Other Friends,"[20] chastizes anthropologists for their parasitic and exploitative relation to the tribes and their failure to aid them in time of political need. "During the crucial days of 1954," for example, Deloria writes, "when the Senate was pushing for termination of Indian rights, not one single scholar, anthropologist, sociologist, historian, or economist came forward to support the tribes against the detrimental policy" (98). In *Custer* Deloria writes in a mordantly ironic and comic manner, but there is very little anger, little that might be called rage. If John Smith—who is, as I have said, as much mad as angry—wants to change the fact that "White people no longer *feared* Indians" (30), Deloria quite rationally and sanely wants white people not so much to fear Indians as to take them seriously, to consult with and listen to them, to support them where outside support might be helpful.

I also want to mention here a text of the period that did not receive nearly as much attention as Deloria's *Custer*, but that is well worth noting in these regards. I am referring to Gerald Vizenor's essay "Why Must Thomas White Hawk Die?" originally published in June 1968. White Hawk, a Dakota and a freshman premedical student at the University of South Dakota, along with a friend, William Stands, had, in the early spring of 1967 broken in to the home of James Yeado, a white jeweler in Vermillion, South Dakota, where White Hawk shot and killed Yeado.

Originally, White Hawk pleaded not guilty by virtue of insanity; then he changed his plea, and pleaded guilty to premeditated murder. Testifying at the trial of William Stands, however, White Hawk both confirmed the fact that he had pleaded guilty to the charge of premeditated murder *and* also insisted that the shooting of Yeado was accidental. White Hawk was sentenced to death, but the death sentence was commuted to life imprisonment with no parole. An orphan who suffered from stomach troubles and had had a head injury in high school, White Hawk, writes Vizenor, "learned not to show his pain and fear and loneliness" (112). Having been marked by whites as a good candidate to model what a successful Indian might be, White Hawk in fact became, Vizenor wrote, "a cultural schizophrenic" (1990b:113). Imbuing his journalism with the imaginative power that would soon be expressed in fiction, Vizenor speculates that, as he grew, "Thomas James White Hawk had given up his right to cry and he was giving up his freedom to dream. His unconscious was a burden of the past," adding, "When he [White Hawk] walked alone *he was bird and animal*" (1990b: 116, my emphasis).

There are some resemblances, I think, between Thomas White Hawk as Vizenor portrayed him and Alexie's John Smith, but I will not develop them further just here. Alexie has been critical of Vizenor's work to the point of disparagement and I suspect the resemblances I have noted are more nearly coincidence than actual influence (although Alexie's first novel, *Reservation Blues*, contains an ex-convict and violent bully by the name of Michael White Hawk, who goes quite mad).

Vizenor, like Vine Deloria in this period, deeply critical as he is of the utter lack of comprehension of Thomas White Hawk shown by those involved in his apprehension, psychiatric examinations, trial, and sentencing, does not express rage and call for retribution. After the death sentence was commuted, Vizenor published "Commutation of Death" in the *Twin Citian* magazine (where the original piece on White Hawk first appeared). His essay concludes, "The next effort on behalf of White Hawk is to find a competent psychiatrist to work with him until the psychiatrist, White Hawk and the society have a better understanding of the disintegration of the *dakota* identity in the Christian world" (1990a: 155).

The year 1968–69 was enormously important not just for Native American activism and nonfiction (and for so much else!), but also, of course, for Native American fiction. But the best-known fiction of that time, like McNickle's earlier work, suggested possibilities for resistance to dominance in ways that not only did not encourage but, rather, warned against the violent expression of rage. Of course 1968 was the year N. Scott Momaday published the novel, *House Made of Dawn*, which received the Pulitzer Prize for 1969, inaugurating what has been called the "Native American Renaissance." Momaday's novel powerfully portrays the disintegration and possible reintegration of a mixedblood World War II veteran named Abel, and makes clear the need to resist the dominant culture in a variety of complex ways. But any rage against the white world on Abel's part is not expressed in conscious acts of violence against it— with, perhaps, one very large exception.[21]

As is well known, Abel kills a white man, an Indian albino, using a knife first to pierce his rib cage, then to disembowel him. Of this, the narrator says,

He had killed the white man. It was not a complicated thing, after all; it was very simple. It was the most natural thing in the world. Surely they could see that, these men who meant to dispose of him in words. They must know that he would kill the white man again, if he had the chance, that there could be no hesitation whatsoever. For he would know what the white man was, and he would kill him if he could. A man kills such an enemy if he can. (95)

Hardly a killing prompted by rage, this is a killing done "naturally," as a matter of course; Abel "killed the white man" and he "would kill the white man again, if he had the chance."[22] In a pioneering essay that seems to have established a consensus, Larry Evers argued that Abel's killing of the white man was a killing of the white—and so disturbing and negative—part of himself.[23] It is hard to deny this. And yet, the particular white man whom Abel kills is an Indian, an albino, and a witch who "*threatened to turn himself into a snake*" (136)—at least according to Tosamah.[24] If Abel is striking a blow against the whiteness within him and the destructive effects of white privilege, the novel does not develop that possibility. *House Made of Dawn* dramatizes a number of important issues and posits subtle means of resistance to dominance. But it does not overtly represent Indian rage, nor suggest that Abel's actions derive from that rage.

In Leslie Silko's *Ceremony*, perhaps the most celebrated Native novel of the 1970s,[25] murderous rage is precisely what must be avoided by the protagonist. In the climactic scene of the novel, Tayo witnesses Emo, Pinkie, and Leroy as they torture and murder Harley. Emo, like Tayo, is a damaged Native veteran of World War II, and earlier in the novel Tayo had attempted to kill him. Now, he must resist the urge to take revenge on him for Harley's death if he is to escape the "witchery" and complete the ceremony that will produce his healing and reintegration into the community. "It had been a close call," the narrator says: "The witchery had almost ended the story according to its plan; Tayo had almost jammed the screwdriver into Emo's skull the way the witchery had wanted. . . . He would have been another victim, a drunk Indian war veteran settling an old feud" (265). That is what the whites would say, had Tayo yielded to his rage and acted violently. As for the Indians, "the witchery would work so that the people would be fooled into blaming only the whites and not the witchery. It would work to make the people forget the stories of the creation" and cause the priests to "cling to ritual without making new ceremonies as they always had before" (261).

Thus Vine Deloria, Jr., the best known and most prolific activist writer, Gerald Vizenor, an activist and journalist, N. Scott Momaday, and Leslie Marmon Silko, probably the best known Native fiction writers of the late 1960s and early '70s, all address the damage done to Indian people by white America and propose measures to resist and undo that violence. But they do not register anything like the anger bordering on murderous rage found so frequently in the writing of African American authors of this same period. This statement is in no way, let me make clear, to suggest that Native American writing somehow lagged behind African American writing. My comparativism is not based on an unstated developmental narrative of progress. As I have said in commenting on the work of Mourning Dove, both the similarities and the differences in the situations and the literatures of Native Americans and African Americans need to be considered. And one of these differences has been the general sense on the part of Native American novelists from the 1960s at least until the '90s—when there is some shift—that the impulse to act on the rage felt by oppressed persons in a colonial situation is something that must be resisted or rejected in favor of some more culturally appropriate action.

It is also the case, of course, that from 1968 until the 1990s, as has been widely noted, the Native American novel has very intensively been concerned with the subject of *identity*—although, as Eric Cheyfitz properly adds, the "central theme of *identity* . . . needs to be understood in relation to the agenda of *sovereignty/land*, which is the strong theme of Native American writing from its beginnings to the present moment" (2002: 4). The identities the mixedblood protagonists of Indian fiction of the past thirty years achieved or failed to achieve are "hybrid" identities, to be sure, but most of them, I want to claim, must nonetheless be called "Indian" identities. I need to establish this point as a way of working toward an understanding of the politics of *Indian Killer*, which are, as I will suggest, a kind of "identity politics."

*   *   *

Louis Owens has quoted N. Scott Momaday as saying that in learning about his forebears, he "acquired an identity; and it is an Indian identity, as far as I am concerned" (in Owens 1992: 13). Momaday's Indian identity and the identities of characters in his novels identified as Indians are doubtless hybrid identities in the broad sense that *any* sociocultural, psychological, or philosophical identity construction (the subject or citizen; the self or person or ego; the subject, *ego* or *cogito*) must always-already be mixed and conjunctural (cf. Philip Deloria on Charles Alexander Eastman, in the preceding chapter). There are no "pure" identities as there are no "pure" races or cultures.

But it seems to me that something more than this is meant by writers like Cyrus R. K. Patell who understand hybridity in the poststructuralist sense of—in particular—Homi Bhabha. Using terminology from the late Raymond Williams (generally hostile to poststructuralism), Patell relates hybridity to "cultural emergence" (3), where the hybrid, if I may put it so simply, appears as some genuinely *new* thing. As Patell uses Williams's terms, the emergent appears more nearly as a break from both residual and dominant values—or, in this case, identities—rather than as a particular extension or inflection of them. (The discussion here, to be sure, resembles recent debates about postmodernism's relation to modernism.) Patell writes, for example, that "John [of *Indian Killer*] is a cultural hybrid, but he is not 'successfully integrated'; he is a cultural hybrid who finds his hybridity intolerable" (4). Patell offers this assessment to make a valuable point about "The Violence of Hybridity in Silko and

Alexie," the title of his essay. But I think Officer Randy Peone,[26] a minor character in *Indian Killer*, has a more accurate diagnosis than Patell: Officer Peone thinks John is schizophrenic.

It is perfectly obvious that schizophrenia can be a sociopolitical category invoked to "discipline and punish." (It was, from the 1950s to perhaps the '70's, also rather irresponsibly recommended by, among others, Norman Mailer, R. D. Laing, Ken Kesey, and a number of French writers as a liberatory response to the constraints of "normality.") But that does not in itself strip the term of diagnostic usefulness as naming a medical condition (or, as in Vizenor's comments on Thomas White Hawk, invoked as a sociopolitical category in the interest of resistance). This is to say that John Smith is strange and troubled in ways that even James Welch's self-destructive Jim Loney (in *The Death of Jim Loney*) or Abel, for example, are not. But even the example Patell gives of Tayo as a successfully integrated hybrid seems to me inaccurate if the hybridity of Tayo's "Indian" identity must be taken as an "emergent" identity in the sense of something thus far unknown—a break or rupture—rather than an adjustment or revision of something formerly fairly well known.

Of course Tayo's Indian identity, like Momaday's, will be different from Indian identities of a hundred, let alone five hundred years ago (which identities, in turn, were inevitably different from those that preceded them by centuries, etc.). All students of these matters are familiar with the frequently cited passage in *Ceremony* in which Betonie explains how the ceremonies have to change (this is reiterated in the brief passage I have quoted above from near the end of *Ceremony*) if they are to be operatively effective in the present. This is not the same thing as Patell's version of emergent hybridity as change.

The point to which Silko has conducted Tayo is *back*, as it were, to a residual or "traditional" identity—an "invented tradition," if one insists, but "invented" only to the extent that this "tradition" involves alterations, changes, and updatings of the traditional or "the same," and not to the extent—to repeat—that it involves the emergence of some genuinely new identity.

We have already remarked in several places that change is in fact a thoroughly traditional practice, and that oral cultures have always engaged in the sort of unnoticed selective forgetting or updating that can permit them to change while yet remaining the same. What is different in *Ceremony* is that changing the traditional in the interest of sustaining the "traditional" has become something one does self-consciously rather than unself-consciously; my quotation marks mean to invoke that self-consciousness. Betonie says that the ceremonies are different though the same; they are "traditional." The traditional person says the ceremonies are the same as they always were, period. But that is probably the major difference between the "traditional" and the traditional, for all that the former is no doubt more discernibly marked by its hybridity than the latter.

Just as Momaday, for all the strands in his cultural formation, can reasonably call his identity "an Indian identity, as far as I am concerned," so, too, can Tayo. So, too, can the man I met in Minneapolis some years ago who told me that once he thought of himself as a Finndian because his father was Chippewa and his mother was Finnish, although now, as far as he is concerned, he is an Indian whose mother was Finnish. Perhaps had he pursued the possibilities of Finndianness, one would have had to confront this as a truly hybrid, a new and emergent identity. An Indian with a Finnish mother is also something new, to be sure, for no Indians had Finnish mothers way back whenever. But given this man's sense of the matter—that he is an Indian, albeit of a different kind—it seems to me a mistake to emphasize the emergent hybridity of his identity rather than its changing sameness, its likeness to rather than its difference from the traditional. Thus, while not denying the hybridity of contemporary Indian identities in the fiction I know, I want to emphasize their Indianness.

Contemporary Indians in literature may express these identities in much the same terms as those we used to speak about critical perspectives on Indian literature in Chapter 1. Novelistic Indian identities, this is to say, may privilege nationalist, indigenist, or cosmopolitan values, and each identitarian position will imply a politics, an *identity* politics. Thus a nationalist character would insist on the centrality of her tribal membership—Cherokee, Lakota, Hopi, Mohawk, Navajo, and so on—to her identity, an identity that is committed to (here is the politics) the fullest possible achievement of tribal/national *sovereignty for her people.* The indigenist will insist on the centrality of a geocentric worldview to his identity, which worldview, differing as it does from that of the modern West, seeks to challenge and alter the epistemology on which colonialism is based and to evolve different social and economic arrangements than those of Western capitalisms or socialisms. To achieve these new arrangements obviously also requires greater degrees of sovereignty for indigenous peoples (thus, again, the articulation of nationalist and indigenist perspectives). Indian cosmopolitans, as I have noted, have tended to be what Anthony Appiah has called "cosmopolitan patriots." Like other "cosmopolitan patriots," Indian cosmopolitan patriots believe they can "take their roots with [them]," and their politics involves the attempt to mobilize tribal values for the project of human liberation everywhere. The liberation imagined will, in all likelihood, nonetheless provisionally need to express itself in terms of the nation and people, and their indigenous, Other knowledge. To adapt the words used by Jean-Paul Sartre in another context, Indian cosmopolitans will live their tribal "particular-ism to the end to find thereby the dawn of the universal."[27] And just as Appiah, Fanon, and even Sartre found these cosmopolitan principles in Africa rather than in Europe, so, too, as we have noted, may Indian cos-mopolitans find their principles in the historical practices of many Native peoples.

Consider once more the example of Gerald Vizenor. In one place or another, Vizenor has written that the tribes are dead; Indians are inven-tions, or simulations; Indians are *indians*, or post-Indians; and so on. Such remarks might be read as rejections of an "Indian" identity in favor of some "emergent hybridity." But the identity Vizenor has elaborately been defining and redefining has at base the deep and unmistakable roots of "tribal" values—which can and indeed must be taken along wherever one may go—to the cities, to Europe, to China, anywhere. These values wish to substitute for Western ideologies of "progress" and "dominance," ideologies of what Vizenor has called "continuance" and "survivance." In these regards, Vizenor may well have provided *Indian* versions of cos-mopolitan patriotism seeking to avoid what Fanon called "the pitfalls of national consciousness."[28]

Patell calls Reggie Polatkin a "half-breed," "culturally hybrid," just as his cousin, Marie Polatkin, is also "culturally hybrid" (4). This is techni-cally accurate, to be sure, but I think it does not help much in under-standing *Indian Killer*. To call Reggie and Marie half-breeds, as our dis-cussion of *Cogewea* should have indicated, makes their situation rather more dire than the situation implied by reference to them as mixedblood. They are mixedblood, to be sure, although like the poor half-breed they suffer from a certain imposed cultural deprivation and its resultant con-fusions: Marie's parents wouldn't teach her the Spokane language be-cause it would do her no good in the world to know it; Reggie's white father wants him to be a good Indian—to think Indians basically vile and vicious. But, as we noted much earlier, Alexie has been very contemp-tuous of those who call themselves mixedblood rather than Indian, "be-cause that's what we are." For him, mixedbloods like Reggie and Marie are simply Indians. Obviously this matter of identity is not that simple—who says, after all, "what we are?" and what if we think "we" are not what some say "we are?" But I would agree: Native American, mixedblood, post-indian, or indian, if one must name these characters' identity, it is Indian.

Thus, of Low Man Smith in Alexie's recent story, "Indian Country," the narrator says, "He was a Coeur d'Alene Indian, even though his mother was white" (2000: 121) Again, the matter is sure to be more complex than that, but it makes little sense to deny such insistence that Low Man Smith is Indian—or, as I have maintained, that Marie, Reggie, and John Smith are *Indian* as well. This is extremely important because, as we have already seen and will see further, in *Indian Killer* whether you are Indian or not may quite literally mean the difference between life and death.

My claim here is that Alexie's novel breaks with the majority of Native American novels from the century's turn through the 1950s, '60s, '70s, and '80s in that it is not about its Indian characters' search for identity—not Marie's or Reggie's or even John Smith's search for identity. It is also not about resisting rage and finding a more culturally appropriate way to express one's pain and anger as a colonized and oppressed person. In one or another, sometimes in both these regards, *Indian Killer* seems to be part of a shift that is noticeable in at least some other Native American fiction of the 1990s.

Vizenor's *The Heirs of Columbus*, for example, is very much about identities, but *not* the identities of the novel's Indian characters, who are untroubled in these regards. *Dead Voices* is about how and where tribal values might best survive—on the reservations or, more likely, in the cities; only in the spoken voice or, necessarily, on the printed page. But its narrator, Laundry, and its focal center, an old tribal woman named Bagese, once more are not concerned with the question of "who they are." They are Indian people of one sort or another, and their problem is how to sustain and make effective the Indian or tribal values—decidedly not enrollment cards or "blood quanta"—that make them who they are.

Something similar may be said of the Indian characters of Leslie Silko's *Almanac of the Dead*, a very different book, to be sure, from any of Vizenor's. *Almanac*, as I have already remarked, is about the latest stage in the ongoing Indian wars against the colonizer, and about how a very diverse "tribe" of revolutionaries might rid the Americas of the colonial order. In the makeup of her novel's tribes, Silko is as broadly cosmopolitan as Vizenor; values indigenous to the Americas are to triumph in the interest of everyone, wherever they may come from. In Silko's most recent novel, *Gardens in the Dunes*, Sister Salt and her younger sister Indigo, of the Sand Lizard people, for all their complex relations with white Americans and Europeans, are entirely secure in their Indian identities. If Tayo suffers as a mixedblood, only to heal himself as an Indian; if Jim Loney suffers as a half-breed, never to become comfortable as an Indian or as a hybrid person; Sister Salt and Indigo have other concerns than "who they are." [29]

In similar fashion, Alexie's novel is not about "hybrid" or even Indian identities; rather, it is about the anger and rage Indian people feel toward whites who have hurt and in the present continue to hurt them. That rage will have lethal consequences. Alexie's novel is about the unsettling and frightening fact that (as Patell quotes Fanon) "decolonization is always a violent phenomenon" (Patell 7), and that "The revolutionary politics that have always been a thread in the Native American novel seem now to be more pressing and aggressive than ever" (8)

Are the politics of *Indian Killer* in fact revolutionary? Anarchistic, individualistic, and terrorist, it might be said that the politics of *Indian Killer* are actually more nearly *counter*-revolutionary than revolutionary.[30] Unlike John, who thinks painfully hard about which white man ought to be killed, the killer acts strictly on his/her/its impulses. The killer seems to choose his victims at random, even once choosing for a victim someone he does not kill. (We have noted that he kidnaps and then returns Mark Jones safely to his home.) Throughout the novel, the killer has acted completely alone, and his/her/its actions—as one might expect, although the killer does not consider this either—produce a backlash of white rage and further violence against Indians.[31]

Vizenor's *Heirs of Columbus*, like *Indian Killer*, also concludes with an image of a dance; its final sentence (there is, however, an Epilogue) is, "The children danced on the marina, and their wounds were healed once more in a moccasin game with demons" (183). Vizenor's children are part of the universal tribe comprising the sovereign nation established by Stone Columbus and the "heirs of Columbus" at Point Assinika.[32] Stone's policy is to accept anyone who wants to be tribal, "no blood attached or scratched," (162) and indeed the community with which we are to identify in *Heirs* is a rag-tag community of crossbloods, whose mongrel ancestors are Columbus, Jesus, Mayans, Jews, Moors, and, thanks to advanced genetic technology, today may even include Europeans who come to Point Assinika for a transfusion of "Indian blood." As I have developed the matter elsewhere, this seems to me the sort of community implied by fictions that belong to what Anthony Appiah has called the second or postnational stage of the postcolonial novel, a community ultimately united on the basis of "an ethical universal, . . . a certain simple respect for human suffering" (Appiah 1992: 155)

Silko's northward and southward marching armies in *Almanac* are not yet in a position to raise the flag over their own sovereign community or to dance in celebration of healing. They are also composed of a rag-tag collection of people: African American, Asian American, Euramerican, Native American. *Almanac* insists that the ancient prophecies are not to be mocked, and that the Americas *will* return to the values of life, the values, that is, of peoples indigenous to the Americas. But Silko is quite clear in acknowledging that these values may be lived by a "transnational," a universal, or cosmopolitan community of people, those committed to—in Vizenor's terms, again—continuance and survivance rather than progress and domination.

The people dancing at the cemetery with the killer, however, are all Indians; and the killer's victims have been—and, it seems likely, will continue to be—whites, in particular those with blue eyes, man, woman, or child. The killer and the Indians who join him are not, as I have said, Native nationalists. The question Indian people regularly pose to John Smith, "What tribe you are?" is not, and, it would seem, could not possibly be raised in regard to the killer. And there is absolutely no attempt to specify the tribal identities of those who come to join him; it is enough to know that they are all Indians. Nor is the killer an indigenist; we have no idea what he/she/it believes or values, or what sort of landscape he/she/it calls home. We know only that he/she/it hates white people for the wrongs committed against Indian people. Obviously the killer will not advocate cosmopolitan values to the Indians who join him; Indians and Indians only are dancing and the single interpretation of the Ghost Dance allowed for in the novel—in this very different from the 1992 INARTF Treaty's invocation of a "new Ghost Dance"—accents its commitment to the destruction of whites.

What politics, then, can we extrapolate from this novel and its ominous final pages? It seems to me that the political position implied in *Indian Killer* is the position I will call Red Nationalism with loose reference to the Black Nationalism of the 1960s. Black Nationalism in part derived from the *négritude* movement of the 1940s in the colonies of France. Professor Patricia Penn Hilden, on reading an earlier draft of this chapter, wittily suggested that what I was trying to describe in Alexie's novel might, perhaps, be called *rougetude*. But *rougetude*—I want to keep that term—must be distinguished from *négritude* in a very important regard. This is because *négritude*, in the influential version championed by Leopold Senghor,[33] in particular, was an African essentialism. It was not, as Hilden points out,

based on the racial mixing that occurred [here] during slavery and colonization. . . . In Africa, black was just plain black and nothing else. Thus any anti-essentialism set in opposition to *négritude* will also not be grounded (*as it must be* with Chicanos and Indians) in the acceptance of mixed race/mixed racialized experience but rather in a more sophisticated understanding that no such thing as a racial essence exists outside the confines of those who created, invested in, and now profit from whiteness as *the* race or the invisible race. (personal communication, November 2, 1989, my emphasis)

What I am calling Red Nationalist *rougetude* in *Indian Killer* is a type of "racism," although it is not based on "racial" assumptions about biology or blood. It most certainly acknowledges the complexities of "mixed race/mixed racialized experience," but it subsumes the particularities of those complexities—here we may well call them hybridities—into the generic, "racial" category, Indian. As I have tried to make the case thus far, the nature and meaning of Reggie's, Marie's, and John's "mixed race/

mixed racialized experience" is simply (!) the complex experience of being Indian. *Indian Killer* suggests that being Indian is *like* belonging to a race, and that the Indian "race" today is filled with rage against whites and attracted to the idea of a murderous expression of that rage. As with Fanon, the colonialist dictum, Force is all the Natives understand! is turned against the colonialists: If they understand nothing else, they will understand murder!

Alexie's *rougetude* or Red Nationalist "racist" politics are, then, as I have already suggested, a form of identity politics. Identity politics of this sort must be seen, as Kenneth Mostern has written, "neither as a solution nor as a problem, but rather as a fact . . . a practice of politics in the United States . . . determined systematically in and by the social field" (32). Inasmuch as "collective political action always supposes a relationship of identification," as Mostern continues, the question becomes just what "relationship of identification" to privilege. In the United States those who are not white cannot escape "racial identification," and so, again, Reggie, Marie, and John are all Indians not so much because they share "Indian blood," or even because they share very much in the way of culture. They are Indians because a racist society treats them as Indians. And their solidarity with one another and with the killer, for all that they themselves do not construe it racially, is nonetheless based on what Anthony Appiah has called "intrinsic racism," the belief "that the bare fact of being of the same race [here, even if you don't necessarily believe in races!] is a reason for preferring one person to another" (1989: 45). Indians in *Indian Killer* are Indians; they know each other as Indians without any special attention to racial mix, hybridity, blood quanta, enrollment cards, or even culture. Yet despite the fact that Indian identity is not racialized by Indians in the novel, it nonetheless acts according to a kind of "intrinsic racism" that leads to a fairly straightforward, if rather sinister politics: Indians for Indians, Indians against whites.

This pan-Indian solidarity is the only "nationalist" content of the Red Nationalist politics of *Indian Killer*. The Indians at the cemetery with the killer are not dancing to achieve a greater degree of sovereignty for any particular tribal people. Any actions these Indians may take is strictly a blow struck in the war between Us and Them. As the first chapter of the novel made clear, this is definitely war; as subsequent chapters make clear, the Ghost Dance is conceived and reconceived as an Indians-only affair—and no "treaty" of any kind is envisioned that might put a stop to the war. The INARTF Treaty called on any non-Natives who would end the Indian wars and participate in the "new Ghost Dance" to make "a major change in their behaviors, attitudes, and values" (Charleston in Lyons 464). But *Indian Killer* does not see that sort of change as a possibility; it is the *fire* this time.

In his brief but extraordinary career as a writer of fiction, Alexie has several times tried to sort out his feelings about the complex and painful question of what sorts of relations—friendly, loving, hostile—might be possible between Indians and whites. To cite just a few examples, in "Imagining the Reservation" (in *The Lone Ranger and Tonto*), we are told that "Survival = Anger x Imagination," and that not anger but "Imagination is the only weapon on the reservation" (150). This follows a story called "The First Annual All-Indian Horseshoe Pitch and Barbecue," which ends with the words, "she held the child born of a white mother and red father and said, 'Both sides of this baby are beautiful'" (148). Nonetheless, a later story affirms that "the most valuable lesson about living in the white world [is]: *Always throw the first punch*" (176).

Alexie's recent collection, *The Toughest Indian in the World*, also can be read on both sides of the matter. The first story, ironically (it would seem) called "Assimilation," has the Coeur d'Alene wife of a white man seduce the darkest Indian man she can find, only, at the end of the story, to return passionately to her white husband. Once Mary Lynn and Jeremiah had explained their relation by saying, "Love is love" (14), knowing that explained nothing. But at the story's end the narrator—this time, I believe, without irony—says, "They loved each other across the distance" (20). In "Class," an Indian lawyer who has never slept with an Indian woman (besides his white wife, he has "slept with seventeen prostitutes, all of them blond and blue-eyed" 43), has a violent adventure in an Indian bar, then returns to his wife. The story concludes with him saying to her—again, I think, without irony—"I was gone. . . . But now I'm back" (56).

The longest and most powerful story in the book, "The Sin Eaters," has its twelve-year-old Spokane protagonist, Jonah Lot (?), dream "about war on the night before the war began, and though nobody officially called it a war until years later, I woke that next morning with the sure knowledge that the war, or whatever they wanted to call it, was about to begin and that I would be a soldier in a small shirt" (76). What happens next is not a dream. Soldiers arrive; they want Indian "blood" in order, as a Dr. Clancy tells Jonah, to save the world (115). Anne Frank is mentioned early (80); the Indians have their heads shaved (96), are herded into cattle chutes (96), and, at one point, fear the possibility of ovens (97). References to the Holocaust are frequent and explicit. The story ends in a manner I find infuriatingly ambiguous and unsatisfying, perhaps the most egregious example I know of Alexie's determination to prefer cleverness to commitment. (But I will claim that *Indian Killer* also will not commit itself to even a tentative resolution of the important issues it raises.) Young Jonah is forced to have sex with a very dark-skinned Indian woman who has already herself been forced to have sex with "five men" (119)—dark Indian men, it would seem—that day. Jonah, who knows he "would survive and live on" (118), finds his "way inside of her," and walks "through the rooms of her," where, as the woman advises, he can "hide" (120). "They wanted our blood," Jonah says, "They would always want our blood." Nonetheless, the story enigmatically ends at a tangent—perhaps I've missed something important—to such issues as the blood wars. "Are you my mother?" Jonah asks. "Yes," the woman answers. Final line: " 'Mother,' I whispered. 'Mother, mother, mother' " (120).[34]

Subsequent stories in the collection portray a happily married Mohawk and Spokane couple ("Saint Junior"), an Indian woman who slept with John Wayne ("Dear John Wayne"), and, finally, a story that several times asks the question, *What is an Indian?* (224ff). The question is posed specifically by Dr. Lawrence Crowell, who was, "according to his vita, a Cherokee-Choctaw-Seminole-Irish-Russian Indian from Hot Springs, Kentucky, or some such place" (224). This gratuitous potshot at Louis Owens[35] develops with the narrator's mother indulging herself in a long and tedious monologue (it is meant to be funny, I think) which mostly conveys contempt for the "white guy who says he's part Indian" (226). Then the narrator's father is brought on to inform Dr. Crowell that he "might be a Native American but you sure as hell ain't Indian" (228).

The story ends by working out the tender relationship between the narrator and his (now) physically helpless father: "*What is an Indian?* I lifted my father and carried him across every border" (238). Nice: but where does that leave us? Maybe we have to go back to an earlier point in the story where the narrator says, "I'm not exactly racist. I like white people as a theory. I'm just not crazy about them in practice" (217). But that doctrine too has its exceptions.

In Alexie's first novel, *Reservation Blues,* Big Mom, a woman of extraordinary power and legendary authority, is more generous. She recommends "forgiveness" (203) rather than throwing the first punch, noting that "the white man has always been better at violence anyway" (208), and wondering, "When are Indians ever going to have heroes who don't hurt people?" (209). Thomas Builds-the-Fire, an important character throughout Alexie's fiction (and, of course, in his screenplay for the film, *Smoke Signals*), worries about the children born to Indian-white couples, "but he also knew about the shortage of love in the world" (82).

Chess Warm Water, Thomas's lover, insists, to the contrary, that a mixedblood child—Chess uses the older, derogatory term, "halfbreed" —is sure to find that "Half of him will always want to tear the other half apart. It's war." And, when she says to Thomas, "let's get married. Let's have kids. . . . Let's have lots of brown babies," Thomas, smiling, responds, "Okay" (284). At the novel's end, Thomas, Chess, and her sister Checkers drive off through the night to the sound of Big Mom's flute playing a note for each of the nine hundred Spokane horses slaughtered by soldiers in 1858, and then "nine hundred, nine thousand, nine million [notes], one note for each of the dead Indians" (306). Consistent with the hopeful tone of the conclusion—of Thomas, Chess, and Checkers it is said: "They were alive; they'd keep living" (306)—Big Mom's music can be imagined as elegiac, commemorative, and also perhaps "forgiving." But that is not likely to be the kind of music to which the killer and the Indians at the cemetery are dancing, as they remember that "the score is about *ten* million to three, in favor of the white guys," so that "This Killer's got a long ways to go" (220, my emphasis).

Meanwhile, even in *Reservation Blues* there is music of a different kind from that of Big Mom at the end, music that might prefigure the music we might imagine in *Indian Killer*. In *Reservation Blues*, Alexie describes Robert Johnson playing a "blues [that] created memories for the Spokanes, but they refused to claim them," "blues [that] churned up generations of anger and pain. . . . Those blues were ancient, aboriginal, indigenous" (174). Those blues made of "The smell of sweat, blood, and cotton" (175) are, of course, the music of Robert Johnson's black forebears. "Thomas listened closely" to those blues, "but the other Spokanes . . . would not speak about any of it. They buried all of their pain and anger deep inside, and it festered" (175). In *Indian Killer* that pain and anger will not be buried and left to fester; it will not be resisted in the interest of completing a ceremony; nor will it be assuaged and healed. Rather, it will express itself in murderous rage against the whites who have hurt both blacks and Indians.

The Red Nationalist *rougetude* on which the "intrinsic racism" of *Indian Killer* is based is almost certainly of the type Jean-Paul Sartre called "an anti-racist racism." As Sartre described it in the essay "Black Orpheus,"[36] "anti-racist racism" was created by "the Negro," who "does not at all wish to dominate the world; he wishes the abolition of racial privileges wherever they are found." And, Sartre adds, "he [the Negro] affirms his solidarity with the oppressed of all colors" (n.p.). Inasmuch as Alexie's Red Nationalist *rougetude* also has as its end the destruction of "racial privileges," one must applaud it; inasmuch as it operates in a manner parallel to an "intrinsic racism," one must at the very least be wary of it, even as a strategic move.

Commenting on Sartre's description of anti-racist racism, Anthony Appiah notes that Sartre saw it "as a necessary step in a dialectic that would lead to the transcendance of racism by an identification with humanity," the sort of thing I have claimed to find in Vizenor's *Dead Voices* and Silko's *Almanac of the Dead*. Appiah continues, however, "necessary or not, it has indeed proved to be the next step: The question now is whether we are ready for the transcendance Sartre anticipated (1989: 58). Fanon also anticipated the transcendance of racism and an end to violence. But this is not what is projected at the end of *Indian Killer*.

In the novel's penultimate chapter, called "Testimony," Marie Polatkin, as we have noted, says that " 'John Smith didn't kill anybody except himself. And if some Indian is killing white guys, then it's a credit to us that it took over five hundred years for it to happen' " (418). Marie then added, " 'And there's more, Indians are dancing now, and I don't think they're going to stop'." She is, as we have also noted, correct; the concluding chapter of the novel finds the killer joined by "A dozen Indians, then hundreds, and more, all learning the same song, the exact dance. The killer dances and will not tire" (420), nor are his fellows likely to tire or "to stop."

The question for the novel and its politics is, What does this mean or portend? It might mean what I believe Marie thought it meant: that an Indian, having begun at last killing white guys after some five hundred years, is not likely to stop, and that other Indians will join the killer in murder. This chapter's title, "A Creation Story," would then imagine a new beginning for Indian people—Creation—to come about through acts of murderous violence directed against a "racially" denominated oppressor, white men. Perhaps such murders may be seen as therapeutic, as described by Fanon, or, like Bigger Thomas's murder of Mary Dalton, as "an act of *creation*" (Wright 366). This Ghost Dance, as Marie earlier insisted to Dr. Clarence Mather, is not "about peace and beauty" (313). The Ghost Dance in *Indian Killer* is about murder as creation.

Is the ending of *Indian Killer*, then, Sherman Alexie's warning to whites? If so, it is a warning quite unlike Fanon's, for Fanon wrote in the midst of revolutionary, nationalist mass agitation in Algeria in the 1960s and of a world in violent process of decolonization. Nor is it a warning like Richard Wright's from the 1930s in *Native Son*, for there does not presently exist any mass movement of the right or left that could mobilize, politicize, and direct Indian rage in the way fascism and communism might then have promised or threatened to do. If this is a warning to whites, I think it is one intended primarily to produce a *frisson*, a shiver—but not much more. Alexie's mostly white readers will shiver—this murder, that murder, any particular murder, only murder in a book. It's only that postmodern turn! And yet I would like to think that there may just be something more to take from the end of *Indian Killer*, although it is a postmodern "more," no doubt.

That "more" has to do with the killer's relation to owls, referred to all through the novel and returned to at the end. Mark Jones, we have noted, the only person to have seen the killer and lived, told the police that the killer was a bird, not a he or a she but an "it." We know that the killer has torn out the eyes of his victim, Justin Summers, "With hands curved into talons" (54), before placing "two white owl feathers . . . on the white man's chest" (54). Finally, on the last page of the book, as the killer "spins in circles . . . , with each revolution, another owl floats in from the darkness and takes its place in the tree," and, after, "The killer gazes skyward and screeches." The book ends, "The killer never falls. The moon never falls. The tree grows heavy with owls" (420).

A bit earlier on that same page, we are told that the killer "believes in all masks, in this wooden [?] mask;" "With this mask, with this mystery, the killer can dance forever." We are also told in this brief chapter that owls are "Birds of prey, birds of prayer" (419). The image of the tree heavy with owls is certainly ominous, and owls in many Native cultures are considered to be harbingers of death. But prayers here seem to be set in rough opposition to "prey" so that these prayers would not be prayers for the enemy's death. Do all or any of these images, all or any of these linkages, the masks, and the mystery, the singing and dancing and owl flights, suggest more than further vengeful killing? The book shifts, here, from the level of sociopolitics to the level of symbol and ritual; if there is indeed something "more" than further murder, we will have to imagine it ourselves. Red is a fearful matter in *Indian Killer*.

Notes

Preface

1. See, for example, Cornel West, *Race Matters*, Kenneth O'Reilly, *Racial Matters*, and Michael Levin, *Why Race Matters*, among others.

2. See my *Ethnocriticism: Ethnography, History, Literature*.

3. The upper case is awkward, to be sure, but I will occasionally use it to indicate the fact that a given first person plural and a third person plural pronoun include not merely designation and number but pronounced difference. Thus: we are many and they are fewer; but, We think one way about some things, and They think another. Some of my upper- and lower-case choices are indeed subjective; Others would write them other ways; still others would write them Other ways.

Chapter 1. Nationalism, Indigenism, Cosmopolitanism

1. I quote Churchill here as a nationalist (and below as an indigenist) although Lakota lawyer John P. Lavelle, in a recent essay, refers to "Churchill's distinctive anti-tribal ideology" (251). Lavelle ascribes to Churchill the belief that "Indian tribes ought to be reviled and actively opposed for employing tribal membership criteria that require an individual to be possessed of a given degree or 'quantum' of tribe-specific Indian blood—typically one fourth—in order to be eligible for tribal enrollment" (252). Lavelle's "blood" logic has its own problems (on the subject of "Indian blood" see Strong and van Winkle 1996, and also Chapter 4 below), and, in view of Churchill's collaboration with Means, it may not represent his position in regard to tribal sovereignty altogether fairly. Lavelle's essay, however, is of great importance in that it cites chapter and verse to demonstrate the errors, falsifications, and misrepresentations that mark and mar Churchill's writings. In the interest of full disclosure, I should note that I have been—along with James Clifton, Sam Gill, Werner Sollors, and others—the object of a particularly distorted and unfair attack on Churchill's part, and so I claim no neutrality or objectivity toward him—although I cite him with no adverse commentary beyond this note.

2. See Wilkinson; Harring; Strickland; P. DeLoria; V. DeLoria and Lytle; and Resnik.

3. As noted, however, a great many Native people do *not* wish to regard tribal membership as comparable to citizenship, a notion, it might be said (and has been

said), that the Indian Reorganization Act of 1934 sought to impose on the tribes. The Native view is not rights-based but nation-people-based.

4. Translation, like anthropology, has historically been in the service of colonialism. But both translation and anthropology today have also sought to take forms that oppose colonialism. See Chapter 3 below.

5. For European meditation on these matters, see Pierre Clastres, *Society Against the State*.

6. For an insightful and moving account of these matters from a personal perspective, see Hans-Ulrich Sanner's "Confessions of the Last Hopi Fieldworker."

7. As ethically distinct from invocations of the nation in support of oppression, for example, as in the last days of apartheid in South Africa, in the Balkans very recently, and currently, it would seem, in Macedonia.

8. See Womack, for example, on Alex Posey and Joy Harjo; Julian Rice on *Black Elk Speaks*; and Shari Huhndorf on D'Arcy McNickle's *Wind from an Enemy Sky*.

9. Or songs, as Donald Bahr, Lloyd Paul, and Vincent Joseph, *Ants and Orioles: Showing the Art of Pima Poetry*, makes clear. See also Larry Evers and Felipe Molina, *Yaqui Deer Songs*, among other studies too extensive to cite.

10. See chapter 5 of *Red on Red*, "Fus Fixico: A Literary Voice Against the Extinction of Tribal Government."

11. For more on the "question . . . whether cultural sovereignty can be seen in the same terms as political sovereignty," see David Murray, "Cultural Sovereignty and the Hauntology of American Identity." The quotation is from p. 237 of that essay.

12. Owens's sentence concludes, however, as follows: "a consciousness and worldview defined primarily by a quest for identity: What does it mean to be "Indian"—or mixedblood—in contemporary America?" (20). Although Owens here subscribes to the idea that there is a common indigenous "consciousness and worldview," for him that "consciousness and worldview" does not inevitably lead to a common indigenous identity.

13. The indigenist sense of difference/distance from Western epistemology has on occasion manifested itself as an attack not merely on social science, as in Vine Deloria, Jr.'s powerful and witty attack on anthropology in 1969, but, as in Deloria's recent *Red Earth, White Lies*, an attack on "science" of every kind. For the claim that science is indeed constituted by worldview, see also Maurice Bazin's "Our Sciences, Their Science," and Clara Sue Kidwell's "Science and Ethnoscience." More forceful is Alan Bishop's "Western Mathematics: The Secret Weapon of Cultural Imperialism." For a sympathetic yet critical review of Deloria's book, see David D. Harris. A devastating critique has been published by H. David Brumble, with a brief and somewhat evasive response by Deloria.

14. See David Abrams for a powerful account of the panhuman need for a relationship to the sensuous "surround." It should be made absolutely clear, however, that "nature" writing of the sort associated with, for example, Wallace Stegner (see Elizabeth Cook-Lynn's *Why I Can't Read Wallace Stegner*), Annie Dillard, William Trogdon (William Least Heat Moon), and Ian Frazier, among many many others, is simply not consistent with what Abrams or Native indigenists mean. For some of the differences between Native people and "the mainstream environmental movement," see Susan Kollin, "Race and Global Environmentalism: Nora Dauenhauer, Tlingit History, and the Poetics of Place." For a review of the exponential growth of ecocritical studies, see William Slaymaker, "Ecoing the Other(s): The Call of Global Green and Black African Responses."

15. Roger Moody's edited book of this name is a collection of essays, not an

anthology of literary texts. The title, however, seems possible for any one of a number of literary anthologies.

16. This phrase occurs in the subtitle of an essay by M. Annette Jaimes. At the College where I teach, however, a course of that name is offered under the departmental heading of "Public Policy."

17. See, for example, David Murray's *Indian Giving: Material and Discursive Economies in Early Indian and White Exchanges.*

18. But see Thomas Schlereth's work, to which I am indebted for some of the Classical, Renaissance, and, in particular, Enlightenment background. For contemporary revivals of cosmopolitanism, see Appiah (1997); Clifford (1998); Gilroy (1993, 2000); Hollinger; Nussbaum et al., Rabinow; Robbins; Robbins and Cheah; Siebers; and Krupat (1989, 1996), among others. Some few of these offer examples of cosmopolitanism other than European.

19. I have discussed my own personal relation to this recognition in "A Nice Jewish Boy Among the Indians," chapter 5 of my *Turn to the Native.*

20. Among Vizenor's many texts, see in particular Part 1 of *Crossbloods: Bone Courts, Bingo, and Other Reports, Landfill Meditation: Crossblood Stories,* the novel *The Heirs of Columbus,* and, most recently, *Fugitive Poses.*

21. Alexie's *The Lone Ranger and Tonto Fistfight in Heaven* is conflicted on this matter, some stories indicating a separatist or exclusionist perspective, others more open to conjunctures. This is true as well in *Reservation Blues,* parts of which are fully cognizant of the value to Native people of relationships or alliances with non-Natives. *Indian Killer,* however, is a book that, as I discuss it in Chapter 5, seems committed to a hostile separatism. Alexie's recent short piece, "The Unauthorized Autobiography of Me," contains a troubling mockery of "mixedbloods."

22. See his *Manifest Manners: Postindian Warriors of Survivance,* in particular, Chapter 1, "Postindian Warriors."

23. Thomas Biolsi and Larry Zimmerman's term "late imperialism" (4) is more accurate as a description of the political situation of contemporary Native American literature than "postcolonialism." Although, as I have argued in my *Turn to the Native,* some contemporary Native American novels resemble a second wave of postcolonial fiction in Africa, there is no "post-" as yet to the colonial condition of Native people.

24. See the collection of that name edited by W. H. Capps.

Chapter 2. On the Translation of Native American Song and Story

1. It may be useful to indicate my understanding of the differences between oppositional and dialectical terms. Oppositional relations are the constructions of logic, deriving perhaps foremost from Aristotle's principles of identity, nonidentity, and the excluded middle: there is "A" and "not-A," which, for any given discussion in which they appear, are to one another as positive and negative. "A" is fully itself: "not-A" is in no way whatever "A" is. Dialectical relations, however, present terms which inevitably overlap and intersect, each needing—or, better, unavoidably including—the other for its own meaning. Differences between terms, thus, are matters of degree not kind. The principle of logical opposition requires that we must choose *either* "A" *or* "not-A," that choice removing from consideration the term rejected; dialectically, we may *emphasize* "A" or "not-A," that emphasis in no way negating the term de-emphasized. (For an interesting discussion of this matter in feminist terms, see Nancy Jay, "Gender and Di-

chotomy.") I have taken the time to make this point because I believe it bears importantly on how we think about translation, informing us, for example, that such a question as, "Is it accurate, is it authentic?" cannot be answered with a simple yes or no. In the same way, it informs us that the observation, "It's lovely, it's powerful," cannot disqualify the question, "Is it accurate, is it authentic?"

2. See my "Post-Structuralism and Oral Literature."

3. The quotation from Spinden appears in Tedlock's 1983 version of this essay in his *The Spoken Word and the Work of Interpretation.* The essay was originally published in 1971.

4. See Bahr's "Oratory."

5. The oldest description of Native poems or songs seems to come from William Strachey in 1612. See Swann (1992: xiv).

6. There are doubtless other of Schoolcraft's song texts that might be chosen, but just here, uncovering the unfamiliar seems less useful than emphasizing what has oft been expressed but not so well attended to. My own discussion will have achieved its best purpose if it persuades the reader to review Dell Hymes's indispensable essay "Some North Pacific Coast Poems: A Problem in Anthropological Philology," first published in 1965, and reworked for his *"In Vain I Tried to Tell You": Essays in Native American Ethnopoetics.* Here is Hymes's retranslation (1981:41) of the Chippewa original:

Flitting insect of white fire!
Flitting insect of white fire!
Come, give me light before I sleep!
Come, give me light before I sleep!
Flitting insect of white fire!
Flitting insect of white fire!
Light me with your bright instrument of flame.
Light me with your bright instrument of flame.

Hymes further comments (42),

Ethnologists *often* can be relied upon; literary versions *often* may be better than literal counterparts; structure may *often* be accessible in translation—but how is one to tell *when?* The only way to tell is by independent control of the results of translation, through access to the original texts, and, preferably, to the linguistic aids necessary for their analysis.

7. See, for example, John Bierhorst, ed., *The Fire Plume: Legends of the American Indians Collected by Henry Rowe Schoolcraft.*

8. See, for example, Powell's *Anthropology of the Numa* and Voth's "Powamu Songs" (my thanks to Peter Whiteley for calling these to my attention). Also working in this period as government ethnologist was James Mooney, whose *Myths of the Cherokee* offers prose translations of an enormous body of texts. Although the original Cherokee texts are not given, there is a glossary of Cherokee words retained in some of the translations and elaborate notes on linguistic and ethnographic matters. Mooney's *Cherokee Sacred Formulas and Medicinal Prescriptions* (revised, completed, and edited by Frans M. Olbrecht, and published in 1932) consists chiefly of "The Swimmer Manuscript," "a small daybook of about 240 pages . . . about half filled with writing in the Cherokee characters" (Mooney in Olbrecht 1932:1). Mooney obtained it from a Cherokee known in English as "Swimmer," and began work on it in 1888. Although these are "medical prescriptions," and therefore obviously not "literature" as Westerners usually think of

it, some of them are sung, and, in translation, look rather like a good deal of the material that has been presented as "Native American poetry." I give an example of Mooney's translations procedures below (170–71; I have not included the Mooney/Olbrecht notes):

ˌɩˈɑ–ɴˌˀɔⁿ	Dɩˈniskɔ·liˈ	Dʋˈnitɫǫ̈ŋǫ̈·ˈ.iˋ			
this-and	their heads	whenever they are ill			

ɑniˈsɢüˈya	ɑniˈlɔˌˤiˈ	|	ʋtsɩˈˤnɑwaˋ	anɔˈˤnɩ·ɢaˈ	| aˈnɪɒɑ·ˈᵘeε̄
they men	they just passed by		beyond-it-stretched	they have come and said it	they (are) wizards

ɑniˈlɔˌˤiˈ	| ʋtsɩˈˤnɑwaˋ	anɔˈˤnɩ·ɢaˈ	| ʋtsɩˈˤnɑwaˈ	ɢɔ̈ˈtɫtɑˌˤaⁿˈ |
they just passed by	beyond it stretched	they have come and said it	beyond it stretched	It (has been) rubbed

ʋtsɩˈˤnɑwaˋ	anɔˈˤnɩ·ɢaˈ	| yᾰˤ
beyond it stretched	they have come and said it	Sharp!

ˌɩˈɑ–ɴˌˀɔⁿ	na.ˈsɢwɔ̈ŋˈ	Dɩˈniskɔ·liˈ	Dʋˈnitɫǫ̈ŋǫ̈·ˈ.iˋ	| ˌɩˈaˈ nɩ-ʋstiˈ |
this-and	also	their heads	whenever they are ill	this so far like

ɔˈɒali-ɢüˈɒli	anǫ̈·ˈskɔ̈tɫ̦ˈ.i	ɒɩᴅzɔˈˤtˤɩstɔ.tiˈ
mountain-he climbs	it (sol.) used to be held in the mouth—H	they to be blown with it

AND THIS IS (FOR) WHEN THEIR HEADS ARE ILL
(*free translation*)

The men have just passed by, they have caused relief,
The wizards have just passed by, they have caused relief,
Relief has been rubbed, they have caused relief. Sharp!

Now that we have William Powers's work on Lakota "Yuwipi" curing songs (e.g., "Text and Context in Lakota Music," *Sacred Language*, etc.) along with the work of his teacher David McAllester (e.g., " 'The War God's Horse Song,' An exegesis in Native American Humanities," among others, it might be interesting to return to Mooney's "prescriptions" not only as ethnography/science but also as poetry/art.
    9. Cf. Burlin:

The interlinear translations here given have been made with care in the hope that the book may be of some aid in the comparative study of the linguistic stocks of the North American continent; yet they are offered as approximate only, for philological accuracy requires full and intimate knowledge of the Indian languages—a knowledge which the recorder [Burlin] does not possess. Whenever an authority on the language of a given tribe has been found his criticism has been solicited, as follows, and the recorder wishes here to express her grateful acknowledgment of the services so kindly rendered. (535)

Burlin's list of "authorities" includes Franz Boas, James Mooney, and the Rev. H. R. Voth, among others.

10. Cf. the following example from Fletcher's "The Relation of Indian Story and Song," from the Navajo (in Chapman 237):

A PRAYER FOR RAIN

"MUSIC BARS"
Song

11. See, for example, Drinnon's general attempt to recuperate Austin's reputation, as well as the approving words of Michael Castro (in Coltelli 102–3ff).

12. Austin's note to this text, in an appendix (173), reads, "The personal song is an expression of a man's own philosophy, or a note of his consummate spiritual experience. It is often sung going into battle, or on the approach of death, in which case friends of the singer will often gather around his bed and sing it for him."

I am no expert on Lakota culture, but I have my doubts about some of this—or perhaps I should only note that Austin's remarks are at best very vague in their ethnographic content. And she gives nothing whatever as a guide to the Lakota original. In relation to my comments on the Cherokee "prescriptions," in note 8 above, it should be said that Austin has indeed reworked four of them from Mooney's literal translations, "with the help of Leota Harris, a woman of Cherokee descent, who had the formulas almost in the original form from her mother." Typically, Austin notes that she refrained from doing her own versions "until [she] had additional material which [she] thought would bring out their poetic values" (173). As typically, she has no hesitation in stating which one of the four "is most poetic in concept." Her standards for determining "poetic values" and "concepts," as expressed in the lengthy introduction to *The American Rhythm*, have not worn very well.

13. See Castro's *Interpreting the Indian: Twentieth-Century Poets and the Native American*.

14. See "Anthropology in the Ironic Mode: the Work of Franz Boas."

15. The "comparative method" in anthropology, if not "literary anthropology" strictly speaking, was attacked by Boas in an influential early paper called "The Limitations of the Comparative Method in Anthropology" (1940) [1896].

16. An early harsh critique is the well-known essay by William Bevis, "American Indian Verse Translations" (1974). William Clements's "Faking the Pumpkin" (1981) also takes the cudgel to Rothenberg, perhaps a bit excessively. Rothenberg has offered a thoughtful and nondefensive defense of his ongoing commitment to "total translation" in Swann (1992). I have suggested that Rothenberg's work may also be seen in the context of criticism, specifically what I call ethnocriticism, quite as well as in the context of translation. See my " 'Literary' Criticism/Native American 'Literature' " in *Ethnocriticism*.

17. As Swann notes, John Swanton's original Indian language text, with a literal, and a free/literary translation is given in Dell Hymes's "Some North Pacific Coast Poems," in which Hymes retranslates it (cf. Hymes 1981:45; Swann 1985:127) as he did Schoolcraft's "Chant to the Fire-Fly."

18. Kroeber's "Turning Comparative Literature Around: The Problem of Translating American Indian Literatures," the essay from which I have quoted, seems quite different from the position he had earlier taken in his introduction to *Traditional American Indian Literatures*.

19. See Bevis's "American Indian Verse Translations."

20. For Hymes's method, and the distinction between "metered verse" and "measured verse," see his "Discovering Oral Performance and Measured Verse in American Indian Narrative," both in *"In vain I tried to tell you"*.

21. If I am not mistaken, Hymes published his first commentary on this narrative (originally recorded by Melville Jacobs and published in 1959) in 1971. He retranslated it in "measured verse" six years later, in the paper cited just above. The version of the story appended to this latter essay differs only in very slight degree from the 1977 verse translation. For an account of the "Literary uses and related versions" of the story, see Hymes (1981:300).

22. See, for example, William Bright (1979), Virginia Hymes (1974), M. Dale Kinkade, Joel Sherzer (1983, 1987) and Barbara Tedlock (1980), among others.

23. For that, see Mattina's introduction to *The Golden Woman*. Wendy Wickwire's edition of the work in English of another Northwestern storyteller, Harry Robinson, is also interesting in these regards. See *Write It on Your Heart: The Epic World of an Okanagan Storyteller*.

24. See, for example, Hinton and L. Watahomigie, eds., *Spirit Mountain: An Anthology of Yuman Story and Song*.

25. There is also a literary translation by Swann (in Bahr 1987:213–14):

FREE TRANSLATIONS (SWANN)

1 (1) Jesus descends to this vile earth.
       Here I descend,
       here I descend,

Descend to this vile earth.
My poor heart,
I don't know what will happen.

26. The examples are cited from a manuscript in my possession. Versions of this material also appear in Bahr, Paul, and Joseph (1997).

27. The phrase is the title of a book by Kenneth Lincoln.

Chapter 3. America's Histories

1. The term is from Eric Wolf, who does not consider Native people to be without history, although for him and for others the history they have is mostly the result of imbrication in world systems.

2. Cf. Donald Bahr: "To my knowledge tribal societies do not have *fictions* in the modern sense of stories that people make up with no pretense or faith that the characters in the story really lived or that the characters' actions really occurred" (1993: 47). Bahr has worked with the Akimel O'odham (Pima) and Tohono O'odham (Papago) of Arizona. For further illustration of this point see pp. 72ff. of my *Turn to the Native*. None of this is to say that *individuals* may not engage in embroidering the truth or inventing tall tales. And, obviously, contemporary Native Americans steeped in or attentive to their tribal traditions write novels and short stories that are in whole or part invented fictions.

3. See Eric Havelock, "Why Was Socrates Tried?" and, much later, *The Muse Learns to Write*.

4. The article cited below by Landsman gives some sense of the issues in regard to the Constitution and the Iroquois Confederacy. On the Walum Olum, see Oestreicher, and for Seathl's speech see Kaiser.

5. After the battle, however, many apparently did recognize the body of Custer, and Cheyenne women, it is said, pierced his ears with awls so that he might hear better than he had in 1869 when he apparently did not hear or heed Stone Forehead's warning to keep his promise not to harm the Cheyenne lest he be turned to dust (see Powell 1: 119–22). Before the Custer battle, Sitting Bull is said to have had a dream in which he saw soldiers falling dead into the Lakota camp, because "these have no ears" (see DeMallie 1993).

6. On the basis of his reading of Dr. Thomas Marquis's *Custer on the Little Big Horn*, James Welch believes that the election of Brave Bear was a joke. Raymond DeMallie (1993) takes the matter seriously from his reading of David Miller's account—in spite of the fact that DeMallie's own original research turned up no reference "to this aspect of the Council in Dixon's papers" (DeMallie 1993: 535 n.3). Miller admitted that Brave Bear, who died in 1932 at age 87, "never had much to say about his honorary distinction as the Slayer of Custer" (262). He also notes that White Bull (see below) told him in 1939 that he had come to believe that he himself was indeed the warrior who had killed Custer and that Miller "was the *first* white man to whom he had confessed" (253). In paintings done between 1890 and 1913, the Oglala Amos Bad Heart Bull represents Crazy Horse killing Custer with a club (Blish no. 183).

7. According to Miller, there are many who might claim to have killed Custer—although both in 1909, and even 1926 there were concerns that the whites wanted to know only in order to punish the perpetrator. Candidates for the honor or the danger of having killed Custer include the renowned Rain-in-the-Face, who both

claimed the deed for himself and also said it had been done by a man named Hawk. There is the Cheyenne, Two Moons, nominated by another Cheyenne, Medicine Bear, and there is the Santee Sioux, Walks-Under-the-Ground, who was known to have been riding Custer's horse after the battle. Others who might be considered are Red Horse, a Minneconjou, Flat Hip and Little Knife, both Hunk-papa, and the "girl warrior" (Miller 210) Walking Blanket Woman, who claimed to have stabbed Custer in the back. (Custer's body, according to the official report of its examination, exhibited no stab wounds.) And, as noted above, Amos Bad Heart Bull reserved the deed for his Oglala relative, Crazy Horse.

8. I am grateful to Raymond DeMallie's "'These Have No Ears'" for alerting me to this example, as well as to the one preceding.

9. Recent work (e.g., Malotki) has shown that to be untrue, but in any case Whorf's perhaps overly famous essay doesn't so much show that the Hopi language has no concept of time as that—as one would again expect—it expresses temporality in a manner very different from Indo-European languages.

10. See James Clifford's "Identity in Mashpee" for a similar and yet very different account of a trial in which an indigenous group had to demonstrate its difference by means of rules which, if successfully adhered to, inevitably negated difference. See also Gerald Vizenor's account, in "Native Transmotion," of the impasses in court in a case pitting the East Lake tribe of Anishinaabe (Chippewa) against the federal government "over the right to regulate the wild rice harvest on the Rice Lake National Wildlife Refuge" (167). Vizenor's account of the crime and the trial of Thomas White Hawk (see below) are also to the point here.

11. See Stephen Tyler's parallel claim in "Postmodern Ethnography."

12. Lyotard and others blame the Enlightenment for the rationalization of terror. Reason has most decidedly been limited to instrumental reason, a techné without a phronesis. But, as Jürgen Habermas and many others have insisted, what is needed is more Enlightenment, not less: a radicalized and inclusionary Enlightenment. One must argue not only against a "withdrawal of fraternity" from other humans, but for the extension of a measure of fraternity to plant and animal species. This tradition is powerful in St. Francis, and also, of course, in tribal cultures. In any case, I hope it is clear that I am in no way comparing Lyotard or Readings to the Nazis.

13. Columbus's *diario* as "abstracted" by Fray Bartolomé de las Casas says: "yo plaziendo a nro senor levare de aqui al tpo de mi parti da seys a .v.al. p[ar]a q deprenda fablar" (68). *Fablar* is an older form of the Spanish *hablar*, and it means "to speak." But it is obvious that *fablar* derives from the Latin *fabulare*, one of whose meanings is to fabulate or tell stories. The translation usually given, that Columbus was taking six Natives to Europe "in order that they may learn to speak," is surely correct—as it is also very curious. Columbus must know that these people do in fact speak *something*, that they make speechlike sounds, that they seem to communicate with one another, for all that *proper* speaking means to speak Spanish or another European (or African—Columbus's pilot Pedro Niño was an African, and Columbus had surely heard Moorish speech) language. It is probably anachronistic to imagine that Columbus might have meant, "In order for them to tell their stories," yet it is linguistically possible. My thanks to Professors Pauline Watts and Eduardo Lago for help with Columbus.

14. See also Peter Hulme's *Colonial Encounters*, among others.

15. See Keith Basso's "An Annotated Bibliography of American Indian Writing Systems." Gerald Vizenor's "Native Transmotion" also has some interesting things to say about Anishinaabe (Chippewa) "writing."

16. I am indebted to Peter Nabokov's important study for these and other examples. Gaur discusses the *mide* scroll held in the British Museum (26).

17. We have more usually taken the wampum strings to be currency (and, presently you can swipe your "wampum card" at the Pequots' Foxwoods Casino to see if you are an instant winner of a "jackpot" sum). Johnson, and, I believe, many eighteenth-century Euramericans who had contact with the Iroquois, understood that that was not the strings' most important function. The entire sentence from Johnson's letter reads as follows: "It is obvious to all who are the least acquainted with Indian affairs, that they [the Iroquois] regard no message or invitation, be it of what consequence it will, unless attended or confirmed by strings or belts of wampum, which they look upon as we our letters, or rather bonds." (264). See also Murray (2000b), chap. 5, "Wampum."

18. See Hertha Wong's chapters "Pre-Contact Oral and Pictographic Autobiographical Narratives: Coup Tales, Vision Stories, and Naming Practices" and "Pictographs as Autobiography: Plains Indian Sketchbooks, Diaries, and Text Construction," for more on the autobiographical dimension of picture writing.

19. I cite, with DeMallie's permission, an unpublished manuscript of his called "Dissonant Voices: Anthropologists, Historians, and the Lakota People."

20. See Diane Glancy's *Lone Dog's Winter Count.*

21. In a fascinating study of Jonathan Carver's 1778 *Travels Through the Interior Parts of North America, in the Years 1766–8,* Paul Alkon notes the similarity between Carver's "relativistic" sense of history and that of the Lakota Winter Counts. "Paradoxically," Alkon writes, "they share this feature [a relativistic rather than absolute notion of time] with the majority of pre-Enlightenment historical writing" (284). Mallery dourly calls Battiste Good "the bad editor of a good work," seeing his personal additions not as serving the purposes of whatever the late nineteenth-century equivalent of hybridity might have been, but rather as the result of "meddlesome vanity!" (1893: 288). Referring to Mallery's publication of the Good winter count in his "Pictographs," Helen Blish (see just below) makes no mention of his negative judgment, although her own estimate is that the Good winter count is "the most extensive *and in some respects* the most significant of all" (25, my emphasis).

22. Drawings 126 to 185 deal with the Battle of the Little Big Horn, and number 183, as we have already noted, shows Bad Heart Bull's cousin, Crazy Horse, killing Custer with a club, for all that Bad Heart Bull was more interested in Major Reno's engagement with the Indians than in Custer's. To put these 59 drawings of the Battle of the Little Big Horn in perspective, it is worth noting that drawings 32–84, 88–97, 100–102, 218–96, and 298–303—146 in all—depict "Sioux-Crow Fights," obviously a subject considerably more interesting to Bad Heart Bull than the Custer fight.

23. In a further note, the Kilpatricks inform us that "The literature ascribes Shawnee as well as white blood to Sequoyah" (196).

Chapter 4. From "Half-Blood" to "Mixedblood"

1. See " 'Indian Blood': Reflections on the Reckoning and Refiguring of Native North American Identity" (565). This fine essay includes a critique of my account some ten years ago of N. Scott Momaday's use of phrases like "memory in the blood"—an account in which I did indeed attack the essentialist dangers of ref-

erences to "Indian blood," but did not, as Strong and van Winkle show, proceed to the "more delicate and complicated task" of resistance they describe. These present "reflections" on *Cogewea* are an attempt more nearly to do so, for all that I remain wary of blood logics, *even* in the interest of "rights and resistances."

2. S. Alice Callahan's *Wynema: A Child of the Forest,* first published in 1891, now has the distinction of being, as the back jacket of the new edition by A. Lavonne Brown Ruoff puts it, "the first novel known to have been written by a woman of American Indian descent."

3. See Brown (1993) for a fuller history of *Cogewea*'s critical reception and for biographical information on Mourning Dove. I would like very gratefully to acknowledge Alanna Kathleen Brown's help with this chapter; its interpretations and opinions, however, are solely my own, as are mine alone any errors.

4. Mourning Dove's own "blood quantum" is not clear. Alanna Kathleen Brown informs me that "In an August 28, 1916 letter, McWhorter refers to Mourning Dove being 3/8 White." But Mourning Dove's claim "to be 1/2 White in a Patent in Fee on her allotment in 1910 in contrast to her claim to be 1/4 White on a later Patent in Fee request in 1921, leaves the issue of parentage and bloodlines ambiguous at best" (Brown, personal communication, September 1998). Miller's research has persuaded him that Mourning Dove was a fullblood who invented her European ancestry. See also Margaret A. Lukens, "Mourning Dove and Mixed Blood: Cultural and Historical Pressures on Aesthetic Choice and Authorial Identity."

5. This phrase has proven attractive. Strong and van Winkle quote it, and a volume called *Loosening the Seams: Interpretations of Gerald Vizenor,* edited by A. Robert Lee, appeared in 2000.

6. See Hollinger on what he calls the "ethno-racial pentagon": African American, American Indian, Asian American, Latino/Chicano, and European American, these categories most specifically deriving from Statistical Directive 15 of the Office of Management and Budget in 1977. Citing much recent work on these matters, Hollinger cogently points out how this pentagon—revised somewhat but still in place—makes Koreans, Chinese, Vietnamese, and Japanese the same, unites the English and the Irish, joins Jews and Protestant fundamentalists, obliterates differences among Puerto Ricans, Hondurans, and Dominicans, as well as disallowing differentiation among American blacks (Jamaicans, Africans, Haitians, etc.).

7. See Zack, Root (1992), Funderberg, Penn, and O'Hearn.

8. Although it appeared too late for me to do more than merely note it, Paul Gilroy's *Against Race* (2000) is also important in these regards.

9. And yet, further work needs to be done before one can feel certain that Eastman is indeed the most appropriate reference here, rather than, say, Carlos Montezuma, Henry Roe Cloud, Arthur C. Parker, or Zitkala Sa, for all that these latter, in varying degree, are increasingly coming to be known. There are also the Reverend Sherman Coolidge, Albert Hensley, Oliver Lamere, Elizabeth Bender, and others who need study.

L. V. McWhorter was in close contact with an eastern friend named McLean who sometimes sent him books. But we do not know, from his letters, whether McWhorter actually had read Eastman, nor do we know from her letters whether Mourning Dove had any particular awareness of him and his work.

10. I have offered a fuller account of these options in the Conclusion to my

Ethnocriticism, most particularly with reference to the work of David Hollinger and Linda Kerber.

11. David Hollinger speaks of cosmopolitanism as "the desire to *transcend* the *limitations* of any and all particularisms" (in Krupat 1992: 240). I have critiqued this form of cosmopolitanism in the Conclusion to *Ethnocriticism*.

12. Although Du Bois's meaning is quite clear, what constitutes a "dark body" — or, in Cogewea, a "tawny hue" — is always relative. Lise Funderberg tells of hearing about how, when her parents went for a marriage license, the clerk in charge recorded her father's race as "Caucasian," only to have him explain that he ought instead to be classed among African Americans (13). David Theo Goldberg writes that he has been "characterized, among other things, as white, European, Anglo, Jewish, and African American" (253). As we have noted, with reference to Goldberg, it was only in the 1970s that the census accepted self-identification. I note but do not engage the question of Du Bois's presumed racialist essentialism in this period or his possible abandonment of anything like essentialism in his later work. Further complicating these matters are the recent studies by Ross Posnock and Wilson J. Moses. See also Robert Reid-Pharr's essay review of both books.

13. See George Stocking, Jr.'s "The Turn-of-the-Century Concept of Race" for an extremely useful account of these matters.

14. Stocking's work is indispensable for a fuller understanding of Boas. See also Cole, Elliott, Handler, M. Harris, Herskovits, Hyatt, Kuper, and Krupat (1992), among others. I am indebted to Michael Elliott for many of these references.

15. Nor, so far as I know, Du Bois along with any of the Native intellectuals who were his contemporaries early in the century. Lawrence J. Oliver, however, commenting on Ah-nen-la-de-ni or Daniel LaFrance's "An Indian Boy's Story," writes that "The Mohawk's narrative is a case study of DuBoisian 'double consciousness'" (801). LaFrance's narrative first appeared in 1903 (Oliver is commenting on a 1990 reprint), the same year as DuBois's *Souls of Black Folk*. But Du Bois's first account of "double consciousness" had appeared in 1897, in a form less poetic than that of *Souls*, but one that more directly bears upon the situation of Native Americans. See Holt.

16. Here, as above in reference to Eastman, I use "fullblood" with a certain unease, given the concerns of this essay. But, as Strong and van Winkle, I, and others have noted, it is not possible to avoid the terms of exactly the (historically inscribed) discourse one would displace. In a manner similar to what Gayatri Spivak has called "the deconstructive philosophical position," one "offers an impossible 'no' to a structure which one critiques, yet inhabits intimately" (794).

17. The "From . . . To . . ." form of title was not unusual in Native writing of this period, for example, the 1915 autobiography by Joseph Griffis (Chief Tahan) called *Tahan: Out of Savagery, into Civilization*. *Tahan* has an introduction by Arthur C. Parker (we shall return to Parker below) in which Parker suggests that it may have been "a ceaseless desire to achieve something better, that civilised and educated Tahan" (9).

18. Hampton educated Indians from the time that Richard Pratt took his first prospective Native students there in 1878. In "the following year a small Indian Department was established" at Hampton that "continued to function with government aid until 1912 and without it until 1923" (Hertzberg 16). Pratt opened Carlisle in 1879.

19. Wald's essay makes a distinction between criticism from the perspective of "ethnicity" (for example, Werner Sollors) and criticism—as here—from the per-

spective of "internal" or domestic colonialism, for example, John Marshall's oxymoronic description, in his rulings in *Cherokee Nation v. Georgia* of 1831 and *Worcester v. Georgia* of 1832, that the tribes were "domestic dependent nations." The earliest—and very sophisticated—comparative work from the "internal colonialism" perspective that I know is that of Robert Blauner (1972).

20. I take the term "postethnic" from the title of David Hollinger's book *Postethnic America: Beyond Multiculturalism*. Although the nuances of Hollinger's "Beyond" and "post-" are occasionally troubling to me, I am much more in sympathy with the position developed here than that in his 1985 essay, "Ethnic Diversity, Cosmopolitanism, and the Emergence of the American Liberal Intelligentsia," which I have criticized, as noted just above, in the Conclusion to my *Ethnocriticism*.

21. Jim also observes that "the firecracker celebration of the Declaration of Independence . . . is not for our race" (59), an echo, although Jim surely does not know it, of Frederick Douglass's 1852 speech, "The Meaning of July Fourth for the Negro."

22. Compare, for example, the epigraph from Langston Hughes to Nella Larsen's autobiographical novel, *Quicksand* (1928):

My father died in a big old house
My Momma died in a shack.
I wonder where I'll die,
Being neither white nor black.

Hughes's speaker, of course, is literally both white and black, as is Larsen's protagonist Helga Crane, whose mother was white and whose father was not. But by 1920 mixed-race persons who were both white and black had to be either white or black, which, of course, meant black (unless they were light enough to "pass"). See Hutchinson for an important critique of recent biographical work on Larsen.

23. To call it that. The novel allows none of the characters anything of an interior life or "psychology" apart from what can be deduced from behavior: for example, someone is cheerful, secretive, or brave because he or she acts in a manner indicative of cheerfulness, secretiveness, or bravery. This is, to be sure, the usual mode of treating character in traditional Native American oral narrative, although not, of course, in nineteenth- *or* twentieth-century European or American fiction.

24. Mourning Dove's younger sister, Julia (1891–1955), was married to a Frenchman. Another sister was named Mary Margaret (1892–1949). The novel does not offer hints as to how M. and Mme. LaFleur will live—whether they will reside in the American west, in Europe, or elsewhere. Is it perhaps relevant to think here of the fate of Hester Prynne's daughter Pearl in *The Scarlet Letter*, whose life—unlike that of her (English-born) mother—can have fuller, nonpuritanical scope only in Europe?

A very particular interest in Europe appears in Leslie Marmon Silko's most recent novel, *Gardens in the Dunes* and in James Welch's *The Heartsong of Charging Elk*.

25. Although the families of both men had already settled the matter by traditional means, in 1882 the Brulé Sioux, Crow Dog was tried and convicted by the Dakota territorial court of having shot and killed the Brulé chief, Spotted Tail. The case went all the way to the Supreme Court, which eventually ruled that Indians were not subject to the laws of the United States but to their own laws, a victory, as we have noted in Chapter 1, for Native Sovereignty. The Major Crimes

Act of 1885 was passed by Congress with the intention of bypassing the ruling in *Crow Dog*, establishing that "federal criminal law could be imposed on those who violated U.S. law" (Harring 138), including Indians. See Harring and also Wilkinson.

26. There is a very substantial literature on the Dawes Act, its intentions and consequences. See in particular Hoxie, Prucha (1973, 1984), Priest, and Hagan.

27. Anonymously published in the same year, 1912, as Mourning Dove completed her first draft of *Cogewea*, James Weldon Johnson's novel *Autobiography of an Ex-Colored Man* presents a sad and moving portrait of a person of mixed black and white parentage who, after witnessing a horrible lynching and finding that he *is* ashamed of the black "race," decides to "pass" as white from then on. His shame at belonging to a "race" to whom such things could be done, rather than any shame at identifying with a "race" that could do such things, and his consequent conscious abandonment of his "race," whatever one may think of it now, must also be read in relation to its historical period—a period just after *Plessy v. Ferguson*, with an upsurge in lynchings and the riots attendant on Jack Johnson's 1910 defeat of Jim Jeffries for the heavyweight championship of boxing. On this latter, see Bederman's harrowing account.

28. As with so many others one casts, for convenience's sake, into monolithic categories, the Red Progressives or assimilationists were by no means all in agreement with one another, nor did all of them maintain the same position as times and conditions changed—although it probably is accurate to say that all continued to believe in the necessity of adopting some form of "civilization" as defined by mainstream America. It must also be recalled that what it meant, for example, for Carlos Montezuma to call for the abolition of the Bureau of Indian Affairs early in the twentieth century is not what the "same" call meant for those who occupied the Bureau in 1968. Philip J. Deloria's book is of much use for an understanding of these matters.

29. Justice Robert Taney in his notorious *Dred Scott* decision of 1857 had adopted the same logic in regard to Indians. An Indian, Taney wrote, who "should leave his nation or tribe, and take up his abode among the white population, . . . would be entitled to all the rights and privileges which would belong to an emigrant from any other foreign people" (in Elliott 1999: 624–25). This was not the case, in Taney's view, for the descendants of slaves. See Elliott, whom I cite further below, for a valuable discussion of the "triangulation" of Native Americans, African Americans, and other non-European Americans.

30. See Roediger, Ignatiev, Brodkin, and Matthew Jacobson, among others. In the early twentieth century, as Shari Huhndorf has pointed out to me (personal communication, October 25, 2000), it was more typical for white men to marry Indian women for the land they controlled, after the Dawes Act, than for Indian women to marry white men as an entree of sorts into "civilization."

31. I discuss "antiracist racism" further in Chapter 5.

32. This is the result of sociocultural rather than racial factors, it would seem. Parker's optimism—I cannot say whether it is real or merely strategic—would seem to echo some quite extraordinary remarks by Dr. Eastman at the first meeting of the Society of American Indians (on Columbus Day, 1911, in Columbus, Ohio!). "In connection with the words of the last speaker, that there has been a great deal of injustice done to our tribes, I wish to say that *really no prejudice has existed so far as the American Indian concerned.* . . . There is no prejudice against our people *in the professions*" (in Hertzberg 69, my emphases).

33. In fairness to Parker, we should again cite Philip Deloria, who follows Parker's career into the 1940s, at which time Parker—perhaps, as Deloria notes, with tongue "something less than firmly in his cheek"—"advised Americans 'to be Indians'" (125).

34. I offer the following citation as illustrative of the enormous difficulties faced by Native intellectuals of the period. In 1919, Zitkala Sa urged Native people to hold "permanently a small portion of their inherited land," because "we cannot really be happy unless we have a small piece of Out-of-Doors to enjoy as we please," signing herself, "Yours for the Indian cause" (in Hertzberg 182). To find the proud author of "Why I Am a Pagan" (1902) writing of the powerful indigenous relation to place in terms of enjoying "a small piece of the Out-of-Doors"— whatever her intended purposes or audiences—seems testimony to the terrible assaults on tribal landholdings during the height of the Dawes period.

35. See for example, Adams, Pfister, and Lomawaima for statistics on the lamented tendency of a number of graduates to "return to the blanket," their premature deaths, and other difficulties. This is not to say that all or even most graduates of the boarding schools entirely regretted their experience.

Although McWhorter's motives were benevolent, his "elevation" of Cogewea's language in his 1922 revision of the manuscript of the novel as a sign of her Carlisle education is entirely misguided. In Hazel Hertzberg's succinct description, "Carlisle was essentially a grammar school with a primarily vocational emphasis" (17). It *did* have college age students who played on its Pop Warner-coached football teams against Yale and Princeton. But eighteen-year-olds at Carlisle might be reading and writing at only a fourth grade level, and it is extremely unlikely that any Carlisle graduate ever spoke in the caricature of Victorian speech that McWhorter attributed to Cogewea.

Moreover, "Carlisle" by the 1920s would hardly signal distinction to white readers (although it does seem to have remained the case that Carlisle graduates in the Indian Service were very highly regarded). As noted above, Richard Pratt, who made the school famous, had left it by 1904, and by 1914 Carlisle was under investigation for financial irregularities. It was closed by the government and taken over by the War Department for military use in 1918. Zitkala Sa taught at Carlisle briefly during General Pratt's superintendency, but she was never a Carlisle student. And the major Native intellectuals of the period—Eastman, Montezuma, Roe Cloud—were all graduates of eastern universities and professional schools.

36. Mourning Dove was an admirer of Collier, and Collier, having read her *Coyote Stories* of 1933, offered her government employment. Although Mourning Dove worked on its behalf, her Colville tribe voted against the IRA reorganization in 1935—electing her, nonetheless, "to the Tribal Council, the first Colville woman ever to win such an office" (Brown, personal communication, September 1998).

37. As Shari Huhndorf has pointed out to me, Mourning Dove's marrying two of the three MacDonald sisters to *atypically* "good" white men is also something of an oddity of the book. What would Mary, in particular, have done if the amiable and apparently unprejudiced French aristocrat had not been dropped in her way?

38. The passage referred to in Vizenor invites "white settlers to dive with mixed-blood survivors into the unknown . . . in search of a few honest words upon which to build a new urban turtle island" (in Strong and van Winkle 564).

Chapter 5. The "Rage Stage"

1. Alexie gives the date only as "the late sixties." But because the protagonist, John Smith, is said to graduate from high school "on time, in 1987" (22), at the age, therefore of about eighteen, the date of his birth must be 1968 or '69. I have called those overlapping years a single "winter" with reference to the well-known Lakota practice of counting years as "winters," each winter being a part of two Western years Although John Smith's actual tribal affiliation remains undetermined, he most frequently identifies himself as Lakota or Navajo.

2. Alexie has criticized the use of "Native American" as a "guilty white liberal term" (in A. Powers 57). His preferred term is Indian "because that's what we are." He has also, as we have already noted, mocked some Native writers' self-reference as "mixedbloods." My usual practice, in accord with that of most critics, Native and non-Native, is to use Native American and Indian more or less interchangeably, although in this chapter I reflect Alexie's preference and more often than not speak of Indians. Shari Huhndorf usefully reminds us that "Native America comprises not only Indians but other groups of indigenous peoples as well, including Alaskan Eskimos, Canadian Inuit, Aleuts, and Native Hawaiians (all non-Indians)" (2001: 1). Although John's Indian mother's fullbloodedness is emphasized, we are told nothing about his father.

3. The boy is named after his adoptive father's father, a German immigrant whose name, unless he had chosen to Americanize its spelling, would probably have been Schmidt. I cannot tell why Alexie chose to name this central Indian character after one of the more famous settler figures of Anglo-American history and myth. Once, Daniel Smith, John's adoptive father, asks a homeless Indian whether he has encountered him. The man responds, "You adopted an Indian kid and named him John Smith? No wonder he talks to himself" (219).

Other names in the novel—Jack Wilson, Clarence Mather, Dr. Faulkner, Buck Rogers—also appear to be of significance, although I cannot say what that significance might be. I suspect the names are either a private joke or a tease on Alexie's part.

4. For example, Judith Bolton-Fasman in the *Christian Science Monitor*. As Professor Patricia Penn Hilden has pointed out to me, John *is* an Indian killer to the extent that he kills himself.

5. Students who have attended the University of Washington tell me it is usually referred to as "U-Dub," short for "U.W." Alexie, who knows Seattle and the University of Washington far better than I do, never has his characters call it that. So as not to confuse the uninitiated reader?

6. The killer has done this "With hands curved into talons" (54), and, as we will soon note, the killer is identified by his one surviving victim as a "bird," or, rather, an "it," not exactly a bird. The narrator never uses a pronoun for the killer (whom the narrator never calls the Indian killer); the killer, therefore, may be thought of as "he," "she," "it," or all three.

7. An early story in Alexie's 1993 collection, *The Lone Ranger and Tonto Fistfight in Heaven*, mentions "Aristotle Polatkin, who was shooting jump shots exactly one year before James Naismith supposedly invented basketball" (45), and Junior Polatkin is an important character in Alexie's first novel, *Reservation Blues*. Sara Polatkin, a Spokane, a newly declared lesbian and a law student, appears in "Indian Country," in *The Toughest Indian in the World*. What relation, if any, the legendary Aristotle and the quite contemporary Junior and Sarah might have to Marie and Reggie Polatkin will only be clear to insiders.

8. Wilson is a former policeman who presently writes novels, perhaps like those of Tony Hillerman, about an Indian detective named Aristotle Little Hawk. The novel he is working on throughout this novel is called *Indian Killer*. Wilson claims to be part Shilshomish Indian, descended from someone named Red Fox. No Indian person in the novel takes that claim seriously, and no one in the novel remarks on the fact that Jack Wilson is the American name of the Paiute prophet of the Ghost Dance, Wovoka. *Why* the ex-cop turned novelist bears Wovoka's English name, why Dr. Clarence Mather is named after one of the foremost Puritan Indian haters, Cotton Mather, or why Dr. Faulkner, the chair of his department, Anthropology, bears the name of a major novelist from the American south I cannot say. *Reservation Blues* briefly mentions a tribal police officer named Wilson who is considered a white man for all that he is acknowledged to have a little bit of Indian blood. Officer Wilson is a reader of Tom Clancy novels.

9. Apparently Native American literature at the University of Washington (and elsewhere) in the late 1960s was taught in the *Anthropology* department, not in the English department or Indian Studies department (which may not yet have existed).

10. John is in some degree following the example of a rather mysterious Indian priest named Father Duncan, whose influence on him has been substantial. John's adoptive parents are Catholics, and what it means to be a Catholic often enters John's mind. *Reservation Blues* says that most of the Spokanes on the reservation are baptized Catholics, and Father Arnold, a white priest on the reservation, is sympathetically presented. There is also a Father Arnold who is "President of St. Jerome the Second University" (173) in the story "Saint Junior" in the recent collection, *The Toughest Indian in the World*. John's "rising" after his suicide may have a precedent in *Reservation Blues* as well, where Junior Polatkin, after his suicide (Junior shoots himself), nonetheless has a conversation with his friend Victor (1995: 289). The search "for an Indian mother" also turns up suddenly, as we shall see, at the end of Alexie's recent story, "The Sin Eaters."

11. The turquoise, of course, suggests a Navajo, or at least southwestern—the pueblos? Mexico?—killer. Although John does not know his tribal affiliation, we have noted that he usually responds, when asked, that he is Lakota or Navajo. In search of his father (or Father Duncan who disappeared into the desert), maybe his mother, exactly *which* desert "John" is headed for from Seattle is not clear.

12. See in particular Shari Huhndorf's "Cultural difference and Colonial Desire" for an excellent exposition of this point.

13. The statistics are not broken down by gender, so I am guessing that males are in the vast majority as perpetrators.

14. The two black men who work the night shift at "Seattle's Best Donuts," frequented by John on sleepless nights, are a handsome younger man, whom John knows as Paul, and an older man "whose great-great-grandmother had escaped slavery by marrying into the Seminole tribe" (99), whom John calls Paul Too. The two Pauls, and Paul Too in particular, bring to mind Paul D of Toni Morrison's *Beloved*, which novel also mentions a Paul A and a Paul E, all once slaves. Morrison's epigraph—"Sixty Million / and more"—uses a larger number than Alexie's homeless Indian quoted above, but it might well serve for *Indian Killer*. The other literary references—that same homeless man says he knows other homeless Indians named Loney, Tayo, and Abel, and John is repeatedly asked by an Indian woman whether he knows Laura Tohe, a Navajo poet—seem to me no more than jokes for those in the know. Here I disagree with Cyrus Patell, who has made some-

thing more of Loney, Tayo, and Abel as listed among the homeless. I return to Patell below.

15. A blurb on the jacket of *The Lone Ranger and Tonto* from the *Chicago Tribune* says, "*The Lone Ranger and Tonto Fistfight in Heaven* is for the American Indian what Richard Wright's *Native Son* was for the black American in 1940." But I can see nothing in *The Lone Ranger* that in any regard bears comparison to *Native Son*— although, as I have said, much in *Indian Killer* does. A blurb on the back jacket of *The Toughest Indian* states, "There is an anger in Sherman Alexie's work that hasn't been seen since James Baldwin." I consider Baldwin briefly below.

16. It had a Foreword by then-Senator Fred R. Harris, highly favorable reviews in the *New York Times, Chicago Tribune,* and *Chicago Sun-Times,* and more than five printings by 1969 alone.

17. According to Vine Deloria, Jr., whose work I will again refer to below, Indians were very enthusiastic about the possibility that Robert Kennedy would eventually replace his assassinated brother, Jack, as president. Robert Kennedy's death, Deloria has written, "completely . . . altered the outlook of the American Indian toward American society" (1969: 193). Clyde Warrior, an extremely important figure in the shaping of Native American political activism, also died in 1968 at the age of twenty-eight.

18. Deloria was Director of the National Council of American Indians and important in defining the concept of Red Power. See Hagan (1979: 170–71).

19. Clyde Warrior was one of the Council's founders, in 1961. The NIYC participated in the Poor People's March on Washington (Vine Deloria, Jr. felt this was a mistake for Indian people) and the occupation of Alcatraz (see below). See Witt and Steiner (220–22) and Smith and Warrior, chapters 4–8 in particular.

20. Originally published in *Playboy* magazine (!), the essay's influence was very substantial, so much so that the 1989 American Anthropological Association Convention held a session called "Custer Died for Your Sins: A Twenty-Year Retrospective on Relations Between Anthropologists and Indians." For papers given at that session and for Deloria's response, see Biolsi and Zimmerman. In a strange diatribe against "anthropology" in toto, Scott Michaelsen seems to complain of Deloria's subsequent qualifications of his earlier take-no-prisoners account, as a renewed commitment to "positivism." See the "Prolegomenon" to *The Limits of Multiculturalism.*

21. The other exception would be Abel's anger at the two white women with whom he has sexual relations, and whom he treats violently. I am not able to say whether this is a projection on to the women of a more generalized anger or whether it is indeed a particular—and generally well-documented—case of specific male rage and violence against women. A good deal of anger against women is expressed by characters in Gerald Vizenor's first novel, *Darkness in St. Louis Bearheart* (1978), and in James Welch's first novel, *Winter in the Blood* (1974). Reggie Polatkin, in *Indian Killer,* also behaves violently to a white woman.

22. In James Welch's recent *The Heartsong of Charging Elk* (2000), Charging Elk, a Lakota in Marseille early in the twentieth century, having been drugged, awakens to find a Frenchman performing fellatio upon him. As his consciousness returned, "he knew what he must do. It was not so much a decision as a resolve" (277). Charging Elk stabs the man in the back and cuts his throat. Then, "two sleeps later, he still felt strong about killing the *siyoko.* It was simple enough— when one comes upon evil, one kills it" (297). I think this is very close to Abel's feeling about the albino.

23. See Evers's "Words and Place: A Reading of *House Made of Dawn.*" It should

also be obvious that those who might be the killer in Alexie's novel are all—with the possible exception of John Smith whose father is not identified—mixed-bloods, so that their rage against whites cannot help but be anger directed at some part of themselves. I thank Professor Patricia Penn Hilden for help with this point as well as others in this chapter.

24. Karl Kroeber's unfortunately neglected essay "Technology and Tribal Narrative" notes in its first sentence that Momaday's novel has been treated "as if the [Pulitzer] award resolved all critical issues," so that "the novel's strangeness as novel has never been adequately investigated" (17). Kroeber observes that "Abel's assumption of a personal 'duty' to kill the 'evil' Albino *violates* the fashion in which the Jemez community would exorcise such a malignancy" (19). He writes that "Abel's inarticulateness reflects Momaday's generic deprivation. The very form of his work testifies to his impotence to impose a symbolic order other than one structured by the culture he would resist, or pass through, to recover a different order, an order that would not use language novelistically" (21). Kroeber recommends to our attention "a more important literary work than Momaday's novel" (22), one that also began to come into being in 1968, Peter Seymour and Anthony Mattina's *The Golden Woman* (1985). For a claim that Momaday's generic problems in *House Made of Dawn* may be taken in a more positive fashion than Kroeber (and I) take them, see Bernard Selinger's learned but somewhat uneasy recent essay, "*House Made of Dawn*: A Positively Ambivalent Bildungsroman."

25. Kenneth Roemer has recently (1999) established that *Ceremony* is, indeed, the most solidly mainstream and canonical Native American novel.

26. There is a "real" Randy Peone. He is a Spokane who in 1989 founded "The Last Name basketball tournament held each year on the Spokane Indian Reservation," which "pits family teams against each other" (*News from Indian Country*, mid-April 2000: 2A). The Peones were the winners in 1998. There is also another fictional Randy Peone; he is a "minister of the Assembly of God" (289) who makes a brief, late appearance in *Reservation Blues*. In the chilling story, "The Sin Eaters," "Randy Peone, the green-eyed Spokane" (94), is a young man, a boy, placed among Indians with second-darkest skin. I will return to "The Sin Eaters" below. "Randy Peone, the blue-eyed Spokane Indian" also turns up as a "star pitcher and shortstop" for the Spokane Little League Warriors (42) in Alexie's recent book of poems and prose, *One Stick Song*.

27. As Chapter 1 has indicated, the sort of "universal" meant here is not, of course, the long-discredited projection of Western male hegemony on to the rest of the world.

28. See "The Pitfalls of National Consciousness," in *The Wretched of the Earth*. That Vizenor on occasion constructs an argument for sovereignty that I have found to be "cultural nationalist" (see above) should not be taken to contradict his basically cosmopolitan or cosmopolitan patriot position.

29. But Indigo and Sister Salt do need to go home to continue to be who they are. This, it seems, is exactly not the case in James Welch's *The Heartsong of Charging Elk*, for Charging Elk can continue to be Lakota, it seems, even without going home. Still in Marseille after many many years, Charging Elk, near the end of the novel, is confirmed in his Lakota identity by the words of a young Lakota man visiting France, "words that filled his heart" (437). The last sentence of the book has Charging Elk walking through the Paris night knowing that "the Moon of the Falling Leaves would light his way" (438). Clearly his roots have indeed been movable.

30. See Fanon's chapter in *The Wretched of the Earth* called "Spontaneity: Its

Strengths and Weaknesses." There is a literature far too extensive to cite on questions of terrorism and individualism as politically useful or counterproductive to colonized or oppressed peoples.

31. White rage is also abundantly present in the novel, from the vicious *ressentiment* of the talk radio DJ, Truck Schultz, to that of Aaron Rogers (Chapter 13 of Part 3 is called "Anger" and it centers on Aaron). Aaron is the brother of the murdered David Rogers, thought to have been killed by Indians (readers of the novel, but no one in the novel, learn belatedly that this is not the case). David and Aaron are the sons of Buck Rogers, an oldtime Indian hater. Why this man is named after a futuristic comic strip character of the time is, again, a mystery to me. Truck Schultz and the Rogerses all have blue eyes.

32. I have discussed these aspects of Vizenor's novel more fully in "*Ratio-* and *Natio-* in Vizenor's *Heirs of Columbus*" in my *Turn to the Native*. We note again the compatibility of a certain cosmopolitan universality with a non-statist tribal nationalism.

33. Senghor, as late as 1993, pointed to the definition of *négritude* in the French Robert dictionary ("The ensemble of characteristics . . . proper to the black race; belonging to the black race"), as representative of the ongoing influence of his view. Aimé Césaire, who coined the word *négritude* in 1939, for long expounded a culturalist view of *négritude* in opposition to Senghor's essentialism.

34. The title of the story refers to an image offered by a possibly deranged man who suggests that what is going on is *not* about blood (105). Instead, he tells of a room where there are rows upon rows of dead white people on whose bodies food has been piled. The food soaks up all the sins of the whites, and the Indians, he says, will be led into the room where they will be forced "to devour those feasts, devour those sins" (107). For the moment, Jonah "believed" (106). And that is all we have of sin-eating.

35. Owens usually identifies himself as Choctaw-Cherokee-Irish. He is from Mississippi, holds a doctorate, and is a professor of literature and creative writing. Alexie has on several occasions mocked Owens, Vizenor, and other mixed-blood Native writers. Owens responds—in *Mixedblood Messages* (see Chapter 6 in particular)—forcefully and intelligently to Alexie's smart-ass, bad-boy cracks.

36. Sartre's essay served as the Preface to Leopold Senghor's *Anthologie de la nouvelle poésie Nègre et malgache.* Sartre seems—there is room for some disagreement—to endorse Senghor's (but not necessarily all of his contributors') notion of a racial essence.

Bibliography

Abdel-Malek, Anouar. *Nation and Revolution.* Vol. 2 of *Social Dialectics.* Albany: State University of New York Press, 1981.

Abram, David. *The Spell of the Sensuous.* New York: Vintage, 1997.

Adams, David W. *Education for Extinction: American Indians and the Boarding School Experience, 1875–1928.* Lawrence: University Press of Kansas, 1995.

Alexie, Sherman. *Indian Killer.* New York: Atlantic Monthly Press, 1996.

———. *The Lone Ranger and Tonto Fistfight in Heaven.* New York: HarperPerennial, 1994.

———. *One Stick Song.* Brooklyn, N.Y.: Hanging Loose Press, 2000. (2000a)

———. *Reservation Blues.* New York: Atlantic Monthly Press, 1995.

———. *The Toughest Indian in the World.* New York: Atlantic Monthly Press, 2000. (2000b)

Alkon, Paul. "Presidential Address: Did Minnesota Have an Eighteenth Century and If So, When?" *Studies in Eighteenth-Century Literature* 21 (1991): 267–89.

Anderson, Amanda. "Cosmopolitanism, Universalism, and the Divided Legacies of Modernity." In Bruce Robbins and Pheng Cheah, eds., *Cosmopolitics: Thinking and Feeling Beyond the Nation.* Minneapolis: University of Minnesota Press, 1998. 265–89.

———. "Realism, Universalism, and the Science of the Human." *Diacritics* 29 (1999): 3–17.

Appadurai, Arjun. "Disjuncture and Difference in the Global Cultural Economy." *Public Culture* 2 (1990): 1–24.

———. *Modernity at Large: Cultural Dimensions of Globalization.* Minneapolis: University of Minnesota Press, 1996.

Appiah, K. Anthony. "Cosmopolitan Patriots." *Critical Inquiry* 23 (1997): 617–39.

———. "The Conservation of 'Race.' " *Black American Literature Forum* 23 (1989): 37–60.

———. *In My Father's House: Africa in the Philosophy of Culture.* New York: Oxford University Press, 1992.

Assad, Talal. "Are There Histories of People Without History?" *Journal of the Society for the Comparative Study of Society and History* 20 (1987): 594–607.

———. "The Concept of Cultural Translation in British Social Anthropology." In James Clifford and George Marcus, eds., *Writing Culture: The Poetics and Politics of Ethnography.* Berkeley: University of California Press, 1986. 141–64.

Astrov, Margot, ed. *The Winged Serpent: An Anthology of American Indian Prose and Poetry.* New York: John Day, 1946. Reprint New York: Capricorn, 1962.

Austin, Mary. *The American Rhythm: Studies and Reexpressions of Amerindian Songs.* Boston: Cooper Square, 1930 [1923].

Bahr, Donald M. "A Format and Method for Translating Songs." *Journal of American Folklore* 96 (1983): 170–82.

———. "Oratory." In Andrew Wiget, ed., *Dictionary of Native American Literature.* New York: Garland, 1994. 107–18.

———. *Pima and Papago Ritual Oratory: A Study of Three Texts.* San Francisco: Indian Historian Press, 1975.

———. "Pima Heaven Songs." In Brian Swann and Arnold Krupat, eds., *Recovering the Word: Essays on Native American Literature.* Lincoln: University of Nebraska Press, 1987. 198–246. (1987b)

———. "Pima Swallow Songs." *Cultural Anthropology* 1 (1986): 171–87.

———. "Whatever Happened to Mythology?" *Wicazo Sa Review* 9 (1993): 44–49.

Bahr, Donald, and Vincent Joseph. 1994. "Pima Oriole Songs." In Brian Swann, ed., *Coming to Light: Contemporary Translations of the Native Literature of North America.* New York: Random House, 1994. 541–63.

Bahr, Donald, Lloyd Paul, and Vincent Joseph. 1997. *Ants and Orioles: Showing the Art of Pima Poetry.* Salt Lake City: University of Utah Press, 1997.

Baldwin, James. *The Fire Next Time.* New York: Dial, 1963. (1963a)

———. *Notes of a Native Son.* New York: Dial, 1963 [1955]. (1963b)

Ball, Milner. "Legal Storytelling: Stories of Origin and Constitutional Possibilities." *Michigan Law Review* 87 (1989): 2280–2325.

Barreiro, José. "First Words." *Native Americas: Akwe:kon's Journal of Indigenous Issues* 13 (1998): 2.

Basso, Keith. "An Annotated Bibliography of American Indian Writing Systems." Unpublished ms. 1971. Arizona State Museum Library, University of Arizona, Tucson.

———. *Wisdom Sits in Places: Landscape and Language Among the Western Apache.* Albuquerque: University of New Mexico Press, 1996.

Basso, Keith, and Ned Anderson. "A Western Apache Writing System: The Symbols of Silas John." In M. Dale Kinkade et al., eds., *Linguistics and Anthropology: Essays in Honor of C. F. Voegelin.* Lisse, Neth.: Peter de Ridder, 1975. 27–52.

Bazin, Maurice. "Our Sciences, Their Science." In Vera Lawrence Hyatt and Rex Nettleford, eds., *Race, Discourse, and the Origin of the Americas: A New World View.* Washington, D.C.: Smithsonian Institution Press, 1995. 231–40.

Bederman, Gail. *Manliness and Civilization: A Cultural History of Gender and Race in the United States, 1880–1917.* Chicago: University of Chicago Press, 1995.

Beidler, Peter G. "Literary Criticism in *Cogewea*: Mourning Dove's Protagonist Reads *The Brand.*" *American Indian Culture and Research Journal* 19 (1995): 45–65.

Berman, Judith. "Oolachan-Woman's Robe: Fish, Blankets, Masks, and Meaning in Boas's Kwakw'ala Texts." In Brian Swann, ed., *On the Translation of Native American Literatures.* Washington, D.C.: Smithsonian Institution Press, 1992. 125–61.

Bevis, William. "American Indian Verse Translations." In Abraham Chapman, ed., *Literature of the American Indians: Views and Interpretations.* New York: New American Library, 1975. 308–23.

Bierhorst, John, ed. *The Fire Plume: Legends of the American Indians Collected by Henry Roe Schoolcraft.* New York: Dial, 1969.

———, ed. *Four Masterworks of American Indian Literature.* New York: Farrar, Straus, and Giroux, 1974. (1974a)

————, ed. *The Red Swan: Myths and Tales of the American Indians.* New York: Farrar, Straus, and Giroux, 1974. (1974b)

————, ed. *In the Trail of the Wind: American Indian Poems and Ritual Orations.* New York: Farrar, Straus, and Giroux, 1971.

Biolsi, Thomas, and Larry J. Zimmerman, eds. *Indians and Anthropologists: Vine Deloria, Jr., and the Critique of Anthropology.* Tucson: University of Arizona Press, 1997.

Bird, Traveller. *Tell Them They Lie: The Sequoyah Myth.* Los Angeles: Westernlore, 1971.

Bishop, Alan. "Western Mathematics: The Secret Weapon of Cultural Imperialism." *Race and Class* 32 (1990): 51–65.

Black Elk. *Black Elk Speaks.* With John G. Neihardt. Lincoln: University of Nebraska Press, 1979 [1932].

Blauner, Robert. *Racial Oppression in America.* New York: Harper and Row, 1972.

Blish, Helen, ed. *A Pictographic History of the Oglala Sioux.* Lincoln: University of Nebraska Press, 1967.

Bloomfield, Leonard. *The Menomini Language.* New Haven, Conn.: Yale University Press, 1962.

Boas, Franz. *Kutenai Tales.* Bureau of American Ethnology Bulletin 59. Washington, D.C.: Government Printing Office, 1918.

————. "The Limitations of the Comparative Method in Anthropology." In *Race, Language, and Culture.* New York: Macmillan, 1940. 270–80. [1896]

————. *The Mind of Primitive Man.* New York: Macmillan, 1911.

Bolton-Fasman, Judith. "One Author's Effort at Myth Killing." Review of Sherman Alexie, *Indian Killer. Christian Science Monitor,* January 6, 1997.

Bourne, Randolph. "Transnational America." *Atlantic Monthly* 118 (July 1916): 86–97.

Brandon, William, ed. *The Magic World: American Indian Songs and Poems.* New York: Morrow, 1970.

Bright, William. 1979. "A Karok Myth in 'Measured Verse': The Translation of a Performance." *Journal of California and Great Basin Anthropology* 1 (1979): 117–23.

Broderick, Therese (Tin Schreiner). *The Brand: A Tale of the Flathead Reservation.* Seattle: Alice Harriman, 1909.

Brodkin, Karen. *How Jews Became White Folks and What That Says About Race in America.* New Brunswick, N.J.: Rutgers University Press, 1998.

Brown, Alanna Kathleen. "Looking Through the Glass Darkly: The Editorialized Mourning Dove." In Arnold Krupat, ed., *New Voices in Native American Literary Criticism.* Washington, D.C.: Smithsonian Institution Press, 1993. 274–90.

————. "Mourning Dove (Hum-ishu-ma)." In Kenneth Roemer, ed., *Native American Writers of the United States.* Detroit: Gale, 1997. 187–97.

————. "Mourning Dove's Chronology." Personal communication, September 1998.

————. "Mourning Dove's Voice in *Cogewea.*" *Wicazo Sa Review* 4 (1988): 2–15.

Brumble, H. David "Vine Deloria, Jr., Creationism, and Ethnic Pseudoscience." *American Literary History* 10 (1998): 335–46.

Bryant, John. "'Nowhere a Stranger': Melville and Cosmopolitanism." *Nineteenth-Century Fiction* 39 (1984): 275–91.

Burlin, Natalie Curtis. *The Indians Book: An Offering by the American Indians of Indian Lore, Musical, and Narrative, to Form a Record of the Songs and Legends of Their Race.* New York: Dover, 1968 [1907].

Callahan, S. Alice. *Wynema: A Child of the Forest*. Ed. A. Lavonne Brown Ruoff. Lincoln: University of Nebraska Press, 1997 [1891].

Capps, W. H., ed. *Seeing with a Native Eye*. New York: Harper, 1976.

Castro, Michael. *Interpreting the Indian: Twentieth-Century Poets and the Native American*. Albuquerque: University of New Mexico Press, 1983.

Chapman, Abraham, ed. *Literature of the American Indians: Views and Interpretations*. New York: New American Library, 1975

Charleston, G. Mike. "Toward True Native Education: A Treaty of 1992. Final Report of the Indian Nations at Risk Task Force." *Journal of American Indian Education* 33 (1994): 7–56.

Cheyfitz, Eric. *The Poetics of Imperialism: Translation and Colonization from "The Tempest" to "Tarzan."* Expanded ed. Philadelphia: University of Pennsylvania Press, 1997.

———, ed. *The Columbia Guide to Native American Literature Since 1945*. New York: Columbia University Press, 2002.

Churchill, Ward. "I Am Indigenist." In *Struggle for the Land: Indigenous Resistance, to Genocide, Ecocide, and Expropriation in Contemporary North America*. Monroe, Me.: Common Courage, 1993. 403–51.

Clastres, Pierre. *Society Against the State: The Leader as Servant and the Humane Uses of Power Among the Indians of the Americas*. New York: Urizen, 1977.

Claviez, Thomas, and Maria Moss, eds. *Mirror Writing: (Re-)Constructions of Native American Identity*. Berlin: Galda and Wilch, 2000.

Cleaver, Eldridge. *Soul on Ice*. New York: McGraw-Hill, 1968.

Clements, William. "Faking the Pumpkin: On Jerome Rothenberg's Literary Offenses." *Western American Literature* 16 (1981): 193–204.

Clifford, James. "Histories of the Tribal and the Modern." In *The Predicament of Culture: Twentieth-Century Ethnography, Literature, and Art*. Cambridge, Mass.: Harvard University Press, 1988. 189–214. (1988a)

———. "Identity in Mashpee." In *The Predicament of Culture: Twentieth-Century Ethnography, Literature, and Art*, 277–346. (1988b)

———. "Mixed Feelings." In Bruce Robbins and Pheng Cheah, eds., *Cosmopolitics: Thinking and Feeling Beyond the Nation*. Minneapolis: University of Minnesota Press, 1998. 362–70.

Clifford, James, and George Marcus, eds. *Writing Culture: The Poetics and Politics of Ethnography*. Berkeley: University of California Press, 1986.

Cole, Douglas. *Franz Boas: The Early Years, 1858–1906*. Seattle: University of Washington Press. 1999.

Coltelli, Laura, ed. *Native American Literatures*. Pisa: Servizio Editoriale Universitario, 1989.

Columbus, Christopher. *The "Diario" of Christopher Columbus's First Voyage to America, 1492–1493*. Abstracted by Fray Bartolomé de las Casas, transcribed and trans. Oliver Dunn and James E. Kelley, Jr. Norman: University of Oklahoma Press, 1989.

Cook-Lynn, Elizabeth. "The American Indian Fiction Writers: Cosmopolitanism, Nationalism, the Third World, and First Nation Sovereignty." In *Why I Can't Read Wallace Stegner and Other Essays*. Madison: University of Wisconsin Press, 1996. 78–98.

Cronon, William. "A Place for Stories: Nature, History, and Narrative." *Journal of American History* 78 (1992): 1347–76.

Cruikshank, Julie. *Life Lived like a Story: Life Stories of Three Yukon Native Elders*. In collaboration with Angela Sydney, Kitty Smith, and Annie Ned. Lincoln: University of Nebraska Press, 1990.

———. *The Social Life of Stories: Narrative and Knowledge in the Yukon Territory.* Lincoln: University of Nebraska Press, 1998.

Crum, Steven J. "Henry Roe Cloud, a Winnebago Indian Reformer: His Quest for American Indian Higher Education." *Kansas History* 11 (1988): 171–84.

Dauenhauer, Nora, and Richard Dauenhauer. "Haa Shuka, Our Ancestors: Tlingit Oral Narrative." *Journal of American Folklore* 103 (1990): 108–11.

Davis, F. James. *Who Is Black? One Nation's Definition.* University Park: Pennsylvania State University Press, 1991.

Day, A. Grove, ed. *The Sky Clears: Poetry of the American Indians.* New York: Macmillan, 1951.

DeFrancis, John. *Visible Speech: The Diverse Oneness of Writing Systems.* Honolulu: University of Hawaii Press, 1989.

Deloria, Philip J. *Playing Indian.* New Haven, Conn.: Yale University Press, 1998.

Deloria, Vine, Jr. "The Application of the Constitution to American Indians." In Oren Lyons, John Mohawk, et al., eds., *Exiled in the Land of the Free: Democracy, Indian Nations, and the U.S. Constitution.* Santa Fe, N.M.: Clear Light Publishers, 1992. 281–316.

———. *Custer Died for Your Sins: An Indian Manifesto.* New York: Avon, 1969.

———. "Intellectual Self-Determination and Sovereignty: Looking at the Windmills in Our Minds." *Wicazo Sa Review* 13 (1998): 25–32. (1998a)

———. *Red Earth, White Lies: Native Americans and the Myth of Scientific Fact.* New York: Scribner, 1995.

———. "Response to David Brumble." *American Literary History* 10 (1998b): 347–49.

———. *We Talk, You Listen: New Tribes, New Turf.* New York: Macmillan, 1970. (1970b)

Deloria, Vine, Jr., and Clifford Lytle. *The Nations Within: The Past and Future of American Indian Sovereignty.* New York: Pantheon, 1984.

DeMallie, Raymond. "Dissonant Voices: Anthropologists, Historians, and the Lakota People." Presented at the Eastern Comparative literature Conference, Emerging Literatures, Emerging Cinemas, New York University, April 1993.

———, ed. *The Sixth Grandfather: Black Elk's Teachings Given to John G. Neihardt.* Lincoln: University of Nebraska Press, 1984.

———. " 'These Have No Ears': Narrative and the Ethnohistorical Method." *Ethnohistory* 40 (1993): 515–36.

Dening, Greg. *Performances.* Chicago: University of Chicago Press, 1996.

Dirlik, Arif. "The Past as Legacy and Project: Postcolonial Criticism in the Perspective of Indigenous Historicism." *American Indian Culture and Research Journal* 20 (1996): 1–31.

Dollar, Clyde. "Through the Looking-Glass: History and the Modern Brulé Sioux." In Daniel Tyler, ed., *Red Men and Hat-Wearers: Viewpoints in Indian History.* Papers from the Colorado State University Conference on Indian History, 1974. Boulder: Pruett, 1976.

Du Bois, W. E. B. *The Souls of Black Folk.* New York: Bantam, 1989 [1903].

Eastman, Charles Alexander (Ohiyesa). *From the Deep Woods to Civilization.* Lincoln: University of Nebraska Press, 1977 [1916].

———. *The Soul of the Indian: An Interpretation.* Lincoln: University of Nebraska Press, 1980 [1911].

Elliott, Michael. 1999. *The Culture Concept: Writing and Difference in Realist America.* Minneapolis: University of Minnesota Press, 2002.

———. Telling the Difference: Nineteenth-Century Legal Narratives of Racial Taxonomy." *Law and Social Inquiry* 24 (1999): 611–36.

Ellison, Ralph. *Invisible Man.* New York: Random House, 1952.

Erdoes, Richard, and Alfonso Ortiz. *American Indian Myths and Legends.* New York: Pantheon, 1984.

Evers, Larry J. "Words and Place; A Reading of *House Made of Dawn.*" *Western American Literature* 11 (1977): 297–320.

Evers, Larry J., and Felipe S. Molina. "Coyote Songs." In Laura Coltelli, ed., *Native American Literatures.* Pisa: Servizio Editoriale Universitario, 1989. 9–38.

———. *Yaqui Deer Songs: Maso Bwikam, a Native American Poetry.* Tucson: University of Arizona Press, 1987.

Falk, Richard. "Revisioning Cosmopolitanism." In Martha Nussbaum et al., *For Love of Country: Debating the Limits of Patriotism,* ed. Joshua Cohen. Boston: Beacon Press, 1996. 653–60.

Fanon, Frantz. *Black Skin, White Masks.* New York: Grove, 1967 [1952].

———. *The Wretched of the Earth.* Preface by Jean-Paul Sartre. New York: Grove, 1968 [1961].

Fleischmann, Anne. "Neither Fish, Flesh, Nor Fowl: Race and Region in the Writings of Charles W. Chesnutt." In Amrit Singh and Peter Schmidt, eds., *Postcolonial Theory and the United States.* Jackson: University Press of Mississippi, 2000. 244–57.

Fletcher, Alice C. "The Relation of Indian Story and Song." In Abraham Chapman, ed., *Literature of the American Indians: Views and Interpretations.* New York: New American Library, 1975 [1900]. 235–39.

Fogelson, Raymond. "On the Varieties of Indian History: Sequoyah and Traveller Bird." *Journal of Ethnic Studies* 2 (1974): 105–12.

Fontana, Bernard. "American Indian Oral History: An Anthropologist's Note." *History and Theory* 8 (1969): 366–70.

Forbes, Jack. "Intellectual Self-Determination and Sovereignty: Implications for Native Studies and for Native Intellectuals." *Wicazo Sa Review* 13 (1998): 11–24.

Foster, Michael. *From the Earth to Beyond the Sky: An Ethnographic Approach to Four Longhouse Iroquois Speech Events.* Canadian Ethnology Service Paper 20. Ottawa: National Museum of Man, 1974.

Funderberg, Lise, ed. *Black, White, Other: Biracial Americans Talk About Race and Identity.* New York: William Morrow, 1994.

Gaur, Albertine. *A History of Writing.* New York: Scribner's, 1984.

Gelb, I. J. *A Study of Writing: The Foundations of Grammatology.* Chicago: University of Chicago Press, 1963 [1952].

Geyer, Michael. "Multiculturalism and the Politics of General Education." *Critical Inquiry* 19 (1993): 499–533.

Ghosh, Amitav. *In an Antique Land: History in the Guise of a Traveler's Tale.* New York: Vintage, 1994.

Gilroy, Paul. *Against Race: Imagining Political Culture Beyond the Color Line.* Cambridge, Mass.: Harvard University Press, 2000.

———. *The Black Atlantic: Modernity and Double Consciousness.* Cambridge, Mass.: Harvard University Press, 1993.

Glancy, Diane. *Lone Dog's Winter Count.* Albuquerque, N.M.: West End Press, 1991.

Goldberg, David Theo. "Made in the U.S.A." In Naomi Zack, ed., *American Mixed*

Race: the Culture of Microdiversity. Lanham, Md.: Rowman and Littlefield, 1995. 237–56.

Goody, Jack, and Ian Watt. 1968. "The Consequences of Literacy." In Jack Goody, ed., *Literacy in Traditional Societies.* Cambridge: Cambridge University Press, 1968. 27–68.

Gotanda, Neil. 1995. "A Critique of 'Our Constitution Is Color-Blind.'" In Kimberlé Crenshaw et al., eds., *Critical Race Theory: The Key Writings That Formed the Movement* . New York: New Press, 1995. 257–75.

Green, Michael K., ed. *Issues in Native American Identity.* New York: Peter Lang, 1994.

Grier, William, and Price H. Cobbs. *Black Rage.* New York: Basic Books, 1968.

Griffis, Joseph (Chief Tahan). *Out of Savagery, into Civilization.* With an introduction by Arthur C. Parker. New York: George H. Doran, 1915.

Grinnell, George Bird. *The Cheyenne Indians: Their History and Ways of Life.* New York: Cooper Square, 1962 [1910].

Hagan, William. *American Indians.* Chicago: University of Chicago Press, 1979 [1961].

———. *The Indian Rights Association: The Herbert Welsh Years, 1882–1904.* Tucson: University of Arizona Press, 1985.

———. Review of Fr. Peter Powell, *People of the Sacred Mountain. Western Historical Quarterly* 13 (1982): 431–33.

Hale, Horatio. *The Iroquois Book of Rites.* Toronto: University of Toronto Press, 1963 [1883].

Handler, Richard. "Boasian Anthropology and the Critique of American Culture." *American Quarterly* 42 (1990): 250–73.

Harring, Sidney. *Crow Dog's Case: American Indian Sovereignty, Tribal Law, and United States Law in the Nineteenth Century.* New York: Cambridge University Press, 1994.

Harris, David D. 1996. Review of Vine Deloria, Jr., *Red Earth, White Lies. Native Americas: Akwe:kon's Journal of Indigenous Issues* 13 (1996): 60–62.

Harris, Marvin. *The Rise of Anthropological Theory.* New York: Thomas Crowell, 1968.

Havelock, Eric. *The Muse Learns to Write: Reflections on Orality and Literacy from Antiquity to the Present.* New Haven, Conn.: Yale University Press, 1986.

———. "Why Was Socrates Tried?" In Mary Estelle White, ed., *Studies in Honour of Gilbert Norwood.* Phoenix Supplement 1. Toronto: University of Toronto Press, 1952. 95–109.

Herskovits, Melville. *Franz Boas: The Science of Man in the Making* . New York: Scribner's, 1953.

Hertzberg, Hazel. *The Search for an American Indian Identity: Modern Pan-Indian Movements.* Syracuse, N.Y.: Syracuse University Press, 1972.

Hilden, Patricia Penn. *When Nickels Were Indians: An Urban Mixed-Blood Story.* Washington, D.C.: Smithsonian Institution Press, 1995.

Hinton, Leanne, and L. Watahomigie, eds. *Spirit Mountain: An Anthology of Yuman Story and Song.* Tucson: University of Arizona Press, 1984.

Hogan, Linda. *Solar Storms.* New York: Scribner, 1995.

———. *Power.* New York: Norton, 1998.

Hollinger, David. *Postethnic America: Beyond Multiculturalism.* New York: Basic Books, 1995.

Holt, Thomas C. "The Political Uses of Alienation: W. E. B. Du Bois on Politics, Race, and Culture, 1903–1940." *American Quarterly* 42 (1990): 301–23.

Hooker, J. T. *Reading the Past: Ancient Writing from Cuneiform to the Alphabet.* Berkeley: British Museum/University of California Press, 1990.

Hoxie, Frederick. *A Final Promise: The Campaign to Assimilate the Indians, 1880–1920.* Lincoln: University of Nebraska Press, 1984.

Huhndorf, Shari. "Cultural Difference and Colonial Desire: The Politics of Tradition in D'Arcy McNickle's *Wind from an Enemy Sky.*" *American Literary History,* forthcoming.

———. *Going Native: Indians in the American Cultural Imagination.* Ithaca, N.Y.: Cornell University Press, 2001.

Hulme Peter. *Colonial Encounters: Europe and the Native Caribbean, 1492–1797.* London: Routledge, 1992 [1986].

Hunter, John Dunn. *Memoirs of a Captivity Among the Indians of North America.* Ed. Richard Drinnon. New York: Schocken, 1973 [1824].

Hutchinson, George. "Nella Larsen and the Veil of Race." *American Literary History* 9 (1997): 329–49.

Hyatt, Marshall. *Franz Boas, Social Activist: The Dynamics of Ethnicity.* Westport, Conn.: Greenwood Press,1990.

Hymes, Dell. *"In vain I tried to tell you": Essays in Native American Ethnopoetics.* Philadelphia: University of Pennsylvania Press, 1981.

Hymes, Virginia. 1974. "Warm Springs Sahaptin Narrative Analysis." In Joel Sherzer and Anthony Woodbury, eds., *Native American Discourse: Poetics and Rhetoric.* Cambridge: Cambridge University Press, 1974. 62–102.

Ignatiev, Noel. *How the Irish Became White.* New York: Routledge, 1995.

Jacobson, Matthew. *Whiteness of a Different Color: European Immigrants and the Alchemy of Race.* Cambridge, Mass.: Harvard University Press, 1998.

Jahner, Elaine. "Traditional Narrative: Contemporary Uses, Historical Perspectives." *SAIL* (Studies in American Indian Literatures) 11 (1999): 1–28.

Jaimes, M. Annette. "Native American Identity and Survival: Indigenism and Environmental Ethics." In Michael K. Green, ed., *Issues in Native American Identity.* New York: Peter Lang, 1994. 133–53.

Jay, Nancy. "Gender and Dichotomy." *Feminist Studies* 7 (1981): 38–56.

Jenning, Francis. *The Ambiguous Iroquois Empire: The Covenant Chain Confederation of Indian Tribes with English Colonies from Its Beginnings to the Lancaster Treaty of 1744.* New York: W.W. Norton, 1984.

Johnson, James Weldon. *The Autobiography of an Ex-Colored Man.* New York: Penguin, 1990 [1912].

Johnson, Sir William. *The Papers of Sir William Johnson.* 11vols. Ed. James Sullivan et al. Albany: State University of New York, 1962 [1921]. 2: 624.

Jones, Leroi (Imamu Amiri Baraka). *Arm Yrself or Harm Yrself.* Newark, N.J.: Jihad Publications, 1967.

———. *Four Black Revolutionary Plays.* Indianapolis: Bobbs-Merrill, 1969.

Jones, Leroi, and Larry Neal, eds. *Black Fire.* New York: William Morrow, 1969.

Kaiser, Rudolph. "Chief Seattle's Speech(es): American Origins and European Reception." In Brian Swann and Arnold Krupat, eds., *Recovering the Word: Essays on Native American Literature.* Lincoln: University of Nebraska Press, 1987. 497–536. (1987b)

Kidwell, Clara Sue. "Science and Ethnoscience." *Indian Historian* 6 (1973): 43–54.

Kilpatrick, Jack, and Anna Kilpatrick, eds. *Friends of Thunder: Folktales of the Oklahoma Cherokee.* Dallas: Southern Methodist University Press, 1964.

King, Cecil. "Here Come the Anthros." In Thomas Biolsi and Larry J. Zimmerman, eds., *Indians and Anthropologists: Vine Deloria, Jr., and the Critique of Anthropology.* Tucson: University of Arizona Press, 1997. 115–19.

Kinkade, M. Dale. 1987. "Bluejay and His Sister." In Brian Swann and Arnold Krupat, eds., *Recovering the Word: Essays on Native American Literature.* Lincoln: University of Nebraska Press, 1987. 255–96. (1987b)

Knight, Etheridge, and other inmates of Indiana State Prison. *Black Voices from Prison.* New York: Pathfinder, 1970.

Koestler, Arthur. *Darkness at Noon.* New York: Bantam Books, 1968 [1941].

Kollin, Susan. "Race and Global Environmentalism: Nora Dauenhauer, Tlingit History, and the Poetics of Place." Paper presented at the Modern Language Association Convention, December 2000.

Kroeber, Karl. 1981. "An Introduction to the Art of Traditional Native American Indian Narrative." In *Traditional Literatures of the American Indian: Texts and Interpretations.* Lincoln: University of Nebraska Press, 1981. 1–24.

———. "Technology and Tribal Narrative." In Gerald Vizenor, ed., *Narrative Chance: Postmodern Discourse on Native American Indian Literatures.* Albuquerque: University of New Mexico Press, 1989. 17–38. (1989a)

———. "Turning Comparative Literature Around: the Problem of Translating American Indian Literatures." In Laura Coltelli, ed., *Native American Literatures.* Pisa: Servizio Editoriale Universitario, 1989. 39–52. (1989b)

Krupat, Arnold. "America's Histories." *American Literary History* 10 (1998): 124–46.

———. "Anthropology in the Ironic Mode: The Work of Franz Boas." *Social Text* 19–20 (1988): 2–13.

———. *Ethnocriticism: Ethnography, History, Literature.* Berkeley: University of California Press, 1992.

———. "Identity and Difference in the Criticism of Native American Literature." *Diacritics* 13 (1983): 2–13.

———. "'Literary' Criticism/Native American 'Literature.'" In *Ethnocriticism: Ethnography, History, Literature.* Berkeley: University of California Press, 1991.

———, ed. *New Voices in Native American Literary Criticism.* Washington, D.C.: Smithsonian Institution Press, 1992.

———. "Post-Structuralism and Oral Literature." In Brian Swann and Arnold Krupat, eds., *Recovering the Word: Essays on Native American Literature.* Lincoln: University of Nebraska Press, 1987. 113–28. (1987b)

———. *The Turn to the Native: Studies in Criticism and Culture.* Lincoln: University of Nebraska Press, 1996.

Krupat, Arnold, and Brian Swann, eds. *Here First: Autobiographical Essays by Native American Writers.* New York: Modern Library, 2000.

Kuper, Adam. *The Invention of Primitive Society: Transformations of an Illusion.* New York: Routledge, 1988.

Landsman, Gail. "Informant as Critic: Conducting Research on a Dispute between Iroquoianist Scholars and Traditional Iroquois." In Thomas Biolsi and Larry J. Zimmerman, eds., *Indians and Anthropologists: Vine Deloria, Jr., and the Critique of Anthropology.* Tucson: University of Arizona Press, 1997. 160–76.

Larsen, Nella. *Quicksand.* New Brunswick, N.J.: Rutgers University Press, 1986 [1928].

Larson, Charles R. *American Indian Fiction.* Albuquerque: University of New Mexico Press, 1978.

Lavelle, John P. "The General Allotment Act 'Eligibility' Hoax: Distortions of

Law, Policy, and History in Derogation of Indian Tribes." *Wicazo Sa Review* 14 (1999): 251–302.

Lawrence, D. H. *Studies in Classic American Literature.* New York: Viking, 1961 [1925].

Lazarus, Neil. "Disavowing Decolonization: Fanon, Nationalism, and the Problematic of Representation in Current Theories of Colonial Discourse." *Research in African Literatures* 24 (1993): 69–98.

Lee, A. Robert, ed. *Loosening the Seams: Interpretations of Gerald Vizenor.* Bowling Green, Ohio: Bowling Green State University Popular Press, 2000.

León-Portilla, Miguel. *Pre-Columbian Literatures of Mexico.* Trans. Grace Lobanov and M. León-Portilla. Norman: University of Oklahoma Press, 1969.

Levin, Michael. *Why Race Matters: Race Differences and What They Mean.* Westport, Conn.: Praeger, 1997.

Lévi-Strauss, Claude, and Didier Eribon. *Conversations with Claude Lévi-Strauss.* Chicago: University of Chicago Press, 1991.

Lind, Michael. "The Beige and the Black." *New York Times Magazine,* August 16, 1998, 38–39.

Lincoln, Kenneth. *Native American Renaissance.* Berkeley: University of California Press, 1983.

Locke, Alain, ed. *The New Negro.* New York: Atheneum, 1968 [1925].

Lomawaima, Tsianina. *They Called It Prairie Light: The Story of Chilocco Indian School.* Lincoln: University of Nebraska Press, 1994.

Lowie, Robert. "Oral Tradition and History." *American Anthropologist* 17 (1915): 597–99.

Lukens, Margaret A. "Mourning Dove and Mixed Blood: Cultural and Historical Pressures on Aesthetic Choice and Authorial Identity." *American Indian Quarterly* 21 (1997): 409–21.

Lyons, Scott Richard. "Rhetorical Sovereignty: What Do American Indians Want from Writing?" *College Composition and Communication* 51 (2000): 447–68.

Lyotard, Jean-François. *The Differend: Phrases in Dispute.* Minneapolis: University of Minnesota Press, 1968.

———. *The Postmodern Condition.* Minneapolis: University of Minnesota Press, 1984.

Mallery, Garrick. *Pictographs of the North American Indians.* Fourth Annual Report of the Bureau of American Ethnology, 1882–83. Washington, D.C.: Government Printing Office, 1886.

———. *Picture-Writing of the American Indians.* Tenth Annual Report of the Bureau of American Ethnology, 1888–89. Washington, D.C.: Government Printing Office, 1893.

Malotki, Ekkehart. *Hopi Time: A Linguistic Analysis of the Temporal Concepts in the Hopi Language.* Berlin: Mouton, 1983.

Marquis, Thomas B. *Custer on the Little Big Horn.* Algonac, Mich.: Reference Publications, 1986.

———. *Save the Last Bullet for Yourself: The True Story of Custer's Last Stand.* New York: Reference Publishers, 1976 [1935].

Martin, Calvin, ed. *The American Indian and the Problem of History.* New York: Oxford University Press, 1987.

Matthews, F. H. "The Revolt Against Americanism: Cultural Pluralism and Cultural Relativism as an Ideology of Liberation." *Canadian Review of American Studies* 1 (1970): 4–31.

Matthews, Washington. "The Mountain Chant: A Navajo Ceremony." In Fifth

Annual Report of the Bureau of American Ethnology, 1883–84. Washington, D.C.: Government Printing Office, 1887. 385–468.

Mattina, Anthony. "North American Indian Mythography: Editing Texts for the Printed Page." In Brian Swann and Arnold Krupat, eds., *Recovering the Word: Essays on Native American Literature*. Lincoln: University of Nebraska Press, 1987, 129–48. (1987b)

Mattina, Anthony, and Madeleine de Sautel, trans. *The Golden Woman: The Colville Narrative of Peter Seymour*. Tucson: University of Arizona Press, 1985.

McAllester, David. " 'The War God's Horse Song': An Exegesis in Native American Humanities." In Charlotte Heth, ed., *Music of the North American Indians*. Berkeley: University of California Press, 1980. 1–22.

McNickle, Darcy. *Wind from an Enemy Sky*. Albuquerque: University of New Mexico Press, 1988 [1978].

Means, Russell, and Ward Churchill. *TREATY: A Platform for Nationhood*. Denver: Fourth World Center for the Study of Indigenous Law and Politics, 1995.

Memmi, Albert. *The Colonizer and the Colonized*. Expanded ed. Boston: Beacon Press, 1967 [1957].

Michaels, Walter Benn. *Our America: Nativism, Modernism, and Pluralism*. Durham, N.C.: Duke University Press, 1995. (1995a).

———. "Race into Culture: A Critical Genealogy of Cultural Identity." In Kwame Anthony Appiah and Henry Louis Gates, Jr., eds., *Identities*. Chicago: University of Chicago Press, 1995. 32–62. (1995b)

Michaelsen, Scott. *The Limits of Multiculturalism: Interrogating the Origins of American Anthropology*. Minneapolis: University of Minnesota Press, 1999.

Miller, David. *Custer's Fall: The Native American Side of the Story*. New York: Meridian, 1992 [1957].

Momaday, N. Scott. *House Made of Dawn*. New York: Harper and Row, 1968.

———. *The Way to Rainy Mountain*. Albuquerque: University of New Mexico Press, 1969.

Moody, Roger, ed. *The Indigenous Voice: Visions and Realities*. Utrecht: International Books, 1993.

Mooney, James. *Myths of the Cherokee*. New York: Johnson Reprints, 1970 [1900].

———. *The Swimmer Manuscript: Cherokee Sacred Formulas and Medicinal Prescriptions*. Rev. and ed. Frans M. Olbrecht. Bureau of American Ethnology Bulletin 99. Washington, D.C.: Government Printing Office, 1932.

Morrison, Toni. *Beloved*. New York: Random House, 1987.

———. *Playing in the Dark: Whiteness and the Literary Imagination*. Cambridge, Mass.: Harvard University Press, 1992.

Moses, Wilson J. *Afrotopia: The Roots of African American Popular History*. Cambridge: Cambridge University Press, 1998.

Mostern, Kenneth. "Three Theories of the Race of W. E. B. Du Bois." *Cultural Critique* 34 (1996): 27–64.

Mourning Dove (Humi-shu-ma). *Cogewea, the Half-Blood; Given Through Sho-pow-tan*. With notes and biographical sketch by Lucullus Virgil McWhorter. Lincoln: University of Nebraska Press, 1981 [1927].

———. *Coyote Stories*. Ed. and illus. Heister Dean Guie, with notes by L. V. McWhorter (Old Wolf) and Foreword by Chief Standing Bear. Lincoln: University of Nebraska Press, 1990 [1933]. (1990a).

———. *Mourning Dove: A Salishan Autobiography*. Ed. Jay Miller. Lincoln: University of Nebraska Press, 1990. (1990b)

Murray, David. "Cultural Sovereignty and the Hauntology of American Identity."

In Thomas Claviez and Maria Moss, eds., *Mirror Writing: (Re-)Constructions of Native American Identity.* Berlin: Galda and Wilch, 2000. 237–56. (2000a)

————. *Forked Tongues: Speech, Writing, and Representation in North American Indian Texts.* Bloomington: Indiana University Press, 1991.

————. *Indian Giving: Economies of Power in Early Indian and White Exchanges.* Amherst: University of Massachusetts Press, 2000. (2000b)

Nabokov, Peter. "Indian Views of History." In Bruce G. Trigger and Wilcomb E. Washburn, eds., *North America,* vol. 1 of the *Cambridge History of the Native Peoples of the Americas.* New York: Cambridge University Press, 1996.

Nussbaum, Martha et al. *For Love of Country: Debating the Limits of Patriotism.* Ed. Joshua Cohen. Boston: Beacon Press, 1996.

O'Connell, Barry, ed. *On Our Own Ground: The Complete Writings of William Apess, a Pequot.* Amherst: University of Massachusetts Press, 1992.

Oestreicher, David. "Unmasking the *Walum Olum*: A 19th-Century Hoax." *Bulletin of the Archeological Society of New Jersey* 49 (1994): 1–44.

O'Hearn, Claudine C., ed. *Half and Half: Writers on Growing up Biracial and Bicultural.* New York: Pantheon, 1992.

Oliver, Lawrence J. "Deconstruction or Affirmative Action: The Literary-Political Debate over the 'Ethnic' Question." *American Literary History* 3 (1991): 792–808.

O'Reilly, Kenneth. *Racial Matters: The FBI's Secret File on Black America.* New York: Free Press, 1989.

Owens, Louis. *Mixedblood Messages: Literature, Film, Family, Place.* Norman: University of Oklahoma Press, 1998.

————. *Other Destinies: Understanding the American Indian Novel.* Norman: University of Oklahoma Press, 1992.

Parker, Arthur C. "Problems of Race Assimilation in America, with Special Reference to the American Indian." *American Indian Magazine* 4 (1916): 285–304.

Patell, Cyrus R. K. "The Violence of Hybridity in Silko and Alexie." *Journal of American Studies of Turkey* 6 (1997): 3–9.

Pearce, Roy Harvey. *Savagism and Civilization: A Study of the Indian and the American Mind.* Berkeley: University of California Press, 1988 [1953].

Penn, William S., ed. *As We Are Now: Mixblood Essays on Race and Identity.* Berkeley: University of California Press, 1997.

Pfister, Joel. "The Yale Indian: The Managerial and Psychological Individualizing of Henry Roe Cloud." Unpublished manuscript, 1997.

Posnock, Ross. *Color and Culture: Black Writers and the Making of the Modern Intellectual.* Cambridge, Mass.: Harvard University Press, 1998.

————. "How It Feels to Be a Problem: Du Bois, Fanon, and the 'Impossible Life' of the Black Intellectual." *Critical Inquiry* 23 (1997): 323–49.

Powell, John Wesley. *Anthropology of the Numa: John Wesley Powell's Manuscript on the Numic Peoples of North America.* Ed. Don D. Fowler and Catherine S. Fowler. Washington, D.C.: Smithsonian Institution Press, 1971 [1868–80].

Powell, Fr. Peter J. *People of the Sacred Mountain: A History of the Northern Cheyenne Chiefs and Warrior Societies, 1830–1879.* 2 vols. New York: Harper and Row, 1981.

Powers, Ann. "Without Reservation." *Village Voice,* October 22, 1996, 57–59.

Powers, William. *Sacred Language: The Nature of Supernatural Discourse in Lakota.* Norman: University of Oklahoma Press, 1986. (1986a)

————. "Text and Context in Lakota Music." In Charlotte Frisbie, ed., *Explorations in Ethnomusicology: Essays in Honor of David McAllester.* Detroit Monographs in Musicology 9. Detroit: Information Coordinators, 1986. (1986b)

Priest, Loring B. *Uncle Sam's Stepchildren: The Reformation of United States Indian Policy, 1865–1887.* New York: Octagon, 1969 [1942].

Prucha, Fr. Francis P. *Americanizing the American Indians.* Cambridge, Mass.: Harvard University Press, 1973.

———. *The Great Father: The United States Government and the American Indian.* Lincoln: University of Nebraska Press, 1984.

Rabinow, Paul. "Representations Are Social Facts: Modernity and Post-Modernity in Anthropology." In James Clifford and George Marcus, eds., *Writing Culture: The Poetics and Politics of Ethnography.* Berkeley: University of California Press, 1986. 234–61.

Rahv, Phillip. "Paleface and Redskin." In *Image and Idea: Fourteen Essays on Literary Themes.* New York: New Directions, 1949.

Readings, Bill. "Pagans, Perverts, or Primitives? Experimental Justice in the Empire of Capital." In Andrew Benjamin, ed., *Judging Lyotard.* London: Routledge, 1992. 168–86.

Ree, Johnathan. "Cosmopolitanism and the Experience of Nationality." In Bruce Robbins and Pheng Cheah, eds., *Cosmopolitics: Thinking and Feeling Beyond the Nation.* Minneapolis: University of Minnesota Press, 1998. 77–90.

Reid-Pharr, Robert. "Cosmopolitan Afrocentric Mulatto Intellectual." *American Literary History* 13 (2000): 169–79.

Resnik, Judith. "Dependent Sovereigns: Indian Tribes, States, and the Federal Courts." *University of Chicago Law Review* 56 (1989): 671–759.

Rice, Julian. *Black Elk's Story: Distinguishing Its Lakota Purpose.* Albuquerque: University of New Mexico Press, 1991.

Robbins, Bruce. "The Weird Heights: On Cosmopolitanism, Feeling, and Power." *Differences: A Journal of Feminist Cultural Studies* 7 (1995): 165–87.

Robbins, Bruce, and Pheng Cheah, eds. *Cosmopolitics: Thinking and Feeling Beyond the Nation.* Minneapolis: University of Minnesota Press, 1998.

Robinson, Harry. *Write It on Your Heart: The Epic World of an Okanagan Storyteller.* Ed. Wendy Wickwire. Vancouver: Talonbooks/Theytus, 1989.

Roe Cloud, Henry. "From Wigwam to Pulpit: A Red Man's Story of His Progress from Darkness to Light." Unpublished manuscript, 1916. American Indian Institute Papers, Presbyterian Historical Society, Philadelphia.

Roediger, David R. *The Wages of Whiteness: Race in the Making of the American Middle Class.* London: Verso, 1991.

Roemer, Kenneth M. "Silko's Arroyos as Mainstream: Processes and Implications of Canonical Identity." *Modern Fiction Studies* 45 (1999): 10–37.

Root, Maria P. P. "The Multiracial Contribution to the Psychological Browning of America." In Naomi Zack, ed., *American Mixed Race: the Culture of Microdiversity.* Lanham, Md.: Rowman and Littlefield, 1995. 231–36.

———, ed. *Racially Mixed People in America.* London: Sage, 1992.

Rosaldo, Renato. *Ilongot Headhunting, 1883–1974: A Study in Society and History.* Stanford, Calif.: Stanford University Press, 1980.

Rothenberg, Jerome, ed. *Shaking the Pumpkin: Traditional Poetry of the Indian North Americas.* Garden City, N.Y.: Doubleday, 1972.

———. "Total Translation: An Experiment in the Presentation of American Indian Poetry." In Abraham Chapman, ed., *Literature of the American Indians: Views and Interpretations.* New York: New American Library, 1975. 292–307.

———. " 'We Explain Nothing, We Believe Nothing': American Indian Poetry and the Problematics of Translation." In Brian Swann, ed., *On the Translation of Native American Literatures.* Washington, D.C.: Smithsonian Institution Press, 1992. 64–79.

Sahlins, Marshall. "Goodbye to Tristes Tropes: Ethnography in the Context of Modern World History." *Journal of Modern History* 65 (1993): 1–25.

——. *How "Natives" Think: About Captain Cook, for Example.* Chicago: University of Chicago Press, 1995.

Said, Edward. *Culture and Imperialism.* New York: Knopf, 1993.

Sanders, Thomas E., and Walter W. Peek. *Literature of the American Indian.* New York: Glencoe, 1973.

Sanner, Hans-Ulrich. "Confessions of the Last Hopi Fieldworker." In Thomas Claviez and Maria Moss, eds., *Mirror Writing: (Re-)Constructions of Native American Identity.* Berlin: Galda and Wilch, 2000. 41–66.

Sartre, Jean-Paul. "Orphée Noir." Introduction to Léopold Senghor, ed., *Anthologie de la nouvelle poésie nègre et malgache de langue française.* Paris: Presses Universitaires de France, 1969 [1948].

Schlereth, Thomas. *The Cosmopolitan Ideal in Enlightenment Thought: Its Form and Function in the Ideas of Franklin, Hume, and Voltaire, 1694–1790.* Notre Dame, Ind.: University of Notre Dame Press, 1977.

Schoolcraft, Henry Rowe. *Historical and Statistical Information Respecting the History, Condition, and Prospects of the Indian Tribes of the United States. . . .* Part 1. Philadelphia: Lippincott, Grambo, 1851.

Selinger, Bernard. "*House Made of Dawn:* A Positively Ambivalent Bildungsroman." *Modern Fiction Studies* 45 (1999): 38–68.

Sherzer, Joel. *Kuna Ways of Speaking: An Ethnographic Perspective.* Austin: University of Texas Press, 1983.

——. *Verbal Art in San Blas: Kuna Culture Through Its Discourse.* Cambridge: Cambridge University Press, 1990.

——. "Strategies in Text and Context: The Hot Pepper Story." In Brian Swann and Arnold Krupat, eds., *Recovering the Word: Essays on Native American Literature.* Lincoln: University of Nebraska Press, 1987. 151–97. (1987b)

Siebers, Tobin. "The Ethics of Anti-Ethnocentrism." *Michigan Quarterly Review* 32 (1993): 41–70.

Silko, Leslie Marmon. *Almanac of the Dead.* New York: Penguin, 1992 [1991].

——. *Ceremony.* New York: Penguin, 1986 [1977].

——. *Gardens in the Dunes.* New York: Simon and Schuster, 1999.

——. *Storyteller.* New York: Seaver, 1981.

Slaymaker, William. "Ecoing the Other(s): The Call of Global Green and Black African Responses." *PMLA* 116 (2001): 145–57.

Smedley, Audrey. *Race in North America: The Origin and Evolution of a Worldview.* Boulder, Colo.: Westview, 1993.

Smith, Paul Chaat, and Robert Warrior. *Like a Hurricane: The Indian Movement from Alcatraz to Wounded Knee.* New York: W.W. Norton, 1996.

Sollors, Werner. *Beyond Ethnicity: Consent and Descent in American Culture.* New York: Oxford University Press, 1986.

——. *Interracialism: Black-White Intermarriage in American History, Literature, and Law.* New York: Oxford University Press, 1989.

Southern Poverty Law Center. *SPLC Report* 29 (June 1990): 3.

Spencer, Rainer. "Race and Mixed-Race: A Personal Tour." In William S. Penn, ed., *As We Are Now: Mixblood Essays on Race and Identity.* Berkeley: University of California Press, 1997. 129–39.

Sperber, Dan. *On Anthropological Knowledge.* Cambridge: Cambridge University Press, 1985.

Spickard, Paul. *Mixed Blood: Intermarriage and Ethnic Identity in Twentieth-Century America.* Madison: University of Wisconsin Press, 1989.

Spivak, Gayatri C. "The Making of Americans: The Teaching of English and the Future of Culture Studies." *New Literary History* 21 (1990): 781–98.

Stevenson, Winona. " 'Ethnic' Assimilates 'Indigenous': A Study in Intellectual Neocolonialism." *Wicazo Sa Review* 13 (1998): 33–52.

Stocking, George, Jr. "The Turn-of-the-Century Concept of Race." *Modernism/ Modernity* 1 (1994): 4–16.

Strickland, Rennard. *Tonto's Revenge.* Albuquerque: University of New Mexico Press, 1997.

Strong, Pauline Turner, and Barrik van Winkle. " 'Indian Blood': Reflections on the Reckoning and Refiguring of Native North American Identity." *Cultural Anthropology* 11 (1996): 547–76.

———. "Tribe and Nation: American Indians and American Nationalism." *Social Analysis* 33 (1993): 9–26.

Swann, Brian, ed. *Coming to Light: Contemporary Translations of the Native Literature of North America.* New York: Random House, 1994.

———. *On the Translation of Native American Literatures.* Washington, D.C.: Smithsonian Institution Press, 1992.

———. *Song of the Sky: Versions of Native American Songs and Poems.* N.p.: Four Zoas Night House Press, 1985. Rev. ed. Amherst: University of Massachusetts Press, 1993.

Swann, Brian, and Arnold Krupat, eds. *I Tell You Now: Autobiographical Essays by Native American Writers.* Lincoln: University of Nebraska Press, 1987. (1987a)

———. *Recovering the Word: Essays on Native American Literature.* Berkeley: University of California Press, 1987. (1987b)

Takaki, Ronald. *Iron Cages: Race and Culture in Nineteenth-Century America.* New York: Oxford University Press, 2000 [1979].

Tedlock, Barbara. "Songs of the Zuni Kachina Society: Composition, Rehearsal, and Performance." In Charlotte Frisbie, ed., *Southwestern Indian Ritual Drama.* Albuquerque: University of New Mexico Press, 1980. 7–35.

Tedlock, Dennis. *Finding the Center: Narrative Poetry of the Zuni Indians.* Lincoln: University of Nebraska Press, 1978 [1972].

———. *The Spoken Word and the Work of Interpretation.* Philadelphia: University of Pennsylvania Press, 1983.

Timberlake, Henry. *Memoirs: 1756–65.* Salem, N.H.: Ayer, 1971 [1766].

Todd, Loretta. "What More Do They Want?" In Gerald McMaster and Lee-Ann Martin, eds., *Indigena: Contemporary Native Perspectives.* Hull, Quebec: Canadian Museum of Civilization, 1992. 74–79.

Trafzer, Clifford. "Grandmother, Grandfather, and the First History of the Americas." In Arnold Krupat, ed., *New Voices in Native American Literary Criticism.* Washington, D.C.: Smithsonian Institution Press, 1993. 474–87.

Trahant, Mark. *The Constitution as Metaphor: Writing About Tribes and States in the New Century.* Working Papers Series in Cultural Studies, Ethnicity, and Race Relations 16. Pullman: Department of American Comparative Cultures, Washington State University, 2000.

Tyler, Stephen A. "Postmodern Ethnography: From Document of the Occult to Occult Document." In James Clifford and George Marcus, eds., *Writing Culture:*

The Poetics and Politics of Ethnography. Berkeley: University of California Press, 1986. 122–40.

Vizenor, Gerald. *Bearheart: The Heirship Chronicles.* Minneapolis: University of Minnesota Press, 1990 [1978]. (1990a)

———. *Crossbloods: Bone Courts, Bingo, and Other Reports.* Minneapolis: University of Minnesota Press, 1990 [1976]. (1990b)

———. *Dead Voices.* Norman: University of Oklahoma Press, 1992.

———. *Fugitive Poses: Native American Indian Scenes of Absence and Presence.* Lincoln: University of Nebraska Press, 1998.

———. *The Heirs of Columbus.* Middletown, Conn.: Wesleyan University Press, 1991. (1991a)

———. *Landfill Meditations: Crossblood Stories.* Hanover, N.H.: University Press of New England, 1991. (1991b)

———. *Manifest Manners: Post-Indian Warriors of Survivance.* Hanover, N.H.: University Press of New England, 1994.

———. "Native Transmotion." In *Fugitive Poses: Native American Indian Scenes of Absence and Present.* Lincoln: University of Nebraska Press, 1998. 167–99.

———. "Thomas White Hawk." In *Crossbloods: Bone Courts, Bingo, and Other Reports.* Minneapolis: University of Minnesota Press, 1990 [1976]. 105–51.

———. "Why Must Thomas White Hawk Die?" *Twin Citian,* June 1968.

Voth, H. R. 1901. *The Oraibi Powamu Ceremony.* Field Columbian Museum Publication 61, Anthropological Series 3, 2. Chicago: Field Columbian Museum, 1901.

Wald, Alan. "'Theorizing Cultural Difference: A Critique of the 'Ethnicity School.'" *MELUS* 14 (1987): 21–33.

Wallace, Anthony F. C. *Jefferson and the Indians: The Tragic Fate of the First Americans.* Cambridge, Mass.: Harvard University Press, 1999.

Wallace, Paul A. W. *The White Roots of Peace.* Philadelphia: University of Pennsylvania Press, 1991.

Wallerstein, Immanuel. *Geopolitics and Geoculture: Essays on a Changing World System.* Cambridge: Cambridge University Press,1991.

Welch, James. *The Death of Jim Loney.* New York: Harper and Row, 1979.

———. *The Heartsong of Charging Elk.* New York: Doubleday, 2000.

———. *Killing Custer: The Battle of the Little Big Horn and the Fate of the Plains Indians.* New York: W.W. Norton, 1994.

West, Cornel. *Race Matters.* Boston: Beacon Press, 1993.

White, Hayden. *Metahistory: The Historical Imagination in Nineteenth-Century Europe.* Baltimore: Johns Hopkins University Press, 1973.

White, John. Review of Traveler Bird, *Tell Them They Lie. Indian Historian* 5 (1972): 45–46.

White Bull, Chief Joseph. *The Warrior Who Killed Custer.* Trans. and ed. James H. Howard. Lincoln: University of Nebraska Press, 1968.

Whiteley, Peter. "The End of Anthropology (at Hopi)?" In Thomas Biolsi and Larry J. Zimmerman, eds., *Indians and Anthropologists: Vine Deloria, Jr., and the Critique of Anthropology.* Tucson: University of Arizona Press, 1997. 177–208.

———. *Rethinking Hopi Ethnography.* Washington, D.C.: Smithsonian Institution Press, 1998.

Whitt, Laurie Anne. "Indigenous Peoples and the Cultural Politics of Knowledge." In Michael K. Green, ed., *Issues in Native American Identity.* New York: Peter Lang, 1994. 232–46.

Whorf, Benjamin Lee. *Language, Thought, and Reality.* New York: John Wiley, 1956.

Wiget, Andrew. "Oratory." In Wiget, *Native American Literature*, 23–25. Boston: Twayne, 1985.

Wilkinson, Charles F. *American Indians, Time, and the Law.* New Haven, Conn.: Yale University Press, 1987.

Williams, Vernon. *Rethinking Race: Franz Boas and His Contemporaries.* Lexington: University Press of Kentucky, 1966.

Williams, William Carlos. *In the American Grain.* New York: New Directions, 1956 [1925].

Witt, Shirley Hill, and Stan Steiner, eds. *The Way: An Anthology of American Indian Literature.* New York: Vintage, 1972.

Wolf, Eric. *Europe and the People without History.* Berkeley: University of California Press, 1982.

Womack, Craig S. *Red on Red: Native American Literary Separatism.* Minneapolis: University of Minnesota Press, 1999.

Wong, Hertha. *Sending My Heart Back Across the Years: Tradition and Innovation in Native American Autobiography.* New York: Oxford University Press, 1992.

Wright, Richard. *Native Son.* New York: HarperPerennial, 1993 [1940].

Zack, Naomi, ed. *American Mixed Race: the Culture of Microdiversity.* Lanham, Md.: Rowman and Littlefield, 1995.

Zitkala Sa (Gertrude Simmons Bonnin). "Why I Am a Pagan." In William L. Andrews, ed., *Classic American Autobiographies.* New York: Penguin, 1992 [1902]. 459–62.

Index

African American literature: and Native writers, xii, 84, 103, 108, 134n15; rage in, xii, 103, 104–5, 108

African Americans: and Du Bois's "double-consciousness," 82, 134n12; race and, 78, 80, 82–83, 85, 133n6, 136n27

Alcatraz, occupation of (1969), vii, 105, 140n19

Alexie, Sherman: identity politics in work of, 115–16, 119; Indian-white relations in work of, 117–19; on mixedblood identity, 21, 22, 112–13, 125n21, 138n2, 142n35; on mixedblood writers, 21, 142n35; and Owens, 21, 118, 142n35; and "post-Indian" culture, 20, 125n21; preference for term "Indian," 138n2; and Vizenor, 21, 107; *Lone Ranger and Tonto Fistfight in Heaven*, 117, 125n21, 138n7, 140n15; *One Stick Song*, 141n26; "Sin Eaters," 102, 117–18, 139n10, 141n26, 142n34 "Unauthorized Biography of Me," 125n21. See also *Indian Killer*; *Reservation Blues*; *Toughest Indian in the World*

Almanac of the Dead (Silko): cosmopolitanism in, 20, 23, 113; Indian identities in, 113, 114; Indian Wars and Ghost Dance in, 102–3, 113; transcendence of racism in, 113, 119

American Indian Movement (AIM), 105–6

anthropology and anthropologists: academic departments of, 22–23, 139n9; and anti-imperial translation, 13, 65–66, 124n4; and art, 26; Boas and, 33–34, 129n15; and colonialism, 124n4; "comparative method," 34, 129n15; Deloria's attacks on, 106, 140n20; and incommen-

surability of cultures, 61–62; "literary," 34–35, 129n15; Native, 6; and Native perspectives, 13; postcolonial, 65–66; radical relativism of, 61–62; researcher-subject relationships, 6–7, 13; "scientific," 34; and separatist nationalism, 6–7; on value of traditional histories, 60

Apess, William, 16, 20

Appiah, Kwame Anthony: on "cosmopolitan patriotism," 12, 17, 111–12; cosmopolitan perspective of, 14, 17; on "intrinsic racism," 116; on postcolonial novel, 114; on Sartre and anti-racist racism, 119–20

Austin, Mary, 32–34, 37, 38, 128n12; *American Rhythm*, 33–34, 128n12

Bad Heart Bull, Amos, 56, 68, 130nn6, 7, 132n22

Bahr, Donald, 27, 130n2; song translations of, 42–46

Baldwin, James, 104, 140n15

Basso, Keith, 11, 51, 74

Battle of the Little Big Horn, 56, 132n22

Bird, Traveller, 57–58, 67, 72–74; *Tell Them They Lie*, 57

Black Elk, 23, 70; *Black Elk Speaks* (Black Elk with Neihardt), 23

Black Nationalism, 115

Black Rage (Grier and Cobbs), 105, 140n16

Blish, Helen, 53, 68–69, 70, 71, 132n21

"blood": in *Cogewea*, xi, 77, 79–80, 95–96; discourse on, 76, 77, 91, 116, 132n1; and essentialism, 76, 132n1; historical notions of, 78–84; and Indian identity,

hybridity: in contemporary Native fiction, 109–12, 115; as cultural emergence, 109–10, 111; Eastman and, 81–82, 90; and racial categories, 115. *See also* mixedbloods; race

Hymes, Dell: on accuracy of translations, 126n6; Clackamas translations, 39–40, 129n21; influence of, 41; Schoolcraft translations, 28–29, 126n6, 129n17; translation methods of, 38–40, 41, 47, 126n6; *"In vain I tried to tell you"*, 126n6; "Some North Pacific Coast Poems," 126n6, 129n7

identity, Indian, 1–2, 92–94, 114–16; and assimilation, 92–93; communal, 7–8; in contemporary Native fiction, 109–15, 141n29; and critical perspectives, 1–2; and hybridity, 81–82, 89–91, 109–10, 111, 112, 115; and identity politics, 111–12, 114–16; and indigenousness, 12, 13, 124n12; and nationalist perspective, 7–8; and separatism, 125n21; and the "traditional," 21–22, 110–11; translation, and principle of, 25–27, 28, 38

INARTF Report. *See* Report of the Indian Nations at Risk Task Force

Indian Killer (Alexie): character names in, 99, 138n3, 139n14, 142n31; compared to other Native novels, xii, 103, 113, 119–20; Ghost Dance in, 99, 101–3, 115, 116, 120, 139n8; hybrids in, 109–10, 112, 113; identity politics of, 109, 112–16, 119; and Indian Wars, 102; "intrinsic racism" in, 116, 139n8; John Smith's Indian identity in, 101, 109–10, 138n1, 139n11; killer's identity in, 99–101, 120–21, 138n6, 140n23; literary references in, 139n14; on mixedbloods and Indian identity, xii, 112–13, 115–16, 125n21; 1960s context of, 98, 104–5, 138n1; owls in, 100, 101–2, 120–21, 138n6; politics of, 114–16, 119, 120; racism in, 119–20; rage in, xii, 99–100, 103–4, 112, 113, 114, 119, 120–21, 140n21, 142n31; Red Nationalism and *rougetude*, 115–16, 119; Seattle setting, 98–99, 105, 138n5; separatism in, 125n21; and Wright's *Native Son*, 104, 140n15

Indian Reorganization Act of 1934, 95, 137n36

indigenist perspective, 10–14; and anti-colonial nationalism, 5, 22; and cosmopolitan perspective, 1, 22–23; as critical perspective, ix, 1–2; and ecocriticism, 13; geocentric worldview and, 10, 11–12, 111, 124n13; identity and indigenousness, 12, 13, 124n12; and identity politics in Native fiction, 111–12; and nationalist perspective, 1, 5, 7, 12–13, 19; and Native American literature, 10–14, 111–12; and non-Native anthropology, 13, 124n13; policies of, 12, 13–14, 124n13; and scientific worldview, 124n13; shared knowledges and, 10–11, 12–13, 22, 124n12; and translation, 13

indigenousness, and identity, 12, 13, 124n12

intellectuals, Native, 19, 134n15, 137nn34, 35

Iroquois, 29, 66, 67, 132n17

Iroquois Confederacy, 54–55, 71

Jahner, Elaine, 7–8, 50, 70

Kagama ruling (1886), 3

Kroeber, Karl, 34, 37–38, 129n18, 141n24

Lakota: Austin's song interpretations, 128n12; on citizenship, 3; and Custer, 55, 56, 70; "Stone Boy" narratives, 7–8, 50; winter counts, 67–68, 132n21

languages, 61–62. *See also* translation, history of

Larsen, Nella, 79, 84, 95, 135n22; *Quicksand*, 79, 95, 135n22

Lazarus, Neil, 4–5, 19

Lévi-Strauss, Claude, 59

Lone Dog, winter counts of, 67

Lyons, Scott Richard, 4, 5, 16

Lyotard, Jean-François, 61–64, 65, 72; *différend* concept, 61, 72; on incommensurability of cultures, 61–63, 131n12; and Lévi-Strauss, 59; and Readings, 62–64, 65, 131n12

Major Crimes Act (1885), 88, 135n25

Mallery, Garrick, 66–67, 68, 132n21; "Calendar of the Dakota Nation," 67; "Pictographs of the North American Indians," 66–67, 132n21; "Picture-Writing of the American Indians," 67

title